Ashley Mullenger is a commercial fisherman working off the North Norfolk coast. She is one of the few women working in the industry and was named 'Fisherman of the Year' in 2022. Advocating for better representation and equality in the industry (only 2% of crew members are women), as well as raising awareness of issues the fishing communities are facing, she has built an avid following online. She shows daily life in fishing and encourages others to take up the profession.

T0385340

MY FISHING LIFE

A Story of the Sea

Ashley Mullenger

With Lynne Barrett-Lee

ROBINSON

ROBINSON

First published in Great Britain in 2024 by Robinson
This paperback edition published in 2025 by Robinson

A CIP catalogue record for this book
is available from the British Library

ISBN:978-1-47214-833-9

Typeset in Garamond Premier Pro by SX Composing DTP, Rayleigh, Essex
Printed and bound in Great Britain by Clays Ltd, Elcograf S.p.A.

Papers used by Robinson are from well-managed forests
and other responsible sources

Robinson
An imprint of
Little, Brown Book Group
Carmelite House
50 Victoria Embankment
London EC4Y 0DZ

The authorised representative
in the EEA is
Hachette Ireland
8 Castlecourt Centre, Dublin 15, D15
XTP3, Ireland
(email: info@hbgi.ie)

An Hachette UK Company
www.hachette.co.uk

www.littlebrown.co.uk

For the Fishermen of the United Kingdom,
Past, Present and Future

Fore

The front part of something, especially a boat

Summer 2021

It's almost 1 a.m. on a mid-July night, and every window in the house has been thrown open to let the air circulate, after a week of temperatures well into the fiery thirties. A cool breeze from the northern hemisphere is steadily making its way down over the country, and most people lie asleep, their bodies grateful for the welcome reprieve the frigid air has brought with it.

In my house the shrill pitch of an iPhone alarm sounds, cutting through the heavy atmosphere like a knife. I wake quickly; I've grown used to shutting it off as fast as possible before it wakes anybody else up. I scoop up the phone and make my way to the bathroom where a pile of clothes I prepared the evening before awaits me. I dress and brush my teeth by torchlight before making my way to the door and soundlessly pulling on my work boots.

Seven minutes after waking up I'm out into the night air and the darkness that envelops me within it. I can feel the breeze playing with loose tendrils of my hair – hair I haven't even brushed, let alone looked at. But it has its uses. Unlike Nige, I can predict what kind of day I'm going to have at sea based on how much that little draught wants to play with it.

Those first seven minutes of my day are completed with zombie-like precision, but I am shaken into life with a turn of the key in the reliable old Hi-Lux. As I bowl along the moonlit back roads, disturbing all kinds of startled wildlife in my haste to get to Wells-next-the-Sea, the last vestiges of sleepiness melt away.

I pull up on the quayside. Bar Nige and the boat, it's now virtually empty. Devoid of the hundreds of tourists who thronged here just a few hours earlier, it's now the sole preserve of the ever-persistent seagulls, who are fighting over the remains of their chip papers. Out on the water, I can see the navigational lights of the other boats already disappearing into the night. Time to join them.

I jump down to the foredeck, dazzled as usual by the searchlight that's mounted on the mast, and tap on the wheelhouse window. Then with a thumbs-up from Nige, I throw off the ropes and push the boat away from the wall. We need to be gone by 2.30 a.m. if we're to stand a chance of leaving the safety of the tidal harbour for what looms beyond: the obsidian void that is the North Sea.

That is where I make my living, and time and tide wait for no man.

Or woman.

Introduction

I never planned to become a fisherman. It came about by chance, when I was twenty, and bored at work, and wanting to try something different, and it started with a single question: 'Does anyone fancy going on a fishing trip?'

That trip – a morning's mackerel fishing from Wells-next-the-Sea in Norfolk – was the start of an obsession that would see me transform from clean-cut office worker to one of the UK's few female commercial fishermen. That day, when local fisherman Nigel took us out into the North Sea, I couldn't have known that he would go on to become my friend, mentor and skipper, and that a few years down the line I would find myself co-owning and working with him on two commercial fishing boats, *Fairlass* and *Saoirse*.

The sea has captivated people ever since humans first set sail on it; its beauty, its potent force, the mysteries it holds. For a select few who make their living from it, trying to understand it – to second guess its ever-changing moods – creates an addiction to salt water that keeps them coming back for more.

My Fishing Life will document the reality of that life, with all the day-to-day drama that is normal for any fisherman, working in arguably the most dangerous of all peacetime professions. I'll show you the physicality and sheer doggedness required to work at sea, and the daily struggles to make an honest living out of a job that relies entirely on the weather and the tides, plus a fisherman's legendary faith in their intuition. And I'll take you on a journey around the changeable coasts of our islands as I travel to bring *Fairlass* and *Saoirse* – from the Outer Hebrides and Northern Ireland respectively – to their new home port in Wells.

But this isn't just my story. It is also a love-letter to the people of our fishing industry: the colourful, weather-beaten and idiosyncratic characters who have dedicated their lives to catching seafood, just as Nige and I do today. It's from them and their stories that I learned respect for their skill and courage, and began to understand how the actions of the past have shaped the fragile fishing industry we have today.

With the marine environment changing – both politically, and as a result of global warming – *My Fishing Life* lifts the lid on what it's like to be one of the country's very few female fishermen. It isn't about romanticising life at sea, or the British seaside. It's the truth; a truth swept up in politics as much as crab pots. A story of poverty, community, friendship, and beloved boats. Of a way of life that's in jeopardy if we don't open our eyes to what is going on beneath the surface.

I want to show you the reality of how seafood finds its way to you. The bravery and strength of the skippers and crew, the early mornings and late nights, the love and care lavished upon the boats from which it is caught. And in this ever-changing, often exasperating, sometimes quixotic line of work, the despair that's part of any fisherman's life. I hope my tale will also do justice to an iconic industry that, while it feeds and impacts almost all of us, remains one of our most mysterious and misunderstood.

Chapter 1

It's 8 p.m. on a miserably cold February night in 2019, and I'm in the wheelhouse of Nigel's boat, *Never Can Tell-A*. From where I sit on the bench seat I can feel her coming down off one wave before rearing back up again to meet the foamy mass of another, its energy dispersing onto the salt-spattered wheelhouse windows and roof. It sends torrents of water down onto the deck behind me, and a sudden salty shower, courtesy of the integral roof vent. Up ahead, beyond the 200 metres lit by the boat's spotlight, will be the white-crested waves that will tell us to ease the throttle. Marked by a West Cardinal buoy, flashing its white light nine times, is the sanctuary of deeper water, where the sea is not trying to make landfall over the shallow sand bar quite so urgently.

I can't recall the last time I felt quite so exhilarated, and at such times I talk – talk incessantly and inanely, a stream every bit as relentless as the waves punching the boat. I talk about the pots, and how muddy they are likely to be now. I talk about the thrill of this being my first proper fishing trip. I talk, at some length, about the weather.

'Shut up Ash,' Nigel snaps at me. 'I'm tryin' to fuckin' concentrate! This is the kinda place you can smash ya boat to pieces!'

I don't need telling twice. Nigel's authority is absolute. But it's not only that; he has always placed his confidence in me and has never asked me to do anything he doesn't feel I'm capable of. So along with the excitement I'm feeling determined: tonight is my first proper chance to prove to Nigel that his confidence has not been misplaced. My natter stops, and the sea sounds rush in to claim the space.

Once we're out into the deeper water Nige switches off the spotlight and we are left in the darkness, with the noise of the water crashing against the hull an explosion of sound over the steady whir of the engine. All we can see ahead now is an ocean of flashing red – the lights of several hundred wind turbines. Were it not for the intermittent glow of Cromer Lighthouse, we could be anywhere, though, since the southern North Sea has become the offshore windfarm capital of the world. The turbines are fast becoming a landmark in themselves.

Although I've been working for Nige since August 2018, this night marks the first commercial fishing trip where I am a necessity, rather than a luxury. Up until this point, I've been mostly ashore doing admin, bait and pots, a job spec I imagine is unique to the fishing world, and is often very physical and sometimes smelly. My role ashore has included pot mending, sorting out all the paperwork and (I have to say, contentiously in some areas) getting my hands on lots of lovely shickle.

Shickle is the name for what's left of a crab after the viable meat has been removed. It makes brilliant bait, and is free, and eco-friendly as well, because what's not wanted for selling goes back to the sea again. It's also available on a strictly first-come-first-served basis, and, being ashore while other fishermen were out fishing, my trick would be to come first and serve myself all the best bits, probably to some people's annoyance.

I would only go to sea when Nige was expecting it to be busy, to lend my luxurious extra pair of hands to him and his sons, as in literally a pair of hands, to riddle whelks. If sorting shickle's a bit whiffy, riddling whelks is, at times, an even muckier business. It begins with a series of fifty or so 25-litre plastic drums with concrete in the bottom, holes drilled in the side, and a mesh on top with an entry hole. The size of that entry hole is crucial. Leave it too loose and you run the risk of any whelks marching in for a free lunch and marching straight back out again, or a hungry seal forcing its head in to steal your bait. Too tight and it becomes a strict one-in-at-a-time policy, and whelks aren't in the business of forming an orderly queue like us Brits. They will lose interest and look for their dinner elsewhere. So the aperture must be set to the optimum size (roughly that of a can of Fanta or a fist) by tightening the drawstring just right.

The whelk (Latin name *buccinum undatum*, hence their nickname of 'buckies' in some parts) is a collective term for several species of carnivorous sea snail. They live in colonies on

9

the seabed, which rarely intermingle, so they evolve to have very different characteristics, including the thickness of shell/amount of meat ratio. They are also picky – there are only certain types of bottom that they like – so as one of the late fishermen of Wells was fond of saying, 'They are where they are and they're not where they're not.' It's true of all species, but with whelks it feels particularly pertinent, as you can go from hero to zero (haul-wise) within a hundred yards.

Once the whelks have been tempted the pots are hauled up, all fifty of them, and quickly, using the onboard hydraulic winch. (Quickly because time, in this endeavour, is money, and if you work out of a tidal harbour, the clock ticks relentlessly.) Each pot is then shaken out over the riddle, a metal table with grading bars, which allows undersize whelks to fall through and find their way back home. But this is fishing, so it obviously doesn't happen all by itself. The process requires a human touch. This consists of pushing and pulling the catch vigorously back and forward over the bars, while also picking out every object that isn't a sizeable whelk, of which there are usually quite a lot: the remnants of bait, hermit crabs, small spider crabs, the odd fish, limpet-covered pebbles and various species of starfish. (Lots of starfish. Sometimes hundreds of starfish. Big starfish, little starfish, medium starfish, two-legged starfish, three-legged starfish, brittle starfish, bright purple starfish – those ones are called Bloody Henry – and even the odd one with ten legs. All of which get flung back over the side like so many tiny Frisbees.) With hands working quickly, you then usher the catch towards the riddle's shoot, sending the viable whelks down to a waiting fish box below. And all this must be done before the next pot and its contents are unceremoniously emptied out in front of you – usually a whole ten seconds later.

Despite having seen the process done time and time again by Jack, Nigel's younger son, who also had to shake the pot before passing it along the line to his dad for baiting and stacking, I had never appreciated how intense and overwhelming the process could be. I am not ashamed to say that it took me a while to keep pace with them all.

'He gave ya two!' Nige remarked one day, grinning at me.

I looked at him blankly, not having a clue what he was talking about. Then looked to Jack, then to Kenneth, Nigel's elder son, scanning their faces, desperately searching for insight. Then, as if it were rehearsed, they all stopped what they were doing, raised their bright-blue-gloved hands and kind of waggled them at me. The penny dropped. One of my hands was definitely working harder than the other, following my dominant hand around like a lost puppy. That piece of wisdom has stuck with me ever since.

Another salty shower smacks me in the face. And as we leave the shelter of the harbour, at 8 p.m. on this scruffy Wednesday night, I hope lots of other wisdoms have stuck similarly well. We are off to work a flood tide, the term we affectionately use to describe going out for the period of time the water in the tidal harbour stays deep enough to allow access, with a view to doing as many pots as possible in that time frame and leaving the fishing grounds in time to get back before the harbour starts to drain. That means we have around four hours: we can enter and leave the harbour just two hours either side of high water, which this evening is around 10 p.m. Tonight's foray is so our whelks can be landed first thing in the morning, in time to be added to this week's pay cheque from the processing factory in King's Lynn.

So it's a must-do, rather than a want-to-do situation. No one would choose to go out so late on a flood tide; with so little fishing time, it'll only be slim pickings. But this January, always a difficult month, has been made even more difficult by a broken gearbox. So if there's a chance to earn some money, Nigel has to take it. He has gear close enough – just a couple of miles out – and though it's dirty, at least it's fast. Get out, earn a few quid, get in again. And with his sons not around it has fallen to me to step up to the plate. There has been no ceremony, no time, just the all-important question he asked me three hours ago: 'Do you think you can bait a pot?'

I had, by now, learned that I was not required to answer this. Nigel never asks me to do anything he isn't confident I *can* do, as I've said. It's more just a polite way of giving me my orders.

Baiting is just one part of the four-step process that is fishing for whelks. First you haul the pots (plus, if you don't have an extra pair of hands, shake and riddle them too), then you bait them, then, lastly, you stack, turn and then shoot them back into the water, ready for their next overnight visitors. The baiting bit – taking each newly emptied pot, putting in a piece of cut-up dogfish and a garnish of dead crab, then closing a drawstring – was something I'd seen Nigel do countless times. So inwardly I was pretty confident that I *could* do it. But I replied anyway, with a more modest, 'Yeah I'll do the best I can.'

12

'Yeah you *can*,' came the instant reply.

So that was me told. And if it was confidence he was after, I decided to show him some more. Stacking the pots was something I'd seen him do countless times too, and I was confident I was strong and able enough to be able to pick them up and put them in their designated places in the boat's pound, so that once the process of setting them back came around, they would pull themselves back over the stern in their correct reverse order. I said so. But that was apparently me overreaching myself slightly. He assured me that baiting would do. And one thing you never do is argue with your skipper.

It's a filthy night to be at sea and growing even filthier as our onboard GPS plotter leads us to the first of our strings. It might not feel like it to us, as we don't know any different, but having such a device is a luxury. Our fishing forebears had no tools to guide them to their pots other than skill and experience in using the information they had at their disposal, namely the time, their compass bearing, and, if coming in when it was dark, whatever lights they had to guide them on the shore. (Prior to plotters, fishing in the dark was obviously pretty rare, save for one determined old salt, Tony Jordan, who would go out with nothing more than the flame of a hurricane lamp as a searchlight, though this wasn't ideal, as when a breeze picked up, it would immediately blow it out again.)

In daylight, local landmarks could, and still can, also provide a decent fix. Luckily, Wells is hard to confuse with any other place. St Nicholas' Church at Blakeney is easily visible from out at sea, as is the town's iconic geography. Its miles of golden sands, lined with beach huts, are backed by a forest of towering pines, and, to the west, the sea-grass-covered sand dune that is Scolt Head.

We're no more than 2 miles out now, and through the dark and mizzle I can see the distant twinkly lights of the harbour and town. I wonder if all those people sitting comfortably in their homes watching telly realise we're even out here, doing what we do. From here it feels like a whole other universe.

The wind is blowing straight in my face and making my nose run, but with both hands wrapped up in the trademark fisherman's blue gloves (about an inch too long for my dainty girlish hands) I only have my jumpered shoulder to wipe it on. Not that I'd be inclined to use my hands anyway. Seeing the grey-brown liquid that oozes from the box of cut-up dogfish in front of me is as much motivation as I need to not touch my hair or face; my hands have been constantly delving around in there, after all.

Up against the clock in a way that's exclusive to working a flood tide, Nige is bringing pots over the block and round the hauler as fast as he can, where he promptly shakes the contents onto the riddle and spins the now-empty pots over to me. While he starts riddling, I grab the pots and put the bait in, lowering it down onto the edge of the bait box as I'm doing so, just as he's taught me. If any part of this can be streamlined, it invariably has been, because every small increment of time saved means extra income. Then it's just a case of quickly pulling up the drawstring, leaving the perfect size entrance for our quarry to crawl in overnight.

That done, it's all action (well, even more action) as Nigel darts round behind me and grabs each baited pot, putting it in its designated temporary home in the pound, all ready to be sent back to the seabed.

It's slightly frustrating watching Nigel doing all the work while I can only look on, feeling under-employed. Because I know I *can* do this. I've seen him do it so much. And I almost tell him, 'Nige, I *can* pick up a pot and put it down again, you know.' But I also know why he won't yet let me.

The process of sending the pots back to the sea floor, 'shooting away', as we call it, is one of the most dangerous parts of the job. It starts with a can, tied to a rope (this is our surface marker for the pots) at the bottom of which is an anchor. Once that anchor gets pulled out over the stern of the boat the process of fishing for your whelks is underway and, like the tide, it's a process which waits for no one. That rope is attached to another length of rope, only this time it's leaded to keep it down on the seabed. After 7 fathoms of rope (there are 6 feet to a fathom), the first pot goes down, which is the last pot you processed. Another 7 fathoms of rope then, followed by another pot, and so on and so forth till, half a mile of rope and fifty pots later, you have a second anchor, which is hooked over a rail, and needs picking up and taking to the shooting ramp, ready to follow the last pot out and secure the string of pots down on the seabed. The last bit of rope (colloquially known as a dhan tow) is pulled by the anchor, and ends with a marker can which remains on the surface, its coordinates ready to be logged in the plotter, so you can easily find your way back to it.

The faster the boat is going the quicker the pots are shot away, which means that the pots are set tighter. This speed is what makes for better fishing. Although we sometimes affectionately

15

call whelks racing snails, they are actually anything but, so it's logical that a slack pot shuffling around on the bottom will make it harder to attract these sedentary molluscs.

But the danger is not wholly about the speed of the operation. Once the process has started, even slowing the boat down will not stop those pots going back to their watery home. It is also absolutely vital that the pots are shot back in the exact reverse order you have just stacked them, because if a pot tries to go before it's supposed to it will result in the gear going away out of order, fouling (the industry term for when a pot or pots end up doing that), and taking multiple other pots with it, which will cause a big bundle of rope and pots to be pulled down the deck too, trying to snag anything in its path on the way.

That 'anything' can – and has – included fishermen. Nigel has never been shy about safety when shooting away, and has always made the dangers very clear. So as I stand in the wheelhouse (I'm in charge of the controls, and an extra pair of eyes while he's out there on deck), I swallow my words. I have by now already heard too many horror stories. A rope tangled round the ankle is a route to certain death if you haven't the space, time, or nous to either pull it free or, if the rope is already bar tight, the sense to quickly kick your boot off so you have sufficient breath to swim back to the surface. The tales told in harbour pubs might include a few tall ones but I'm mindful that most of them aren't. And any skipper who has had to locate and haul a drenched and spluttering crew-member back from the depths will not, cannot, ever forget it. Traditionally, so I'm told, the fisherman in question, having returned with no less than his life, will buy the whole house a

16

drink. Devastatingly, many never got the opportunity, which chills me to the bone, and will never lose the power to put a lump in my throat.

A fishing trip of this length – four hours, give or take – will, if we're quick, allow us sufficient time to haul four of our fifty-pot strings, or passes, which are conveniently organised in straight lines on the seabed, close enough together to allow us to shoot one string away and not be too far from the next set. It's a little bit like mowing a bowling green lawn, with each pass the equivalent of a stripe.

Our four runs made, it's then time to turn around and head the couple of miles back to the harbour entrance. Now we're done, and no longer in need of the deck lights, the blackness is absolute, allowing me to appreciate the stars in all their magnificence. And though I'm slightly distracted by needing a wee (fine in summer, but not an option under four layers of clothing), all my senses feel alive, almost supercharged, in this environment, which has a beauty and a majesty and a power all of its own.

I realise too just how normal this now feels. This vast body of water, me and Nige working alongside each other, the sense of teamwork and partnership, and the fact that, throughout, so little's needed to be said. I no longer have a sense that anything ground-breaking is happening. Because it isn't. Call me Mrs Slightly Overconfident, but this just all feels completely natural.

But the North Sea must send us on our way again. To this day I hate a following sea on the bar, but, with the pots set, that is what we must face again, and this time it's even more hairy, and now feels wholly *un*natural. As perhaps it would, because it's a complicated situation. There are sand bars in all kinds of coastal settings globally, and ours is part of one that extends the length of the North Norfolk coastline. Running east–west across the harbour entrance, it dries out completely at low tide every day.

Northerly wind makes waves that run in a southerly direction, and due to the North Norfolk coast being exposed to wind that's been blowing in that direction for some 2,000 miles, all that energy makes its landfall where the water shallows up over the bar. So though the tide is going out the waves are coming in, two opposing forces – wind and tide – that are having an argument.

And there is a great deal of energy involved. So rather than us steaming along and banging into the waves, the sea is now pushing us where *it* wants to go. And as we approach the shallower water the waves start curling up and starting to bare their white teeth, because now they are trying to break. At such times you can do only one thing: put your faith in your boat and your skipper. And respect the sea. Never, ever push your luck.

Nige sees us safely back by midnight and we tie up for the night, but not before I grab the chance to have that much-needed wee before he does a final sluice down of the deck. And as we scrabble back onto the quayside, we spot a familiar human form sitting on the quay. It's one of the old guys who's seen it all, heard it all, and done it all. He also seems a little worse (or better, depending on your perspective) for drink. 'What the fuck are you doing out at this time?' he booms at us, causing a late loitering seagull to spook and take flight. 'Who d'ya think the pair of you are – the Bat Gang?' he chortles, flapping his arms helpfully to illustrate.

He has a point. Doing that flood tide was challenging. But it was necessary. Boats are costly things to run, and need maintaining and servicing, especially at this lean and unforgiving time of year. And so what that we probably only hauled two hundred quid's worth? What I've earned in experience is pure gold. So I'm back to wittering. 'So, did I do well, Nige?' I ask him.

'Yeah,' he says. No more. But that's all I need from him. Nigel's not one for putting a bow on it.

Making my way back to my car, hungry, freezing and exhausted, I realise that I'm likely to get no more than five hours of sleep, as I have to be up at 6.30 a.m. tomorrow, to unload our catch and get the boxes on a van to the processing plant at King's Lynn. Even so, I can feel a distinct bounce in my step, as I have just discovered something important about myself. I have just found my passion. My happy place.

Maybe my preconceptions were wrong. Maybe a woman *can* do this job.

Maybe I can.

Chapter 2

'Do not look back to port once the vessel has left the quayside'

Looking back to port implies that you are not truly ready to embark on your voyage and therefore risk not completing it and bringing about bad luck to the crew and the vessel.

It's a balmy July Tuesday in 2011, and I'm working my summer gig aboard a 10-metre boat called *Sunbeam 3*. I'm in my cut-offs (more accurately, my tiny hand-made 'hotpants' – courtesy of Nige, my personal tailor) and I notice, when she's steaming out to our regular fishing haunts, that our customers are full of chat and feeling blissful. Blissfully overwhelmed, that is, by the special serenity you can only find in the wide-open nothing that is the sea. All is good. We reach our mark and the boat is taken out of gear, where she drifts in the tide. How she sits in the conditions depends entirely on the forces of mother nature and even on a calm day she will, at the very least, gently nod as she bobs around, hoping to pass over a shoal of hungry mackerel.

That's what boats do. They roll. Sometimes it's a graceful lull side to side, others it's a persistent battering, with your field of view changing quickly from sea to sky and back again. If gills are going to turn green, it's now.

Thankfully, I've never been seasick. I always had it in the back of my mind in the early days, however, that if I was, I would have to carry on regardless. I know the odd fisherman that suffers from it occasionally, but they are in a very small minority, and the few that do basically chuck up and keep going. To me, that sounds like a massive inconvenience and pretty grim. So, arguably, I chose the right career.

~

But how did we get here? I have gone charging ahead again like a bull in a china shop – to quote my mother, who I know is immensely proud of me. I also know that, cast-iron stomach or otherwise, it's a career she wouldn't have picked for her elder daughter, no matter how out-there my vocational choices had been.

And they were, by the way, pretty out-there. As a child I aimed high, if somewhat randomly, in that I quite fancied being either an astronaut or a vet, but by the time I was in college, I was a little more down to earth. I had a summer job at a place called The Amazing Maize Maze, where one of my main responsibilities was to don a pair of wings and a special little green dress, and be one of the resident fairies. Since it mostly involved larking about, with the odd break for a rollup with my counterpart in the pink dress, it felt like a fun way to earn some extra money. It was seasonal, however, and once I got back to college, I realised it might not sustain my high-octane lifestyle, as that involved actually putting petrol in my metallic blue Ford Ka – tricky on a part-time fairy's wage.

I got further down to earth shortly after leaving college, when it became clear – to my mum at least – that my lack of a career plan (I was still working out how best to put my A levels in drama and film studies to good use) was no barrier to getting gainful full-time employment. Handily, one of her friends ran a local butcher's shop and abbatoir, and was in need of a new shop assistant, so she put a word in and by the following Monday I was already donning my white jacket and apron, all thoughts of becoming the next West End lead in *Chicago* on hold.

I'm not sure I ever really considered butchery as a career path, but it was an experience I really enjoyed. It was great working for a small local family firm, and the chance to see the whole process of food production, from field to table, gave me real respect for both the people and the processes involved.

Back with Mum however, and with no maritime connection in our family, why would she ever think that this would be the path I'd choose to tread? It's very common for fishermen to inherit the trade through family but I didn't even live by the sea growing up, let alone have any concept of it as a place where people went to work. It wasn't until I was twelve that Norfolk became home and up to this point going to the seaside was a treat reserved exclusively for the summer holidays. Memories of being bundled into the car in the early morning to make the couple of hours' drive (or four-and-half *Blue Peters* away, as Mum would always tell me and my sister Camilla, as we had no concept of time at this age) to the North Norfolk coast to spend a day at the beach. I'm sure eight-year-old me, busy making sandcastles with her sister, would have been dumbfounded if she knew that her future was already lapping at her toes and threatening the very existence of the sandcastle she had just so lovingly created.

Like many young adults without a clear idea of what they wanted to be when they 'grew up', at the age of twenty-one I fell into the career in which I would spend the next eight or nine years. Starting out as a Resident Liaison Officer in the plumbing and heating sector, I cut my liaison teeth by being the first point of contact (or 'battering board' as it was colloquially known) for angry tenants with – you guessed it – no plumbing or heating. I eventually became supervisor of the Planned Installations Team, which felt a little less ear-bashy and confrontational, but as it still involved a great deal of pressure (both actual and mental) I liked to spend my free time outdoors.

My colleagues felt similarly, and were a similar age to me, so we naturally socialised outside work. I specifically remember one day saying aloud in the office, 'Shall we do something fun and different next weekend?' My co-workers having all said yes to the idea, it was left in my capable hands to suggest what and where. To this day, I haven't the foggiest where such a random idea came from, but out popped: 'What about sea fishing, then?' Little did I know that I was about to make a Google search that would change the course of my life and career.

Fate sometimes works in completely logical ways. I typed in 'Norfolk sea fishing' and up popped *Norfolk Sea Fishing*, a link to a website offering 'Chartered Sea Angling Trips from Wells-next-the-Sea (half day or full day)', one of the seaside destinations of my childhood. So the following weekend, at 8 a.m. sharp, me and four colleagues were boarding a boat called *Sunbeam 3*, for a three-and-a-half-hour trip catching mackerel with skipper Nigel and his son Kenneth.

I remember Nigel's first utterances: he wasn't slow in passing comment on one of my colleagues' footwear choices, as he watched her gingerly edge her way down the rusty ladder that was bolted to the sheer stone face of the quay wall, and which ended about 3 foot shy of the rails that ran the length of the boat's open deck.

'Brilliant,' he said, for all to hear. 'Flip flops.'

Still, with the welfare of his paying clients obviously paramount, he and Kenneth courteously held her steady and got her safely aboard. (Being outdoorsy, my own footwear received neither comment nor need for assistance – phew.)

To my landlubber's eye, *Sunbeam* looked practical enough: she was around 10 metres long, and looked like a cross between a workboat and something with a little more poke, a bit like a speedboat. She was light blue, made of fibreglass, with her name emblazoned across her transom, and her deck had a big rectangular raised platform which housed the engine and provided a comfy place to sit. The wheelhouse, which was forward, sat three people comfortably and was equipped with a gas hob, an oven, and lots of screens – the information on which I didn't understand. There was also a cabin forward of the wheelhouse, which housed two modest bunks, plus a toilet with a seventies-style floral curtain for modesty. All in all it was perfectly fit for the job and a nice place to spend a few hours at sea.

Nigel gave us his safety briefing, air-stewardess style – just swap the heels for a pair of Reebok classics, and reimagine the hand movements. The engine already running, the ropes were then thrown, and we were slowly moving away from the harbour.

I had seen Wells' iconic crescent-shaped quayside many times, but never from this vantage point. The tide was still only just getting started at this time, so the boat, and her passengers, sat low in the quay basin, and the buildings that spanned its length seemed to peer down at us. Once upon a time these would have hummed with activity, as they went hand in hand with whatever was going on at sea. As I remembered my mum telling me and my sister, they hadn't always been swanky seaside second homes or flashing neon arcades. The granary, for instance, whose elevated gantry still dominated the skyline, was once where they loaded up malt grown in Norfolk to be shipped over to the Netherlands for making beer.

We made progress through the twisting channel of Wells harbour and the buildings steadily became smaller. The noise of the town was now replaced by the steady din of the engine and the chittering of the seabirds on the tidal saltmarsh, whose musky smell was now fresh in my nostrils. We then rounded the berm, where the yellow tin lifeboat house sat, and were soon passing the beach, destined for the mystery of the expansive green-blue beyond.

The beach at Wells is cherished by those who know the area and, for those who don't, once seen never forgotten. This is partly, as I said earlier, because of its geography. The harbour actually sits a mile inland from the fairway – the fairway is where you always have water, whatever the tide is doing – so the harbour is dry for more of the time than it's wet. (This is why our window for opportunity is only two hours either side of high water, twice in every twenty-four hours.) Heading out to the open sea is the channel we use, beside which is what we call the beach bank, which is flanked by a long footpath. The path is a three-quarter-mile rat run from the town to the beach, and in high season, as it was that day, often shoulder to shoulder with tourists.

The tourists' patience is always rewarded, however, as what they find at the end of their trek is, by any beach standard, magnificent. Not for nothing has this vast sandy haven won multiple awards. It's also designated an Area of Outstanding Natural Beauty, not least because it's backed by that tall pinewood forest, which also acts as a brilliant windbreak from our prevailing south-west winds.

It was a bright, sunny day, and as we motored past the beach, it was filling up with those high-season tourists, who were staking out 'their spot' for the day. I felt we were special. We were going beyond, while they could only sit gazing in awe at the sparkling mass of brine before them.

It was just as glorious out there as I had anticipated and something changed inside me, like a light switch being turned on; I felt this overwhelming sense of acceptance in the environment, and an unexpected feeling that my soul was complete. Feeling the now unmistakable tug tug tug of mackerel as they voraciously gobbled up the glittery hooks we offered was exciting, sure, but this was more than just an angling addiction. Just like the emerald greenish-blue mackerel, I too had been dazzled; in my case by the glittering majesty of the sea.

~

By the time the trip was nearly over and we were well into our return voyage, I had already secured another for the following week. This time, however, it was for eight hours targeting tope. I was already intrigued.

'What are tope?' I asked Nigel as we entered the harbour.

'Small shark,' he replied, as if that was the only information I could possibly require.

'How small?' I asked. It seemed the kind of intel I needed to know.

'Eyes like small dustbin lids,' he replied.

He was joking, of course, but even if he hadn't been, with the exciting prospect of a *Jaws* moment on my next day off, wild horses couldn't have dragged me away.

This time, with none of my mates having the same day off as me, I'd be tagging along with some other random customers. Looking back, being a young woman on her own with a boatful of people I didn't know, apart from Nigel and Kenneth who I had only known for a few short hours ... it's fairly odd? Maybe, subconsciously, I needed to confirm that what I felt at the weekend *was* real.

It was a grey chilly day, the fishing was slow, and though the one tope we caught turned out to be more the size of a small dolphin than of a man-eating Great White, it didn't matter. The spark was still there. Some fourteen years later I can safely say that whenever I have needed clarity, reprieve, or space to think, the open sea has always provided the best medicine.

This routine continued for some months that summer until one day Nigel said, 'Ash, don't worry about ringing up and booking – just turn up when you like. You're no trouble.' Which, in hindsight, was a very kind thing to do, and the foundation of one of the strongest friendships I've ever been privileged to experience. It was also, to some perhaps, an odd one. In fact, I asked Nigel yesterday, while writing these words, if he'd thought I was a bit weird wanting to go out and fish with him as often as I did.

In true Nigel style, he said 'No.' But he went on to tell me that he could see from the outset just how much I enjoyed it. And what it meant to me. And that was good enough for him, for which I am very grateful. If he hadn't been so welcoming and encouraging I would not be where I am now.

I was soon invited to sit in the wheelhouse with him and Kenneth, who answered all my silly questions and fed my insatiable need to learn. *Where are we going? What's that screen with all the red blips? How do you know where we are? Where did the boat come from? How did Nigel end up doing this for a living?* It clearly didn't put them off, thankfully. It wasn't long before every so often Nige would call on me to help some of the customers with their bungled-up reels (usually caused by not listening to his very clear instructions), to unhook their fish, or give Kenneth a hand gutting them on the way in. Like it or not, they were stuck with me now, and I fished for free.

The pull of the sea, over the following winter, didn't leave me. So when, early the next summer, Nigel asked if I'd like to help him out as Kenneth had got another job, it felt as if I'd died and gone to heaven. Only trouble was that I still had a full-time job, so could only help out on weekends and by using my annual leave.

That summer was the next step on my unofficial apprenticeship but when the next rolled around it was becoming clear that it was time to say a 'long goodbye' to my former life. As much as I desperately wanted to, I could not take any more time off work than I had allowance for, so I asked my manager for three months off over the summer. Audacious, yes, but the answer, predictably, was 'no'. I went back to my desk, in a huff that my dream had been snuffed out, and (seriously, who did I think I was?) started drafting my notice. At that point the conversation changed, plus my job: I was given a new post where I'd only work two days a week in the summer, and resume full-time hours in October.

I was elated. That third summer I was living the proverbial dream – long days at sea in the sun, gutting goodness knows how many thousands of mackerel (earning myself the classy nickname of Gut Girl along the way), untangling birds' nests in reels and wrestling lots more small sharks, while highly impressed punters looked on. I also had a killer tan that was the envy of all my pasty deskbound colleagues. October was going to come hard. But not as hard as November, when Nigel told me that he was planning on selling *Sunbeam 3* and going to work full time on a commercial boat.

I was gutted. It would be hard to have to accept that from now on I would be back in my own swivel-chair-bound reality full time, and that the Jekyll and Hyde existence of the previous three summers was now over. But I was also grateful for the absolute privilege of having been able to peek behind the curtain of this magical world (at least to me) that few people ever got to properly see; as in living it, rather than just observing.

Nigel and I remained friends, and when he started to run a boat, the *Terry William*, for one of the skippers in Wells, I would sometimes go along and watch them haul whelk pots on the hot days, sunning myself from the wheelhouse roof.

Which was nice, but I accepted that chapter of my life had closed. That it was time to 'grow up'. To knuckle down and do 'grown-up' things. So, though I missed it, I was determined to be grown-up about it, accepting every invite and appreciating every moment, seeing it for the occasional thrill I thought it now was.

'Thought' being the operative word.

Chapter 3

'Bananas on a boat are bad luck'

Believed to have originated in the 1700s when bananas were transported from the Caribbean. If a vessel was lost in transit, floating bananas on the surface implied that they were responsible for the sinking.

The screech of a seagull – my annoying text message alert – breaks through the din of the office, much to the aggravation of my surrounding team. I'm currently sitting at my desk, consumed by a spreadsheet, but I slide open the notification from Nige, confident that whatever he has got to tell me will, at the very least, give me a few moments of welcome distraction.

Think I have broken my pelvis, the text reads.

What? I instantly text back. *How? Seriously?*

I am met with an all-encompassing *Yeah*.

Well if you can walk without passing out in pain, I tell him, *it's not broken.*

Quick as a flash: *Can't walk.*

By now, following the sale of the *Terry William*, while I'm still stuck in the nine-to-five slog Nigel has been whelking with his friend, Andy Mac, on his boat, the *Two Brothers*. Mac is arguably one of the most successful fishermen in Wells. At the tender age of twelve he would regularly dip out of lessons to go fishing, which might go some way to explain that. They are still at sea, and it turns out, via a series of several texts, that while he was dragging a stack of fish boxes (some 200kg in weight) with a metal hook, the fish box handle gave way and landed him on his hip. Despite standing up and falling back down twice, and then trying to 'walk it off' (Men! Am I right?), he finally conceded defeat and dragged himself back to the wheelhouse, where he committed himself to the sick bay (i.e. the bench seat) and all fishing operations for the day ceased. They are now steaming back to the harbour, having had to wait for the tide, and once they arrive Nige is to be stretchered off by ambulance to King's Lynn hospital. He tells me he really doesn't want any fuss.

Since needing to call an ambulance obviously constitutes fuss, by the time they arrive back at the harbour there is a welcoming party of about twenty people waiting, including the wind farmers and the harbour staff, as well as the ambulance and coastguard.

Nige's next text, once tucked up for the night on the surgical assessment unit, is to tell me he has broken his hip. He's not happy at having, as he puts it, to 'wear a dress', but is cheered up when I arrive fresh from work and bearing goodies: a crate of full-fat Coke, some fags, and an electronic cigarette (just in case); I know he will be climbing the walls for nicotine.

Less than a week later, plated and pinned, he is out of hospital and back at sea.

~

Despite me no longer working for Nige, we seemed to be in one long conversation, sometimes not talking for a few weeks, but always picking back up exactly where we left off. There were many occasions in the four years that followed the sale of *Sunbeam* where I would duck out early from friends' birthday parties and social gatherings because an invite to sea *always* took precedence, whether it was on the private angling boat Nigel skippered for some friends, or to spend the day being mesmerised on a commercial fishing boat he was on.

By January 2016, Nigel had decided it was time he owned another boat. Except this time it was to be a commercial fishing vessel. To the untrained eye, a boat is a boat – some are big, some are small, some look slick, lightweight and nimble, while others appear heavy, resilient, and domineering. New boats gleam and shine as they gently pull against their mooring ropes, like young racehorses in a stable, while the older boats carry the visual patina of use, and sport war wounds from far-flung unknown battles. It's horses for courses; every boat is designed for the task for which it has been built.

The commercial use of boats comes in many formats: cargo shipping, passenger ferries, pilots, tugs, survey, commercial leisure, and fishing vessels, to name a few. Despite the varied nature of their use they share one common theme: regulation. Different regulations for different uses, but regulation none the less.

Before you can even think about operating commercially, and getting your boat on the all-important fishing vessel register, you must jump through a large number of hoops. A fishing vessel is not the same as other kinds of vessels. It is bound by a very long, complicated (and sometimes contradictory) set of rules, all of which must be complied with if it is to be able to sell what it catches.

Good luck finding a *My First Fishing Boat for Dummies* (or, for those of a certain age, a Haynes manual), however. The best/only practical guidance out there in your quest to owning a fishing boat is best gleaned from those who have seen the rules and processes evolve over time. And it takes time, lots of it, to learn it. It's a journey of discovery that has taken me over a decade, and while I share it with you now, I'm still learning. I suspect I always will be.

Having been and enquired about a few other contenders, Nige had found a boat he really liked the look of. The only trouble was that it was up in Whitby, and he had no confidence in the reliability of his (traumatised, after a life of borderline abuse) vehicle, aptly known as his 'fucked truck'. I therefore got a call from him asking me to bunk off work to drive him and his sons up there to look at it.

Waiting at the Hardwick industrial estate in King's Lynn for their chauffeur to put on a sickly voice and call her boss (sorry Laurence, if you're reading this) stand Nige and his two sons. Unmistakably his, they too both sport the blonde hair and blue eyes of their father. By now both Kenneth and Jack have been working as commercial fishermen both in Wells and further afield: Fishguard, Portsmouth, Padstow and Scotland, to mention a few places. However, with the prospect of Nigel buying a fishing boat for them all, naturally they have found their way back to Wells.

36

I have known Kenneth since my first trip. Jack, however, four years younger than his brother, I didn't meet until he was fourteen and came to stay with his dad during my summer sabbatical at sea. I remember collecting him from King's Lynn one afternoon; a very skinny shy boy in a tracksuit, with what can only be described as a skinhead/mullet/rat tail, very gingerly sat himself down in my car. (I wish he had stayed that shy and quiet, frankly . . .) Jack is cheeky, but you can't help but love the lad. Fatigue, however, transforms him into an epic diva, and believe me when I say this boy can, and will, sleep anywhere.

Kenneth is altogether different, very similar to his father, quick-witted, logical and fiery, but with a much longer fuse than the youngest of the trio. Both of them are capable of cutting you to the bone, fast, but as soon as it's done, it's over and forgotten.

Fuelled with coffee and excitement at the prospect of boat shopping we hit the road, bound for Whitby. After a couple of hours' driving, and having been traumatised by the banter of the two twenty-somethings in the back, we make a pit stop at Bridlington harbour, not only for a harbourside fry-up but, as most fishermen like to do, to take a nosey at what's doing in other harbours.

Arriving in Whitby an hour later we have some time to kill so we find a home away from home in the Fleece, a pub with a terrace that overlooks the tidal inlet of Whitby harbour. From here I can make out a plucky-looking red boat on the opposite side of the river. Built of oak and larch in the early eighties in this very town, she is a traditional clinker hull and measures in at 9.9 meters long. At that time I didn't fully appreciate the significance of the length and why she was 10cm shy of being 10 metres long. However, everything in the fishing industry is done for a reason, and after reading this book you too will understand why that 10cm shortfall is so relevant, and why it represents decades of bureaucracy.

~

'What does the name mean?' Jack whispers to me as we stand in front of their prospective new boat. The name *Never Can Tell-A* is painted across both her wheelhouse roof and her arse, and, like her glossy new paint job, gives the impression that she has been well loved. 'I don't know,' I tell him, and make a mental note to see if I can find out. Though unless you can find the original owner or builder, it must obviously fall to perception.

Nigel, meanwhile, is busy making his way down a ladder on to her with Kenneth and the current owner. While Jack and I stand in the biting cold up on the quayside, they go through the finer details of her fixtures and fittings, her engine, her hauler, her electronics and licence – both seller and buyer, I notice, playing their cards close to their chests. It's not until we are back in the car that everybody springs into animated conversation, weighing up the pros and cons. Lovely big flush deck, but no shooting door, meaning the pots would have to be shot away over the side somehow. Not the safest way to undertake the most dangerous job on the boat. The electronics, GPS plotter, radar, autopilot and echo sounder are only a year old, but the hauler isn't suitable, so that will need to be changed. She is being sold with her pots, which Nigel doesn't need. There is also a budget to consider.

Having been looking for a boat for a while now, Nigel chews over putting in an offer. She is, after all, the best he has found within budget and is a better boat than the others he has seen. After weeks of back and forth-ing with the seller, Nigel's offer is accepted and some six weeks or so later, it's time to bring her to her new home in Wells, a task Nige entrusts to Kenneth and Jack. The journey of around 102 nautical miles should take somewhere around fourteen hours at a steady 7 knots. All that's needed is another drive up to Whitby the day before, to exchange funds and sign over paperwork, a trip I don't offer to get involved in. I am still aghast that I have phoned in sick once already – it's something I would never, ever do, and can only put down to a temporary, ocean-based mania.

The deal done, the plan is for Nige to drive back to Wells and for the boys to set off on *Never Can Tell-A* in the morning, hopefully timing it right to arrive at Wells with the tide. But not before a night on the town in Scarborough, obviously, celebrating their new charge (the night life was better in Scarborough, apparently). The evening's escapades are still a blur to this day (at least to me, as enquiries have been met by a brisk 'I can't remember' from all three of them); however, Jack still carries a (hopefully not permanent) reminder. It takes the form of a missing front tooth, allegedly knocked out by his brother.

The trip down passes without incident, despite Jack being in agony and Kenneth in the doghouse as well as the wheelhouse, and the following weekend I make my way to Wells to get properly acquainted. Jack's question about the name *Never Can Tell -A* is still niggling at me. I don't find out the answer but have since decided the 'A' in *Never Can Tell-A* is probably slang for 'her', which seems appropriate; because with this boat you never could. She really did as she pleased. Stubborn to the core, she was better than her master, and she was sure to remind you of this regularly. She met her match with Nige though, because he is equally stubborn and refuses to be beaten.

~

For the next two years, *Never Can Tell-A* played only a peripheral part in my life as I would catch up with Nige only once a month or so, and often just for a natter and a drink. I felt I got to know her, however, as there was barely a meet-up when he wasn't regaling me with the latest nautical nightmare. On one occasion this included the saga of a replacement engine.

I have since learnt that replacing an engine is not actually as frightening as it sounds, providing of course that the engine is an identical (emphasis on identical) swap and that you have the assistance of some heavy lifting equipment. Unfortunately for Nige, despite buying a replacement Ford (from Wales) of the same model, he found the sump was a completely different shape and depth, meaning that upon offering it up into the bilge the engine and its feet would not sit on its engine beds in the boat and protruded far too high to close the engine hatch. What to do? He got it lifted back out and attempted to use the sump from the old engine. Sadly this did not fit. £1,600 later a new sump was fitted but this too needed to be adapted by a local metal worker.

I wish I could say this was where the drama ended, but upon running it up, the oil pressure was terrible. So that engine was hoisted back out. Luckily Nigel found another Ford and, after marinising it himself (having robbed the necessary parts from his other engines before they went to the scrap heap) it was finally lowered in. But his joy and relief that the engine now sat in its proper position were short lived. It had a water leak, which also blew the head gasket.

For the most part Nige can fix most things, often with little more than a piece of twine and determination. But this was a job he had never undertaken and 'head gasket' always sounds terminal to most people. Luckily, Wells is blessed by many mechanically capable fishermen, most of whom will offer their advice and assistance (normally manifesting itself in the form of a question atop the quayside – 'Problems?' – while you're contorted in a bilge with a plethora of rusty tools scattered around the deck). One of our most cherished mechanical gurus is Carl, and it was he that time who came to Nige's rescue. Before he was a fisherman, Carl was a mechanic and there isn't much he can't fix or adapt, to get you out of a jam. Carl has a golden heart and a big soft spot for animals. And because he *always* has a dog biscuit in his pocket for his canine quayside visitors, he is on first-name terms with almost every dog in the town. (Nige and myself would be nowhere if it was not for the skill, knowledge and kindness of this man, for which we are eternally thankful.)

Despite her unpredictability and appetite for engines, gearboxes, starter motors, alternators and batteries (believe me, the list of mechanical mayhem could fill its own book) you couldn't not love this quirky little wooden boat. She was arrogant,

41

bordering on cocky, but she had good reason to be. She was an amazing sea boat, so forgiving, and she knew what to do better than you did. Okay, she wasn't fibreglass and modern like the rest of the fleet at Wells, but her seakeeping qualities were superb.

In 2018 Nige and I met up for one of our weekend catch-ups over a cooked breakfast. I was no longer working for the original plumbing and heating firm but had a similar job in the private plumbing sector. I was feeling completely unenthused about my career and how I felt I just lived the same routine day after day, month after month: wake, work, eat, bath, sleep, repeat. The lack of lustre in me was clearly showing.

'What do you need to live a week, Ash?' Nige asked casually.

Truthfully I didn't know. I was financially comfortable so it was hard to pluck a figure out.

'Er . . . not sure, why?' I said, puzzled.

'Well, can you work it out? Reckon I got a job for you.'

I laughed. What on earth did he think I could offer? Despite my passion for the life I immediately told him what I believed to be true: that much as I'd love to spend my time back at sea, I could not *be* a commercial fisherman.

I meant it. I thought being a woman, and having no experience of commercial fishing, meant I would not be physically capable or skilled enough to do it, and that I'd potentially endanger others on board.

I said so to Nigel.

'Look, I got jobs ashore I could use a hand with,' he countered. 'Mending pots, sorting bait, paperwork, and on the nice days you can come out and jig up some mackerel to sell.'

Now that was a whole other kettle of fish. I had a choice to make. Though my heart had already written my resignation, my head haunted me with the practicalities. Despite a weekly wage being agreed, I already knew fishing was highly unpredictable. Could I afford to take the risk? I had a good job, a steady salary, a pension, paid annual leave ... I would lose all of that. I would also be taking a huge pay cut, but I felt no trepidation. Life is too short to be miserable in what you do. If it didn't work out, I could always find another nine-to-five existence elsewhere.

My notice went in the following morning. My manager was shocked, but knowing that she could not compete with my life's passion, she accepted my resignation. What an overwhelming leap of faith I had taken.

My team were stunned and full of questions. This was, after all, a career U-turn. I had always known a steady income, I started and finished at the same time every day, and the weekends were mine to enjoy. All of that was going to change, but I was heartily sick of office life. The same routine, the same stresses, the same office politics and the same argument about who had left their stinking three-day-old tuna salad in the shared fridge.

Yup. I gave it all up for a life around whelks.

Chapter 4

'Do not say the word pig at sea'

A man sitting by the Sea of Galilee, consumed by evil, begged Jesus to take the evil from him and give it to the herd of swine that sat atop the cliff above. Upon doing this the herd became crazed and threw themselves into the sea to drown.

That first night in February 2019 – that dark, and very stormy, and utterly exhilarating night when I really fished for the first time – came about because of a mechanical fault. Though it's odds on that it would have happened sooner or later anyway. Increasingly, as I mended pots, filed paperwork, and sorted shickle, the call of the sea was becoming louder, much like the muted eerie roar of the waves that hammer the beach after a northerly blow. It's a sound that can only be heard in the dead of night, when the town is quiet and lifeless. Local legend has it – or so Mac told me – that it's the lost souls of mariners calling out in purgatory. But that engineering setback, and accompanying hole in our profits, was both a baptism of fire, and also my fast pass to the job which is now so indelibly written on my heart.

So let me take you back to January, which is always a difficult month anyway. Christmas is put back into the loft for another year, and having to dust off the motivation you left on the quayside in December is always going to be difficult. But we were all back in the working routine, pretty much, and looking forward to the whelk season ahead.

Which was reasonable enough, but boats obviously don't get such memos, or perhaps they get other ones, ones saying 'high priority: scupper plans!' (pardon the pun). I was busy sorting ropes out on the quayside when Nigel called me. He was away for the day, visiting his mum. Back in Wells, meanwhile, the rope I was sorting had been there since before Christmas, the untangling of half a mile or so of damp, gritty tows being one of those jobs you tend to put off. Tangled rope is, unfortunately, an occupational hazard, usually because a tripped anchor has taken your gear for a walk and left it to Poseidon to shuffle about as he sees fit.

I'd been at it for a couple of hours when Nigel called, and, having just encountered an unwelcome gift from a passing dog (thanks for that, considerate owner. Thank goodness for gloves), was happy for the chance to take a break. It was bad news, however. He got straight to the point, telling me that Jack and Kenneth, who were out fishing that day, had called him to say that *Never Can Tell-A*'s gearbox was toast. 'So, what's it like down the end?' he finished, casual as ever, even though I knew not being there to direct operations was killing him.

He meant the end of the harbour, so I took a look and could see there was white water there, following a nor-easterly blow. This meant the harbour entrance was likely to be scruffy too, so, to be his eyes, I drove down to the beach so I could keep a look out from the coast watch station, which is higher up than the beach and gives a view of Holkham Bay and the harbour entrance.

By now I also knew *Never Can Tell-A* was being towed in by another boat. A rule of thumb among fisherman is that you call one another for help before anyone else. You don't call out the coastguard if you can possibly help it. This is a matter of pride in the industry (the lifeboat is *always* the last resort; we are professionals) but recently, following rule changes that have blindsided many, it's also because it's been used as a tool to target boats for safety inspections, which, though necessary, are becoming increasingly illogical and conflicted, not to mention being emotionally and financially draining (more of which later). So it's a case of fellow fishermen always helping each other out; if someone needs your help, you help them, whoever they are – even if it means setting aside personal feelings. Everyone appreciates that we work in a dangerous environment and petty grievances are nothing compared to the wellbeing of our community. I think that makes us professionals too.

For those who don't know, towing a boat is not at all like towing a car, because with a car, if you need to, you can apply the brakes. The sea gets involved too, in a way a road cannot, continually snatching at, then slackening the tow rope. So what you often do, to mitigate for these multiple opposing forces, is insert a car tyre into the middle of the tow rope, to act as a buffer and take up some of the tension.

If you've ever seen a boat using a tyre as a fender (which they're great for ... and also free of course) it's because these elemental forces can really pack a punch. The Bible story of Samson and Delilah centres around Samson's great strength, so it's not surprising that the upright posts that are used for mooring and towing are named after this powerful being; second only to the keel, the samson post is one of the strongest parts of a wooden boat. It will give you some idea of how crucial those tyres are if I tell you that just from those forces, I have seen a samson post snapped clean off.

Having reassured Nige by text, as he'd asked, that they had indeed 'got a tyre in', I was able to follow the boat's progress all the way into the harbour, and report that she was safely over the bar. Once there, with the big waves and other sea dangers behind her, she was able to be hipped up and, for the last bit, towed alongside her rescuer, before being safely lashed to a pontoon in the harbour, where we could make our repairs at any state of tide.

Now, with *Never Can Tell-A* safely tied up in the harbour, both Nigel and I were hard at work on our respective mobiles, urgently trying to source a replacement gearbox, since the boys had already told us the existing one was unrepairable, and our own inspection (well, Nigel's) had confirmed that.

There is never a good time for something to go wrong on a boat, but this was a particularly bad time to be tied up. All produce is seasonal, and whelks are no exception. Though we fish them year round, there are always peaks and troughs, and January, blessed with its frigid sea temperatures, is one of the better times to be targeting them, since cold water gives them a bit of a free rein; with no crabs around they're out of the ground.

So finding a new gearbox *was* urgent. Luckily, we sourced one from a local boat supplies retailer (the last one they had in stock), who confirmed it would be in the next day.

Changing a gearbox is a job that most fisherman will do themselves. It's true that a few will pay others to deal with their repairs, some because they are in a position to afford that luxury, others because they don't know how to do it themselves. I'd love to be able to pay someone to do it – who wouldn't? – but if your boat breaks down offshore, you need to understand how things work if you're going to have the best chance of fixing them, or at least cobbling something together to get you home out of the bits and bobs box, a familiar ally on *every* boat.

At this point in my life, however, it's probably fair to say that I knew as much about boat mechanics as I did about quantum physics – which is to say, not a lot. And that's no exaggeration. Despite being a tomboy growing up, as evidenced by my constantly cut knees and general enthusiasm for getting dirty, I still had no interactions with engineering, engines, or any other mechanical gizmos . . . though this might have been partly because I was a very clumsy child, so my mum sensibly kept me away from tools. As a teenage girl, I also imagine I was not unusual in following peer pressure to care more than I should have about how I looked.

It all fascinates me now, of course, partly because I've realised just how thrilling it is to find out how things work – if there is a night school running anywhere for people with an interest in old six-cylinder diesel engines, sign me up right now – and partly because I understand it all better, having learned so much from Nigel, and from the wisdom and experience of other fishermen. Though that's only been achieved by breakdowns such as this one, from patience, watching, asking, handing over spanners, and, perhaps the greatest lesson of all, living by Nige's ethos of refusing to be beaten. And that's no motivational quote to be stuck up on a bedroom wall; you cannot *afford* to be beaten because if the prop isn't turning you're not earning. The boat is your tool. There's is no other means of creating income. You will never fully appreciate the significance of a cold lifeless engine until it stands between you and your next pay packet.

It being January, the need for income was even more pressing than usual and with the boys having unaccountably made themselves scarce, I was the only helper available. Still, Nige knew he could rely on me to turn up and try my best, and the good thing was that changing a gearbox isn't that mechanically complicated. What makes it difficult is that space on a small fishing boat is always at a premium, and gearboxes are bloody heavy! Working below deck and supporting both yourself and the weight of a gearbox in a confined slippery bilge is painful, dirty, tiresome and a job for two people at the least. And even if one of them wasn't exactly bristling with expertise, I was at least hungry to learn.

The following day, one of my first shore duties was to pick up the shiny new red gearbox and make my way over to Wells so we could change it. So, dear reader, if you ever find yourself needing to change a PRM gearbox on a six-cylinder Ford, the process, roughly speaking, is as follows . . .

First up, smoke a cigarette to prepare yourself for the task ahead. Second up, the shaft that runs from the back of the gearbox through the hull to the propeller has to be disconnected. This shaft is connected to the gearbox via a coupling that absorbs the vibration and impact of the gearbox, and is connected by twelve bolts which, in our set-up, are crippling to undo due to the compact nature of the bilge in *Never Can Tell-A*. However, once the twelve bolts are out and the shaft is forced back away from the gearbox, it can be unbolted from the engine via the bell housing, and its spline pulled back from the fly wheel, essentially freeing it, ready to be lifted up and out.

I have breezed over the process in a couple of sentences but in reality this was hours of swearing, cramp and struggle – and all this *before* we had even lifted the old gearbox out, which, for purposes of accurate visualisation, weighs the same as a giant panda (yes I did google it).

It doesn't need to be lifted far. Only just over a metre up to the deck. However, I have yet to meet anybody who can deadlift a gearbox while standing in a slippery bilge at an awkward angle. It is also vital that it is not dropped, the fear being that a drop from height would end up putting a hole straight through the bottom of your pride and joy and primary source of income. So Nigel and I did what Nigel and I so often do, and engineered something to make the job as easy as possible. With no winch or pulley, we had to improvise our own, using a stack of fish boxes either side of the open engine hatch, with a scaffold bar spanning the gap, and a rope on the gearbox.

We made necessarily slow process. Starting as low as we could, we began raising the scaffold bar, fish box by fish box, at all times keeping the giant panda steady. Eventually, once the two towers were high enough, it was suspended at deck level, where between us, taking the strain on either end of the bar, we could wrestle the gearbox onto the deck.

The more than averagely attentive reader will probably realise at this point that there is another giant panda involved in this process. This one needs to be manhandled from a truck, deposited into a fish box, then dragged, via a rope that's attached to the fish box, downhill (thank God) to the boat. The manhandling then continues, to get the gearbox on board, then the whole scaffold pole and fish-box tower process must be done in reverse.

Fast forward three days, and we were £2,500 worse off, but at last had a shiny new gearbox in the boat, so we took her out for a test run in the harbour.

This did not go quite as planned. It wasn't long before we worked out that something wasn't right; the boat was running but the speed was all wrong. It was at that moment that Nige realised he had made a mistake, and an expensive one, too. In truth, though, it wasn't totally Nige's fault. Gearboxes normally have an identification plate on them, and *Never Can Tell-A*'s, which pre-dated his ownership of her, did not. So he was forced to take a fifty-fifty guess.

When you buy a gearbox you must choose the ratio you need, and Nigel was pretty sure that he needed a 2.5:1 ratio; in layman's terms, that means that for every two and a half turns of the engine the gearbox will spin once. What he *actually* needed, it turned out, was a 2:1 ratio. With a 2.5:1 ratio it would take us an eternity to get anywhere. It was now we realised that, despite us having run the gearbox for less than fifteen minutes, it could not, even for a lower price, be returned. Worse than that, the 2:1 ratio gearbox we needed was out of stock, and had no expected arrival date.

The only option now left to us was to buy a used gearbox for five hundred quid, which was being advertised in the outer reaches of Scotland. With a 1.5:1 ratio, it still wasn't what we needed, but would at least work better than the one we currently had, as it would provide more torque, meaning we wouldn't have to run the engine as hard.

After over a fortnight of waiting, and a logistical nightmare (the transport company, at one point, even lost it for ten days), we finally had a replacement, and could look forward to dragging ourselves through the torment of changing the gearboxes again.

It was far from ideal to put a used, unknown piece of mechanical equipment into Nige's precious boat, but what other choice was there? With little more than tumbleweed rolling around in our respective bank accounts, there was no weather forecast too grim, and no time too unsociable. If there was fishing to be had, then we had to grab our piece of it.

And so it was thanks to that broken gearbox that I was presented with an opportunity to cast off the shickle shackles that had for so long left me bound to the shore.

Chapter 5

'Never take flowers on a boat'

Flowers were believed to be an omen of death, likewise seeing
a vicar or priest before leaving the harbour.

Having a working boat again is great, but now we need to continue
to make up for lost time, while the whelks are still hungry for the
bait in our pots. But for that we need crew. Kenneth and Jack have
never been the most reliable or consistent in that regard and have
been known to take long spells of absence. They're right when
they say never work with family.

It's been three years now since Nige bought *Never Can Tell-A*,
and though he's had his ups and downs, business has been
reasonably stable. It's also been seven months since I gave up my
office job and, to my relief (though I'm that stubborn, I was going
to make a success of it whatever), I have yet to be hauled off to
debtor's prison. In fact I am not missing the comforts of a decent
income nearly as much as I thought I would. (I'm not even really

missing having a regular 'payday' – in this new industry of mine, 'payday' has become a moveable feast. You can't pay someone if the weather or a breakdown means you haven't earned.) Turns out the real value in life comes from being happy. Who knew?

It's during the evening immediately after that dark, stormy, and oh-so exhilarating night that an unexpected text comes in from Nige.

Think I'm gearing myself for a period of you and me while the lads sort themselves out, it reads.

Well you know I'll turn out, I reply. Much as I don't want to try and take Kenneth and Jack's place, I'm feeling excited at the prospect of potentially becoming essential rather than just an occasional stand-in. So I send another text. *Reckon you'd let me stack pots if that does happen?*

Probably gonna have to 😂 comes the answer, quick as a whip.

So Nige might be crying laughing at the prospect, but I do have to, because both his sons are currently AWOL, or to use the terminology of my former career: on a 'period of unauthorised absence'. And though I know Nigel's derision is only in jest, he and I both know I do still have a lot to learn. Given this new situation, I will have to learn fast.

There is a rigid order to stacking pots due to the nature of the pound and ramp, a system which enables the safest possible way of shooting away when a boat lacks a shooting door. Shooting doors are very common on newer potting boats, or boats that have been refitted, and take the form of a hole cut out of the transom. This is one of the safest ways of discharging pots back to their watery home.

As you might remember, *Never Can Tell-A* has no such modern refinement, so Nige contracted the fabrication of a metal pound and ramp, to his own specification. This means the pots can be stacked within it, and then be pulled safely over the stern with very little human input. In fact, the only thing he needs to do is throw the can over to start the process, and, just before the last pot is about to go, put the second anchor on the ramp at the end.

Never Can Tell-A's pound and ramp is composed of two sections. The pound, a big metal tray with foot-high walls, sits square in the middle of the deck, and is bolted to a ramp which sits at a 45-degree angle, its end supported by the gunwale (pronounced 'gunnel') on the stern. The beauty of this system is that in poor weather the pots stay put.

An aside here: however practical, the system is not infallible, as I have subsequently witnessed myself. Ropes can, and do, still get jammed where they shouldn't, in this case on a section of the pound that was probably overdue for a spot of remedial welding, and had a very small section of jagged edge. Needless to say, the rope was successful in finding that tiny area of jagged metal on its way over the stern of the boat. This caused the whole pound section to lift up on end and promptly fly straight over the stern after the final anchor. Nigel's anger was so intense it was practically emanating from his very pores, and I feared even breathing too loudly. Though we never expected to see it again, when the lads were out fishing the very next day, incredibly, there it was, still jammed up with the dhan tow, hanging in the tide like a discarded barn door. (Proving that despite appearances to the contrary and a theme that will run through this entire book, sometimes we *are* blessed with good luck.)

I have since learned that without a pound (which is how we fish now we have a boat with a shooting door), stacking pots on an open deck in heavy weather requires great creativity to ensure that they don't fall over if the boat takes a roll. If they do, it can result in me being absolutely berated, as, more often than not, it causes gear to go away foul, which is dangerous. An analogy which might help describe exactly why is to imagine an orderly queue stretching halfway down the street (not hard, I don't think, as we Brits do love queuing). It's at a toy shop and it's the last shopping day before Christmas; a shop assistant comes out and says there are only six Furbies, or Tamagotchis, or Teletubby dolls left (insert madly hyped toy of your choice here). The kind of chaos that would then ensue, and the huge bottleneck that would result, is exactly what happens if you don't stack your pots in order.

Yet it's worse. Not only does the rogue pot take a load of other pots with it, it also takes all the ropes that go with them. This results in a complete clusterfuck of rope and pots hanging from the hauler the next time you try to work them. All of which constitutes precious time lost and could prevent you from getting round all your gear.

Having watched Nige and the lads stack pots on many, many occasions (particularly during the previous summer when I'd often be called upon to help do the riddling), in theory I know exactly what I'm doing. And once we're actually at sea, the day after having this conversation, I get this great sense of pride in finally feeling I'm contributing – or, as I tend to say, I feel proper.

It's an unexpectedly bright, sunny day, and though we all know it's generally warmer at sea, it feels particularly balmy for February. The sea too is cooperating, being only peppered with wavelets, making my job as the rookie that much easier. It's the perfect sandbox, in fact, for me to learn in.

As we start hauling, I become aware that Nigel's treating me ever so slightly differently; a lot differently, in fact. Where the hauler usually spins so fast that the bolts are a blur, it's spinning so slowly today that I can actually count them. I wouldn't dream of saying anything (not then, anyway – I do now) but it makes me all the more anxious to prove to him pronto that I *can* do this, that I'm not made of glass.

Even so, I'd be a fool if I wasn't nervous. As the first of the pots are unceremoniously flipped over to my 'department', I am pleased and surprised at my own strength and capability; they seem lighter and less cumbersome to handle than I imagined. Are they, or have I developed more muscles grunting bait about than I thought? Whatever their weight, though, it's that orderly queue that's at the forefront of my mind. *Don't fuck up, Ash, don't fuck up, Ash, don't fuck up, Ash* is now the mantra spooling through my brain.

Those nerves are also why I'm constantly mithering at Nige. And always, with every pot, the same question: 'That pot there's right? Isn't it?'

'Yeah, yeah,' comes the answer, and yet again, every time, until it gets to the point where I realise he's saying 'Yeah' but isn't even looking round to check.

At first, realising he's doing this makes me twitchy. If he can't see what I'm doing, how will he know if I do it wrong? But by the time we've hauled the three hundred-odd pots in the six strings we're doing today, I realise it means that he trusts me. And knowing Nigel trusts me is like giving me permission to trust myself. It's a really good feeling. As we head back to Wells, to unload and head to the Fleece for a routine beer, I get this powerful sense that Nigel's genuinely proud of me. (Although he'd never say as much, obviously.) And that he's not surprised by how well I've done, which speaks to me even more.

~

In the weeks that follow that first day when I felt I could genuinely call myself a commercial fisherman, I begin learning at a rate of, ahem, knots. Yes, I've learned how to quickly and efficiently put dogfish and crab in a pot, but there is obviously *so* much more to fishing for a living than this alone. And the very next thing I learn will sound equally obvious, since it's that everything is done for a reason. And the reason at the heart of that truism is a very logical one: energy.

Fishing is a very physical occupation and working with tides means days are invariably long, as they are always dictated by the moon. So I quickly learn that brute strength, though helpful, is not the be-all and end-all. What you need is stamina, and plenty of it. On a boat out at sea, even if that sea is as flat as a witch's tit, you use energy just standing still. (Funnily enough, in this respect, rough weather can be your friend, since you can often use the boat's rolling motion to your advantage.) Though rarely are you ever standing still. On one day, for instance, I realise I have clocked up 7 miles just walking around on deck, on the endless rat run back and forth, putting pots in their place. With the working day sometimes running to fifteen or sixteen hours (and sometimes in blistering heat, with no shade), expending unnecessary energy is just plain dumb. And I probably am dumb, at least at first, because it takes a while for me to realise that when Nige pulls me up for the way I do things, it's precisely because I am wasting the precious energy that I'm still going to need to call on hours later – and not just at sea. Even when we are back in Wells harbour, there is plenty more work to be done to unload the day's catch, not to mention loading the bait on to the boat for the next day.

An aside here: two thirds of the time unloading the catch involves the use of a crane, fixed to the lorry owned by our buyer, Lynn Shellfish, and which lifts four boxes of whelks onto it at a time for us. However, at busy times, when they have no such luxury available, it's a two-person job that needs doing by hand, with Nige and I transferring the boxes – which, by the way, each weigh over *50 kilos* – one by one, up 6 feet of quay wall. These then *still* need transferring onto the back of a tail-lift (more affectionately known as a snail-lift), due to the fact – 😵 😞 🧎 – that they had no choice but to send a tail-lift, since they were out of all the lorries with the cranes.

Working at the quayside, which is obviously a regular aspect of the job is, for me at least, also a pretty sociable affair. The harbour really comes to life when the boats start coming in after a day at sea, and form a natural focal point for people who are out and about; holed up in an office with just your colleagues, this definitely isn't. I already know that, of course, having cut my teeth doing the bulk of the ashore duties, and with Wells being a tourist destination rather than just a fishing port, us fishermen, and what we do for a living, are also tourist attractions; something to look at for holidaymakers who are crabbing off the quay wall, or ambling around eating those ubiquitous fish and chips.

The fish we all eat comes via fishermen. And just like the fish and chips, fishermen are considered iconic, and it's sometimes at the expense of the fishermen themselves. They – no, *we* – are often used in the mass media to represent all that's wholesome and hardworking. In advertising, and beyond that, the fisherman becomes both a concept and a stereotype. They are portrayed as working class, salt of the earth, materially un-aspirational (you never see a fisherman used to advertise a Porsche, even though there are a fair few that can and do own luxury cars). On the other side, there *are* a good few who are struggling, but at the same time there is every shade in between. And without wanting to bang my chest too much, that *really* annoys me, because it's both wrong, and repressive.

It will be no surprise then that, if tourists do engage me in chat, I am always keen to correct misconceptions and offer a whistle-stop tour around our corner of the fishing industry, and that's whether they've expressed interest in having one or not.

I'm also female, of course, which makes me even more of a curiosity, and gives me a greater platform than most, and one that's not always related to the 'grubby blonde girl, big tits and denim shorts' vibe. My friend Jo and I have often joked that I just have one of those approachable demeanours. I always have had, and it long pre-dates my career. I just seem to have something in my face or my expression that makes me a target, particularly whenever some tour guide or other is in need of a volunteer (read 'victim') for audience participation. (My appearance in the dock for piracy in the London Dungeon circa 2015 is still talked about in certain circles.)

Maybe it's also for this reason that I am regularly lynched by tourists and passers-by on the quay (sometimes to Nigel's annoyance, as it slows down the loading or unloading process, and the pub is invariably calling). The questions tourists ask me have by now become so predictable that I have debated getting a T-shirt printed. Or maybe several. All saying 'Yes, they're whelks', 'They will mostly end up in Korea', and 'Would I ask you how much money YOU earn?'

I also regularly get asked where exactly we fish, from tourists who want to delve deeper. Is it 2 miles or 30? Do we all have our own patch? The simple answer is no, but nothing in fishing is simple, particularly when it comes to regulations. There are areas of the sea that are off limits to certain gear types: there's no beam trawling allowed, for example, in certain marine conservation zones (MCZs), and all fishing is prohibited in areas closed for wind farm development (more of which later ...). The rest of the sea, however, is free for anyone to fish, for any kind of seafood, at least in principle. In practice, because our waters are so heavily potted, few trawlers would entertain it – there wouldn't be any sense. They would likely tow straight through some of the fifty thousand pots on the seabed at any time, and the resulting mess and danger would be off-the-scale chaotic. (There is a beam trawler fleet that catches brown shrimp off the Norfolk coast, but that's been going on so long now that both potters and trawlers know to keep out of one another's way.)

This just leaves the competition between pot fishermen. You can set a pot pretty much anywhere you like, and we all have certain grounds we work at certain times of year. But fishing, by its very nature, is highly competitive, so if you're doing well, word soon gets around, and where you'd previously had the spot to yourself, you might one day find another can bobbing on the surface, and know you have acquired company. When this happens, good sense dictates that you try to work with them and, in practice, some you can and some you can't. Most of the time, a long-evolved system of non-verbal communication suffices to keep everyone friendly, but occasionally, tempers fray, and so, sometimes, do ropes, as interlopers have it made clear that they are getting too close.

Methods of this escalation are both inventive and varied. To stitch up someone who has shot their string over our gear, a favourite of mine when whelking is to tie a knot behind the button in the drawstring of one of their pots, so that when they haul it next they will have to spend ten minutes unpicking it before they can slacken the mesh to empty the pot. (No small thing when out at sea with freezing hands.) It's customary to leave a can of beer or a packet of sweets as a reward, but not before having first taken their rent, as in emptying the pot of catch. A scaffold pole threaded through a rival's dhan tow can also cause major inconvenience, as it means them having to cut their rope, which, in turn, means allowing the string of pots that were attached to it to sink back to the sea floor, and them then having the hassle of grappling them back up, as the end marker can and its rope to the anchor now lie on the deck separate to the pots. (We will have a grappling lesson later.)

Such mischievous tactics tend to keep everything friendly, and everyone is aware that there is a red line that's very rarely crossed. If you cut someone else's gear, or have some of your own cut, it's considered serious enough that it's time to find somewhere else to fish, even if you were there first. Nobody wants to lose gear.

(It's probably worth noting that what we have to deal with in Norfolk is nothing compared with tales I've heard from other ports, up to and including boats being sunk by having holes drilled in their hulls overnight, and one fisherman's own car being attached by a chain to the stern of his boat. It wasn't till he'd steamed out to deep enough waters that he felt the weight of whatever, inexplicably, they seemed to be towing. That must be some prime fishing ground!)

The one question I'm *really* glad to hear, and do hear, if only rarely, is 'How are things with the fishing industry after Brexit?' It's perhaps worth noting here that where the Brexit campaigns led, the British media quickly followed, tapping into that stereotype I mentioned earlier on, homing in on the fishing industry, and making fishermen the poster boys of Brexit, despite fishing contributing only a tiny percentage to our GDP. Sadly, however, it's way too big a question to answer on the quayside, unless the person asking has a full understanding of the industry and the upheavals (or, more accurately, botched facelifts) of the last fifty years. If there's one reason I'm writing this book that sits above all others it's that, hopefully, in doing so, I can offer those insights. And piecemeal, in much the same way as I've had to learn it, so it doesn't feel too much like homework.

Well, hopefully . . .

Chapter 6

*'Never set sail on the first Monday in April,
as this is the day that Cain slew Abel'*

There has been a port at Wells-next-the-Sea for over six hundred years. And although it's been a fishing port throughout, its main commercial purposes have changed. For long stretches of its history, as well as ship building (the remnants of the shipbuilding timbers can still be seen at low water), its main commercial use was in the transport of malt and grain, hence that granary on the front I mentioned earlier. The fishing fleet that today dominates the main quay has only been the focal point since the 1980s. The fishermen had, of course, always been here. But with the decline of the big cargo ships coming into the town, they had an opportunity to expand and claim that space.

Considered by many to be the unpolished gem of North Norfolk, Wells is a very pretty place, hence the many tourists who flock to it annually. The lie of the land means the harbour forms a rough L shape, with the quay being the horizontal and the vertical part being the long passage out to the beach and open water. In the middle of all this sits the salt marsh, with its many labyrinthine creeks, and which is covered with sea lavender and samphire.

There are all kinds of pots on the quay (or, in modern parlance, 'Instagram content'), and plenty of tourists to be found standing by them, scratching their heads, as they try to work out which is which. Multi-coloured fish box towers also abound, like giant outdoor Lego has been strewn about by an equally giant child, amid randomly placed bundles of rope and rusty anchors, fishermen being famous for not throwing *anything* away, not if it might come in handy at some point. There is only a four-hour window of access to open water from Wells-next-the-Sea (six if you are in the outer harbour). As the ebbing tide loses its westerly-bound energy at the end of its six-hour cycle, the sand bar that guards the harbour entrance begins to submerge and the direction of flow in the water changes. With the start of the flood, it now takes an easterly course and as the tide finds its way through the channels that run alongside the beach, Wells harbour begins to fill with water.

The flooding tide will continue to push the level of water up for two more hours until high water. At this point, with the flood continuing to run urgently at the harbour entrance, it will pull the water back out again on its way ever eastward. For the next two hours, the harbour begins to drain, as fast as if somebody has pulled out a plug. It is somewhere in this four-hour window, that occurs twice every twenty-four hours, that we and all the other fishing boats – about a dozen in all – must make our departure.

Perhaps I should take this opportunity to draw you a mental map. And let's start, ahem, with the buoys. In Wells, the buoy that marks the area that always stays wet, and therefore demarcates the beginning of the route into the harbour, is called a West Cardinal buoy. (Or, as we call it locally, the Fairway buoy, named after the previous big red and white one it replaced years back, which now sits on the roundabout by the beach car park, slightly dented after being run into by a fishing boat . . .) A Cardinal buoy is a navigational marker, and a West Cardinal buoy's message is 'keep west of me'. Similarly, a North Cardinal buoy says 'keep north of me', a South one says 'keep south of me' and so on.

Understanding navigational markers could fill up a chapter on its own, being a big part of any sea-goer's education. Just as you cannot safely drive a car without understanding how traffic lights are sequenced, neither can you safely navigate any waterway without similarly learning the rules. (There is also a kind of 'highway code' for the sea globally, called the International Collision Regulations – colregs for short – but we'll get onto that a bit later.) The different Cardinal buoys are easy to identify, via both how they look and the lights they show. One of the first things Nige ever taught me, and which I now use to teach others, is that when it comes to Cardinal buoys, 'West has a waist'.

On top of each yellow and black-banded buoy are two triangles, and in West's case they sit tip to tip, the fat part of the lower one at the bottom, and the upper one inverted, giving it the look of an extreme hourglass figure. East is the opposite – clearly more cakes than corsets – and with North and South both the triangles point up or down, to denote their respective ways. It's a logical system, as it is with their lights, which flash according to the layout of a clock-face: North shows one continuous white light, East flashes three times, South flashes six times, and West flashes nine. In darkness, it's those nine flashing lights in the distance that let us know the commute's nearly over and we're almost home.

Back on the way into Wells, and starting from that West Cardinal buoy, there's soon another buoy, this time called a Yellow Special Mark. There is nothing about the look of it that is even remotely special, but it's still an important component of the buoyage as it marks the beginning of the sand bar. So, given that boats love everything except being dry (or run up on the sand bar, which, in parts, is like concrete), when approaching the harbour early on the tide, or in poor weather, it's essential to pass it to port. It's then time to shape up for Number 1, the first starboard mark, which flashes green and has a silhouette like Thunderbird One. Having passed that to starboard, it's on to Number 2, which is red and sits opposite, and flanks the entrance to the channel that will take us into the harbour.

Having followed the reds and greens that mark the safety of the channel, we continue past the beach and outer harbour into the place we call the Pool, and make a sharp turn to starboard, to cut across to the beach bank. It's then a straight run south into the quay basin.

I've already mentioned that we work with the tides, but it's in a more complicated and logical way than it perhaps sounds. It makes sense to work every kind of tide to your advantage, as it's obviously efficient to save precious time and money. But to do so, you first have to understand them, and there are all sorts of variables to consider. To put this in context, when we are out fishing, one of my jobs is to put the boat up to the can, so it's best placed for Nigel to gaff it, and begin the process of hauling in the dhan tow and anchor. This will involve lots of different calculations. To manoeuvre the boat into the best place to do this (and where it will hopefully stay for the duration of hauling the string) I need to position her so that that she's headed straight into the tide (and that's true whatever the tide is doing). If it's up our arse we'll be past the can before Nige has any hope of gaffing it; being against it gives us gives us optimal control.

I also need to know how strong the tides are that day, i.e. are they springs (which are very strong, as the moon is at its fullest), or are they neaps? (Neaps are much weaker and smaller.) This will affect how much power I'm going to need.

There is also a second variable to consider. The average beach-goer tends to see tides as being in or being out. In reality, however, it's not an in-out, hokey-cokey-style situation; there's a flood and an ebb and, as well as the direction being dependent upon your location, the water doesn't just 'come in and out', it follows a journey around a compass. So though flood does fill and ebb does take away, during transitional periods the direction of the tides will not necessarily be the opposite of the other. Knowing your tides, therefore, is another key part of any seagoer's apprenticeship.

The third variable – the weather – is, of course, unpredictable, so requires both intuition and learning. If I'm headed for a can, and it's, say, a windy day, I have to use both skill and instinct to find a balance between the sometimes competing forces of both the

71

tide and the wind. Not to mention knowing how my boat's likely to behave, since every boat responds to those forces differently.

And once that can and the anchor are in, the fun begins, because correcting for those variables is not a one-time-only operation. As we work a string, whoever is on the hauler has to make constant corrections to the boat's speed and angle, to allow for the ever-changing relationship between all those variables. The extent to which we have to do this obviously depends on what sort of weather we're working in. Some days are a dream, and it's easy to get into a rhythm; in layman's terms, calm days, which are a treat. Even windy days can be manageable and relatively easy to work, if the wind and tides seem to be working in your favour. But no two days are the same – how could they ever be? – so you essentially have only two weapons in your armoury: experience (there really is no short cut to this), and a kind of symbiotic relationship with your fellow crew. In our case, Nige relies on me to respond quickly to the need he identifies, both the blatantly obvious and the more nuanced calls, and I need to be both listening and learning. Every trip out adds to my repertoire of situations to be dealt with, making it easier for me to play my part the next time.

Another common misconception I've noticed among the non-nautical is that, for many of them, 'weather' fits into pre-defined boxes. For my mum, for example, if it's going to be sunny, this is filed under 'Ash will have a lovely day'. Fair enough. If I were ashore, this would almost certainly be the case. Out at sea, however, it could be gloriously cloudless, and 36 degrees, but if the wind speed is high it's going to be bloody hard work, since neither hauling gear, nor the state of the sea, are remotely affected by sunshine.

Anyway, ditto clouds, ditto rain, ditto hail, ditto sleet. Ditto – you're getting the picture now – snow. When it comes to hauling gear and shooting pots, when we talk about weather, we mostly mean wind.

Though we must give our friend fog a special mention. Fog, navigationally, is a nightmare. Thick fog is disorientating. (And that is an understatement.) Trying to find your way when faced with a blank wall of grey is never going to be easy. But it also, especially if you concentrate too hard, does very funny things to your eyes – kind of sends them all glittery. I've never actually experienced snow blindness but I think it must similar. You have to keep blinking and looking away to reset your vision, or you completely lose your depth perception. It's especially challenging when going in and out of harbours as, even though you still have your GPS plotter, that will only take you so far. The fine-tuning's done visually by spotting the channel markers. If you can't see them, you might put yourself and the boat (and other people) in danger.

The following names have been changed to protect the innocent. A fisherman I know well, a very experienced one – let's call him Fisherman 1 – left a very foggy Wells harbour in darkness one night and only managed to get a short distance up the channel before meeting the spongy marsh and inadvertently shoving the front end of his boat onto it. He was followed out of the harbour a while later by a second fisherman – let's call him Fisherman 2 – who saw Fisherman 1's predicament on his own way out.

Fisherman 1's radio immediately chittered. 'Follow me, my man!' said Fisherman 2 confidently. 'I know the way out!'

Grateful for the intervention, Fisherman 1 knocked his boat astern, off the marsh, and began following his helpful companion.

A moment or two later the radio once again chittered. And on both boats this time. It was another fisherman on his way out (we could call him Fisherman 3 but we don't need to spare his blushes – he's called Danny). The mirth in his voice was unmistakeable.

'I don't think you do, boys!' he chortled. 'You've just passed me on your way *back* to the quay!'

It bears mentioning that these were two *very* experienced fishermen. Doesn't matter how experienced you are, fog can *always* catch you out. In terms of getting pots from the seabed, however, it makes absolutely no difference. Assuming you've found your way out to open waters in the first place.

Being human, and also British, I have much more to say about the weather. Unlike the sea, I am affected by *all* kinds of weather. As is Nige. Though he would never countenance revealing the presence of such kryptonite in his life, he is no more impervious to nature's curve-balls than I am, and we both have to cope with it accordingly. On blisteringly hot days, when you are doing your work, as always, in thick PVC oilskins (unless you are Horris, who we'll meet later, who opts for working *au naturel* at such times, bar his boots), this might involve rigging up a makeshift shower from wherever we can fix up our seawater hose (or deckwash), or just constantly dipping a baseball cap into the water.

Quick aside, as I think about just how stifling it is to wear a life-jacket on a hot day (heat exhaustion anyone?). It has recently

74

become mandatory to wear a life-jacket at all times when working on deck. I cannot deny for one second that life jackets save lives so, theoretically, it's obviously a good thing. However, life-jackets come with their own set of risks. Both anchors and pots can get caught in the straps, and the consequences are potentially deadly. Can you imagine what it might be like to be pulled into the sea because of your life-jacket, and have that same life-jacket, because it will be trying to get you back to the surface, making it harder to reach down and free yourself? This is true even if it isn't the life-jacket that was responsible for you going in. It makes getting yourself untangled nigh on impossible whatever. Fishermen are now being targeted by spotter planes over this issue, and fines for non-compliance are hefty. There are ever more frequent prosecutions over the issue too, and fishermen are angry that their control over their and their crews' safety has been summarily taken away from them.

Anyhoo . . . on icy-cold days, when it's bitter enough to freeze a witch's tit, it's simply a case of constantly making like a penguin, by wearing multiple layers, and furiously flapping your arms and hands against your body; a lovely little tip that Nige learned from Pops, one of Wells' most highly respected elder fisherman, now gone and who will always be greatly missed. I'm sad I never got the chance to know him better before he passed, but knowing his wisdoms live on through the generations is a comforting thought – and true, I'm sure, of fishing communities everywhere.

This technique, however, doesn't stop your nose from running, and dealing with what comes out is a never-ending exercise in finding new and inventive ways to dispatch streams of stringy snot without using your hands.

Driving rain, however, bar a gale, is probably my least favourite weather, because there is nothing you can do about horizontal, stinging rain, except try to keep your head down and endure it. And it does feel like endurance, particularly if you're female and have long hair. Doesn't matter how carefully you try to tie it back – on a windy, rainy day it always finds a way to channel the rain straight down your face.

~

In my first three months as a *bonafide* member of Nige's crew, I feel I'm learning so much, and in so short a space of time, that I am the proverbial sponge (a sea sponge, in my case), absorbing every nugget of information he is giving me. I still have masses to learn, obviously – I am still learning now and always will be – but the feeling of being capable, through knowing things, is astonishing to me. At no time in my previous life and career has that sense of acquiring skills and knowledge been so profound. The sense is heightened even more by knowing that this knowledge is essential. It's not something I can jot down in a notebook, to refer to later; this is knowledge that I need to reach for every single day when I'm working, and at times when no notebook, or equivalent, might be around. It could, not to overstate, save my life one day.

It's not just my brain that's getting a workout, either. My body has been learning as well. It amazes me daily just how fast it has learned what to do. Muscles have begun forming in places I didn't even know muscles existed, and I am developing a sixth sense – a kind of automatic muscle-instinct – knowing when to move, how to move, how to streamline an operation, and how to use different areas of my limbs and body, to share the load when I'm doing something very physical. I've never done yoga, but I'm developing the vital skill of balance, a process which I don't even have to think about, really – my body just seems to know what to do to keep me upright and productive on a platform that never ever stops moving. I'm long used to being on the water now, courtesy of those many, many fishing trips, but this is a whole other level of physicality, which requires so much more of my body, on every front: quicker reflexes, a stronger core – brute strength, period. I can see it, too, every time I look in a mirror. My shoulders are broader, my arms feel much more muscly, and I just have this sense now of being physically capable.

Not that being a woman on boat isn't without challenges. And not just in the brute-strength department. Whereas men come to work with the advantage of a built-in drainage hose, us girls, annoyingly, are a little more compact, with no easy way to relieve ourselves *al fresco*. So, having been spoilt on *Sunbeam*, which had a private flush toilet, one of my first lessons on *Never Can Tell-A* was how to do exactly that on a boat that had no such luxury. And not just in terms of privacy – she had no toilet at all.

There was no great discussion about this. The first time we were out I said, 'Nige, I need a wee,' and his answer was 'Okay, I'll look the other way then.' I've been squatting down and weeing on the deck ever since and I consider myself something of an expert. Though at times I'm wearing several layers of clothing, plus my oilskins, I have perfected my position to such a level of skill that I

77

have never once got wet, even on the scruffiest of days, when Nige, ever the gentleman, will assist me in my endeavours, by running the boat with the weather so I am as comfortable as possible, to avoid splashback from either sea or wee.

All of this, I realise, has changed me. I used to work in an office, where I had to be presentable, and conform to a standard of looks and of grooming to which, mostly unthinkingly, I complied. The sea has liberated me, because she doesn't give a shit what I look like. Which is just as well in some ways. One unexpected 'bonus' of this new line of work of mine is that I have by now become a connoisseur of mud. It comes in different colours, with different smells, and all kinds of consistencies – there is dry mud, and wet mud, and slimy mud, and sticky mud, all of which have their own distinct properties, the result of their unique chemistry and location. All of them, however, need removing the same way: arms in to mid-forearm, get your fingers in and scrape, grab as many handfuls as time allows for, and chuck the soul-destroying stuff over the side. Or, if there's unlikely to be any whelks in the mud-soup, just tip the pot up, bang it hard against the outside of the hull and let gravity do the rest. Either way, it's a mucky business, though as Nigel says, where there's muck . . .

However careful you are with mud, which is in fact not very, it gets splattered all over the place. Over the boat, obviously, but also all over you, and however hard you scrub (clothes, hair, skin and even teeth) the revolting smell follows you around. Though, annoyingly, you only really notice it when you walk into the warmth of the pub at the end of the day.

It's particularly comical, in our case, as the closest pub to the boat, the Golden Fleece, an old fisherman's hostelry, is now a more upmarket, and therefore more fragrant place. And a welcoming one too. When someone on TripAdvisor, a while back, complained about our slightly pungent presence (and our colourful language, but that's a whole other story) the lovely landlord immediately had the review removed.

Even where I might have retained vestiges of that sense of having to conform to the tedious female stereotype of presenting myself a certain way, a small boat, by its nature, is the opposite of private, so you have absolutely no choice but to be yourself. In fact, you just *have* to be that comfortable with one another in such a small, high-stakes workspace that you might as well be standing there baring your soul. If you get upset in an office, you can escape – to the loo, to your computer screen, to the canteen or car park – but aboard a boat there is nowhere to go. If you don't bring your whole self, your true self, to the party, you simply cannot make any of it work. Happily, I've quickly learned that it's impossible *not* to do this, and this has freed me from the shackles of the female beauty standards that oppress women and girls everywhere. This doesn't mean that there aren't times when I enjoy making an effort, getting dressed up, piling make-up on, and doing my hair. But that's *my* choice. And I honestly can't tell you how good that feels. Plus cutting out the grooming means I can shave twenty minutes off the start of my day. Twenty minutes of extra kip. *Result.*

~

With two tides in the day to take advantage of, and Nigel and I now forming our own capable team, by April, with the boys having reappeared (now all the maintenance has been done), we decide to operate on straight turnarounds with them. This suits us well. Nige's sons, given their youth and strength, can haul upwards of five hundred pots, and he and I can work maybe three to five hundred, in our respective twelve-hour shifts.

Our working times change daily as the tide moves through its fortnightly pattern of springs and neaps. We may start at 8 a.m. and be finished by 7 p.m. and the lads will then turn out to work through the night, landing the following morning ready for us to start the process again, but an hour later. We continue on this never-ending wheel until we are stopped by weather or (yet more) maintenance.

At such times *Never Can Tell-A* breathes a sigh of relief (you really can almost hear it), having been worked non-stop for days on end. The sea is open twenty-four hours a day, seven days a week, but just because you can access it at any time of day doesn't mean it's sustainable for one poor little wooden boat to do so.

And, talking of sustainability, if we wanted to, we could. Whelks, along with crabs and lobster and other less commercially desirable species, are what are known as 'non-quota' species. This means we can catch as many of them as we wish. Quota species, on the other hand (for example, cod, mackerel, plaice, haddock, and sole) can only be caught in limited quantities, based on stock levels and location, as well as 'track record' (i.e. you've caught them historically).

Which is not to say that fishing for 'non-quota' species isn't managed, as well as governed by various regulations. It's also self-managed, because fishermen aren't stupid, and obviously care about sustainability – fishing only at a level consistent with being able to maintain the population – and thereby ensure future stock levels. To over-fish harms everyone, them included. This is a good spring, however, and stock levels are healthy, and benefiting from this with our round-the-clock regime sees us all financially better off.

We're all aware, though, that it's pretty brutal on *Never Can Tell-A*. If we don't want to court disaster, something has to change. It's time to think about getting a second boat.

Chapter 7

'Redheads are considered unlucky – if seen prior to a voyage one must speak to them before they speak to you'

It's mid-May and I'm sat in the Fleece with Nige, while he is transfixed by his phone. I know it will either be XC Weather, BBC Sport, or FindaFishingBoat.com that has his attention. He hands his phone to me. FindaFishingBoat then. And on the screen is another wooden boat, a beautiful blue one. Being a sucker for the aesthetic of a wooden boat, I'm instantly drawn in and scanning the ad to find out more. She's called *Fairlass*, and she's ticking all the boxes.

'She's lovely, Nige,' I say, handing his phone back. 'Where is she?'

'Scotland somewhere, I think. I'm thinking about it. We can't continue to run *Never-Can-Tell-A* non-stop. It's too hard on her. I want you and me to work her and the boys run something else. If you're interested, there's an investment opportunity for you too.'

This makes me prick up my ears. Though, in fairness, it hasn't come completely out of the blue. In recent weeks, albeit separately, Kenneth and I have both had 'the chat' – about how Nige isn't 'going to be around for ever', and how all of us are going to have to pick up the reins, if the business is going to have a viable future. Nige is only in his fifties so it seems a bit premature, even if he does always tell me that he's unlikely to make three score year and ten. I beg to differ. To me, at least, he seems immortal. But now this has come along as an option, why *not* now?

'How much is it up for?' I ask him.

'Dunno. Price on application.'

'You already emailed him?

He nods. This is Nigel to a T. Of *course* he has already enquired about the boat.

~

A few days later we have a figure that's around £88,000 for the boat, including the licence (more of licences later; they are a huge part of commercial fishing), which is reasonable, and achievable, as long as we carry on working as hard as we are. And, since Nigel's impatient to beat any competition, we have a plan to make a road trip to Scotland, where she's based, so we can see her in person. I've never been to Scotland before and it's somewhere I've always wanted to go, but this isn't just Scotland, this is edge of Scotland and then some. The Isle of South Uist in the Outer Hebrides.

Of course, we choose the bank holiday weekend at the end of May to take a look, so I am on at Nige to book the ferry in advance. He's having none of my 'Little Miss Organised' nonsense, however, and assures me that we have nothing to worry about. So I take his word for it but, as we set off on the Friday, I am anticipating a slow, tedious journey. The roads are quiet, however, and we make good progress, plus I'm fizzing with excitement about the quest we've undertaken; I am actually on a trip to potentially buy a share in a fishing boat.

We make good time to Glasgow, and then head west to Mallaig, where we can pick up the ferry to South Uist. The roads change now, becoming gradually thinner and less predictable; where we've spent most of the journey on wide roads with pleasant but undramatic scenery, here the roads feel almost as if they are an intrusion and shouldn't be here, so wild and intense has the vast mountainous landscape become. Living where I do, with all those big skies and largely flat vistas, this feels totally alien, and I'm shocked at how overwhelmed and tiny it makes me feel.

Having left Wells at 5 a.m., we arrive at Mallaig Ferry Port around ten hours later, along with what looks like a couple of hundred other cars. Of *course* there are a couple of hundred other cars there – it's the Bank Holiday. And while we have no trouble booking onto the next ferry to South Uist, the lady in the ticket office cannot get us back on the Sunday morning as planned. Instead, brandishing a huge map, which she scribbles on as she talks, she suggests we take the ferry to the island of Barra on the Sunday, and then get the Monday morning ferry from there back to the mainland at Oban.

Slightly cross now, in one of those 'I fucking told you so!' ways, I stomp back out to run this hiccup past Nige.

He smothers a smirk. (And this despite him knowing *full well* that this is his fault.) 'I *told* you we should have booked the ferry, Ash,' he says.

I manage not to lose my rag with him – nothing is going to spoil my Scottish adventure – and a couple of hours later, we are at the ferry port on South Uist, where *Fairlass*'s owner, Iain, is there to meet us. He has already booked us a B&B for the two nights we're going to be there, so after dropping our bags, we head for food at the Lochboisdale Hotel, the only place we can get a meal at this hour, South Uist being little more than a staging post for holidaymakers on their way to the better-known islands of the Hebrides.

I try to book accommodation for our unscheduled night on Barra, but soon give up. It seems nothing is available (surprise surprise) for the Sunday, so while Nigel samples a selection of the various whiskies on offer, I make peace with the reality that it's almost a given that we'll spend Sunday night sleeping in his Vauxhall Vectra.

The following afternoon, as scheduled, after a short drive across the causeway to Eriskay, we arrive at the harbour under skies that are uniformly grey. Iain's already been out to sea on her, catching crabs, and is just returning as we get out of the car. As we watch *Fairlass* make her way into Eriskay's natural harbour (little more than a sheltered cove with a pontoon), neither of us speaks. She has such grace and presence as she cuts though the deep, clear water, her bow wave an undulating white froth, churning brightly against the royal blue of her hull. She is stunning and in that instant I feel a deep connection with her. Nigel too. I just know it. He doesn't even need to say so. And as she arrives we exchange a glance whose meaning is clear. In our hearts at least, we have both already bought her.

We make our way down the gangway and along the pontoon, and Iain, who we both take an instant liking to (and who we still count as a friend), beckons us aboard to take a better look at her. He doesn't want to sell her, he tells us, but simply cannot find crew for her, and she is too big for him to work single handed.

We sympathise. And when he takes us out for a sea trial, the feeling is even stronger. I'm used to the dimensions of *Never-Can-Tell-A* and though *Fairlass* is only a metre wider and longer, the scale of her makes me feel safe and cocooned, a feeling that's even stronger when I go into the wheelhouse. It's a hard thing to describe but, just like when you go into someone's house, sometimes there is an atmosphere that makes you feel at home. *Fairlass* is so obviously cherished, as well. It's clear Iain works on her constantly. And we can see why he loves her because she is everything we want in a boat. But she's not for us, she's for Kenneth and Jack to work, and I'd be lying if I didn't admit that at this point I'm a tiny bit jealous.

When we return to Nige's car, I send Kenneth a picture. 'She's beautiful,' he texts back. This opens a barrage of questions from both Nige's sons, which we answer for the most part, but agree to sit down and discuss when we get back to Wells.

Having said goodbye to Iain we head straight to the local pub, which, seemingly oddly, is called the Politician and is full of all kinds of memorabilia. It turns out it's not named after some feted local MP, however, but after the SS *Politician*, which sank

87

on her way to Jamaica in 1941, laden with forty-thousand cases of whisky, all of which was 'rescued', along with the crew. It turns out it's the subject of a famous film called *Whisky Galore*, first made in 1949, and again in 2016, and we both resolve to watch it when we get home. It's our own craft, however, that is our main preoccupation so we sit down and unpick our thoughts. There is so much to love, and only a few things we'd change. Iain fishes mostly for crab and lobster, where our quarry is predominantly whelks, so we'd alter some of the set-up around the hauler, and incorporate a riddle. We also agree that before committing to anything we must first address the licence, because *Fairlass*'s is Scottish administered, which might have implications if we bring her back to work in English waters. It's a complication that we need to be 100 per cent sure about, so my first job on our return will be to find Horris, our resident expert in such matters, and pick his brains, but I feel sure it's all workable, and I get into bed that night full of anxious but positive excitement.

On Sunday morning we're both itching to get home to Wells and start the process of hopefully taking ownership of *Fairlass* but, equally, our delay doesn't feel like such a hardship, as the stop on Barra gives us the chance to explore another Hebridean island, and see a bit of their fishing set-up as well. Again, it's tiny, but just as it was on Eriskay and South Uist, fishing dominates in a way that it can't do in Wells, as it forms such a huge part of the area's heritage and economy.

However, that doesn't mean that the local fishing industry isn't under threat. Even as I've been writing this book, there has been a proposal for Scotland to close 10 per cent of its seas to HPMAs

(Highly Protected Marine Areas). Of course we need to protect our marine ecosystems, but the way this was planned would have suffocated the livelihoods of the islanders of the Hebrides. These are isolated communities, which depend entirely on the fish-rich sea that surrounds them. To choke them out of existence, to essentially make them extinct, is reminiscent of the highland clearances in the eighteenth and nineteenth centuries.

They are, however, fighting for their survival. Such was the strength of feeling that a home-grown folk-rock group, Skippinish, were inspired to write a protest song about it. Sung by a local fisherman, it contained lyrics so powerful that it struck a chord with fellow fishermen everywhere. And not just with fishermen. It also moved the nation, reaching No. 6 in the iTunes chart, and inspiring the general public to sign petitions and to lobby their MPs.

To everyone's great relief, it seems to have worked. Rishi Sunak, the current prime minister, has recently called for the Scottish government to make a U-turn on their HPMA plans, and hopefully a better, more workable outcome is pending.

There is some tourism up here, but in only a small select way, so we count ourselves lucky to find a place to spend the night: a recently renovated, and very swanky, hotel. It's eye-wateringly expensive but when it comes to it we cave; neither of us can face a night sleeping in the car, and that, along with the view of the beach and the ridiculously beautiful turquoise water, makes it impossible to resist.

There is only one snag. Though there isn't an advertised dress code as such, it's clear our two-day-old clothes wouldn't cut it if there was. As it is, no one says anything when we enter the restaurant, Nige in his 'ready for the washing machine' jeans and me in ripped skinnies and steel-toe-capped boots. But there's no escaping the fact that every other diner's eye is on us, and not in a hospitable, friendly kind of way. This is not the kind of local scenery they have paid for.

Things don't improve as we settle down to the local langoustines, which we agree are phenomenal. We eat them as they should be eaten, with our fingers and a bib, as the Europeans would – not fannying about, as other diners do, with silly and inefficient cutlery. We also appreciate just how much work and skill goes into catching these succulent little nephrops, so, between us, every last morsel is devoured, the last bits sucked clean from every carapace.

Unfriendly looks have by now become glares, and were we insecure types we'd feel self-conscious. As it is, we feel nothing but pride in our fellow fisherman and, for some of those diners, a little disdain. I wonder how many really think about how their own delicious seafood found its way onto their plates. Do they realise it's via people exactly like me and Nige? People who look like us, dress like us, work just as hard as we do, and would probably not choose to pay way over the odds just to sit in a posh dining room with a pretty view. *We* are the more privileged ones here, I realise. The fabulous food and the jaw-dropping scenery is, for us, just a perk of the job.

If that night is a high point, the following morning sees me in reflective mood on the five-hour ferry ride back to Oban. It's one thing to contemplate becoming part-owner of a boat, and just doing that is a pretty big thing in itself since it will involve both a scary financial commitment and a perhaps even scarier responsibility. At this point in my life this constitutes a profound change, as it will be my biggest responsibility to date. Unlike my car, which requires little more than regular servicing, I am going to be part-responsible for a big expensive piece of equipment which will be working daily in a highly dangerous place. To keep her functional and seaworthy, and always fit for purpose, will require constant monitoring and maintenance. It's not like jumping in a car and, if it breaks down, it's a case of 'Hey-ho, call the AA' – this is a much more serious business. Out at sea you are often a long way from help, and therefore far more vulnerable.

I'm also entering a world of complicated rules and regulations, and, as with income tax, ignorance of them is never an excuse. If we don't comply with them, our livelihood will be at risk, even if sometimes we definitely don't agree with them.

Obviously my partnership with Nige means I have a lot of wisdom and experience to call on and, as I've learned over the time we've been working together, also a further wealth of knowledge in the wider fishing community. It being mostly such a giving and mutually supportive one, much of that information is freely available.

There is no substitute, however, for learning things yourself, both mechanically, and particularly in my case, in terms of the paperwork and administration. With my background in office work, I'm not intimidated by communicating digitally, and by sheer dint of my age – being in my thirties, I'm what I think is probably called an 'elderly millennial' – neither am I fazed by the lightning speed in which tech is changing everything. This encompasses every aspect of what we do and how we do it, from the way we navigate at sea (which is welcomed by all) to the way it is soon going to be compulsory, and enforceable by law, to use an app on our phones to record our catch. Which, by the way, has had the industry in uproar.

It's a lot to take in, and as the water passes beneath us – so clear that you can see down to what must be 3 fathoms – I feel a growing sense of clarity myself. To be worthy of this thrilling new chapter, and of *Fairlass*, I must study. Not just the here and now of what we must and mustn't do, but the history of how things came to be as they are, which, to my untutored mind, feels highly intimidating, just by virtue of the fact that it all seems so scrambled. Just how did the fishing industry come to be such a muddle of seemingly contradictory rules and regs?

Perhaps it's time for me to riddle some riddles.

Chapter 8

'Wear gold earrings'

Not so much a superstition but believed to ward off seasickness due
to pressure points in the ear. A gold earring could also afford you a
proper burial, should your corpse wash up ashore.

When I say the word 'fisherman', what image does that conjure?
A man in his fifties, perhaps, with white hair, a far-from-white
nicotine-stained beard, tattoos long blurred into leathery sun-
ravaged skin, a distinctive walk, and the smell of the sea emanating
from every weather-beaten pore? That's Horris, one of the most
respected fishermen in our community.

Horris blew into Wells on a fresh sou-westerly, his arrival into
the harbour on an unfamiliar boat piquing the interest of several
of the local old salts. This was back in the early noughties, and in
a place like Wells, where certain factions tend to the parochial,
an unfamiliar fishing boat rocking up would have immediately
set tongues wagging. Andy Mac, however, being such an open-

minded, golden-hearted soul, was quick to throw this intriguing character a rope.

That the man's boat was called *Zephyr* seemed fairly appropriate, since it had travelled from its port of registration over in Lowestoft. Horris hadn't drifted off course, however. He was in search of new fishing grounds. With quota fishing becoming ever less viable as an option, he'd decided to try his luck with the non-quota species that were accessible from Wells, having heard there was good fishing to be had, particularly brown shrimp, his preferred catch. Wells was, and is, also in the minority in the UK fishing industry in that, being one of the smaller commercial harbours, it doesn't take a cut of everyone's haul.

Quickly installed, he soon became a familiar face in the Fleece, except for the fact that you could only rarely actually glimpse his face. For a fortnight he would take up a position in the same corner and remain incognito, behind a copy of the *Fishing News*. Now and then (presumably when something intriguing came up between the fishermen at the bar) he'd glance over the top to check them out, but mostly kept himself firmly to himself.

A few months down the line, Andy Mac asked him why he'd been so seemingly aloof. 'I wasn't,' he said, in his forty-a-day rasp. 'I was just sussing you all out.'

Horris soon became part of the furniture. A man of few words but many facial expressions; he could put you in your place with just a glance, or a minuscule elevation of one shaggy eyebrow. He was also a looker – you could tell that, in his day, he must have been right handsome, and had the twinkle in his eye to bear that out. He was also as well known for falling asleep, Guinness in hand, as for his many jaw-dropping tales and sea shanties. Because he had, it seemed, already been everywhere and done everything, which, as well as being entertaining (he was matchless at telling a story), meant he was an invaluable source of fishing knowledge. This was particularly true when it came to fishing history and legislation. Having started fishing in his teens, Horris began his career in the early seventies, which was a very different time in the industry. Back then, a fisherman could go to sea for a fortnight and, if he was prepared to work hard, and in what were difficult and dangerous conditions (fishing is still considered to be the most dangerous peacetime occupation), earn enough to buy a small house. And this wasn't even as a fishing boat owner – this was just as crew.

There was a big, big change in the offing however, with the advent of the Common Fisheries Policy. There had been previous big shifts in the commercial fishing landscape with the beginning of the Cod Wars with Iceland in the fifties, and the implementation of the Sea Fisheries Act of 1967. Arguably, however, the Common Fisheries Policy (which was ratified in 1973 and evolved over the next decade) was, in the minds of many fishermen, the biggest divide-and-conquer move in fishing history. We are still paying the price for it now.

A short (and hopefully not too boring) explanation. Dear old Ted Heath signed us up to the EEC, which saw us join a common marketplace with Europe. As a result, all the fish, in all European waters, essentially became everyone's. Free movement, if you like, for fishing boats. The trouble was that while our fleets weren't interested in fishing in other member states' waters, the seas around the UK, the biggest multi-species fishery in the world, were now fair game for one and all.

Despite the UK having already started to restrict fish landings to conserve stocks, we were now legally obliged to manage fish stocks in the same way the EEC did, via a Total Allowable Catch (TAC) system, regulated by quota and evidenced by sales notes from fish buyers. This required European fishermen who fished on 10-metre boats and over to use logbooks to record their catches. This ensured that TACs and quota were not being exceeded. The situation was complicated further because, as a result of us joining the CFP, by 1985 we too had adopted this strategy, and logbook reporting was compulsory for UK-registered boats as well.

This development is precisely how the divide-and-conquer aspect of this works. The rules only applied to 10-metre boats and over because boats that were under 10 metres were deemed not big enough to have any kind of significant impact on fish stocks. (Back then an under-10-metre boat was smaller, and less powerful, and her size obviously limited how much catch could be stored aboard.)

Managing quota was, and still is, no easy task. One of the management tools used was something called 'track record', where a boat would be given its quota based on what it had caught in the previous three-year period. This obviously meant fishermen were keen to catch all their quota; in a use-it-or-lose-it scenario, they had to, if they were to be sure of not losing that quota for the following year. You may have heard the term 'ghost fishing' in the mass media, a term that today refers to abandoned fishing gear that's still polluting the sea. (And, as anyone who's seen what gets washed up on some of our beaches already knows, is still very much capable of killing wildlife.) Back in the nineties, however, the term had an entirely different meaning. Allegedly some fishermen (with the assistance of some very creative buyers, and some complacency among fisheries' officers) would overinflate their catches to ensure that their fishing rights were not lost for the following year's quota allocation.

With regulation and corruption both rife in the over-10-metre club, it's no surprise that the under-10-metre fleet was looking like an attractive option. They were largely unhindered, unregulated, and for the most part left alone. They could voluntarily submit catch records and didn't have to worry about the hassle of quota and logbooks. So it's little wonder that, during all the drama of the above period, many fishermen thought 'Fuck this', and jumped to join the under-10s.

Many simply sold their boats, and some were even eligible for 'decommissioning', an effort to reduce the capacity of the over-10-metre fleet by the government, which saw them offer cash payouts to fishermen if, along with meeting certain other criteria, they scrapped them instead. In some extreme cases, to bring them under the 10-metre threshold, fishermen even chopped the bow off their boats. (If you have ever seen a fishing boat with a snubbed nose look – now you know why). They could even, if they wanted to, simply screw it back on again, as any 'removable structure' wasn't counted as part of the boat's declared length. Clever, huh? Invent a rule, someone will always find a workaround. The same applies today to 'cat catchers' (a piece of kit I'll introduce you to later).

These developments resulted in the investment and upscaling of the under-10-metre fleet, which, in a very short space of time, became the majority fleet – a fleet partly made up of what were colloquially now known as 'super under-10s', or 'rule beaters'. To this day the under-10s dominate the fleet, with a split of 80/20 per cent.

The sweeping changes didn't stop there. In 1999, to combat the 'ghost fishing' phenomenon, the government in their wisdom decided to abandon the track record approach to issuing quotas. They instead moved to a 'fixed quota allocation' system (FQA) which gave fishermen guaranteed access to 'their' quota. It was now 'owned' by the fishermen and was calculated based on their landings between 1994 and 1996.

Another technique to manage quota adopted by the UK was the establishment of 'Producer Organisations' (POs). Think of it as a members' club, that will assist in the selling of your fish; anything from transport and logistics, representing fishermen as an organisation, support with safety on board your vessel, training, marketing catch, grant application assistance, and even financial support for buying new boats. Their biggest task by far, though, is managing their members' quota.

POs are recognised quota-management bodies that are allocated quota from the government, to then dole out to their members, thus making the job of managing quota more flexible for their fishermen (and, of course, easier for the fisheries administrators of the UK). Quota can be bought sold and traded between POs as needed, and they will of course take a percentage of the financial value of their members' catch.

But how does one gain access to this club, and become part of what is known as 'The Sector'? Back then, FQAs were your ticket in. Pretty exclusive, huh? I'm not even sure that membership is more inclusive these days, but having access to enough quota is essential if you're to maximise the value of your day at sea. This may, however, mean buying or leasing additional quota from 'their' pool.

As you've probably worked out, navigating the complicated over-10-metre boat landscape had become a big headache. So, as a result, joining the under-10-metre fleet became ever more attractive as they could essentially still do their own thing. Yes, they had catch limits set for them in 1999, but as this was not effectively monitored, and no formal reporting mechanism had been put in place, it went unregulated aside from the odd port visit from a fisheries inspector. Some fishermen *did* log their catches, having seen the FQA rollout and the importance of track record, but others didn't, which impacted them later down the line. But we will touch on that later.

It wasn't until 2005 that the shit really hit the fan, with the implementation of the Registered Buyers and Sellers Act. This required any buyer of 'first sale fish' (the term being exactly what it describes) to register their purchase, with full traceability, to the relevant fisheries administrator. This development threw up an unexpected fact; that the under-10-metre fleet was catching way more than anybody realised.

The consequence of finding this out was, to put it bluntly, panic. All of the quota had been given away to the big boys and though they had to find a way to regulate the under-10-metre fleet, there was only 2 per cent of the entire UK quota left to share between them. (WTF?) Since then, to be fair, they have done a lot of work to try and make the under-10s' allocation of quota fairer, but, bottom line, real fairness is still a pipe-dream for many of us, while privatisation *of a public resource* is, I am sorry to say, still, all these years down the line, alive and well.

It really is no wonder that Horris's old vans (both of which are sadly no more) had 'Defra Sucks – But they ain't no Fisherman's Friends', and 'Wot no Quota' spray painted on the side of them.

~

So, back to Horris, who I manage to track down in the Fleece (obviously) in the hopes of picking his brains about the licence situation with *Fairlass*. Bottom line is that though anyone can go fishing, if you want to sell your catch commercially, you must have a licence, and if you buy a boat without one you can't use it to work. So first you need to do one of two things: buy a boat which already comes with a licence, or go to a broker or private individual and buy your own.

Though it's not quite as simple as that. No new fishing vessel licences are being issued, hence buyers who are looking to licence a fishing vessel are required to first source an 'entitlement' (the term for a licence that's been 'dis-aggregated', i.e. one no longer attached to an active fishing vessel; one that has been decommissioned, de-registered, sold or sunk). The entitlement you need will depend on what you're buying, but essentially you need the tonnage (the weight of your boat) and kilowatts (the engine power) to match it. The price of entitlements, the sum you will have to pay for the right to apply for a new licence, varies depending on market forces.

Horris has already given me a primer on all these licensing complexities, so I'm not a complete rookie here. I also know that licensing, taken across our entire fishing sector, is constrained by the finite nature of the whole. To clarify: for both the over-10s and under-10s there is a total for kilowatts and a total for tonnage, and the totals for both, across their respective fleets, must not exceed either individual total.

What I don't know, however, is how all this is affected by the fact that *Fairlass* is registered in Scotland, is over 10 metres, and under Scottish administration. Is the licence that comes with her likely to be complicated? Might it even be worthless to us in England?

'Has it got shellfish?' Horris asks me, while Nige goes and gets him a pint. (Horris is old school; he won't ever let a woman buy him a beer.)

I nod. 'Why?'

He confirms what I already thought – that that's a good thing, because it will allow us to commercially fish for crab and lobster on *Fairlass*, as we already do on *Never Can Tell-A*. It's also a 'bolt-on' to the licence (the same as species like bass and scallops would be), which means it will be worth more if we ever come to sell it. Like buying a car and getting all the optional extras. (These 'bolt-ons' have been generated via the old track record system, by the way, and hike the price a licence is worth, which has a negative effect on young fishermen trying to get into the industry, and who often can't afford them. And don't forget, as far as the government is concerned, licences have no monetary value, so they are unlikely to sort the mess out any time soon!)

'And what category is it?' Horris also wants to know.

'Cat A,' I tell him, trying to sound knowledgeable. All I really know at this point is that category A licences are the best ones. (It allows the licence holder to catch pelagic stocks of fish, such as mackerel and herring, and hence will require quota. Cats B and C, as you'd expect, aren't quite so good.)

'Be careful,' Horris advises. 'You need to check with the MMO, because there's a history, when it comes to transferring licences between administrative ports, of them downgrading them while they're at it.'

'Why?' I ask, because this seems the obvious question. The MMO stands for Marine Management Organisation, the government body responsible for the whole marine environment around our shores, including managing fish stocks, licensing and quota, plus, conceivably, any commercial activity that happens within the marine space, from dredging or construction of a seaweed or wind farm, or any other offshore structure. Why would they downgrade a licence for no reason?

'Huh,' he says rolling his eyes. 'Why do *you* think?'

I consider the question. And it's not just the question, is it? It's everything I've already learned myself about the story of our industry. No wonder men like Horris have so little faith in the powers that control us.

His expression confirms it. 'And make sure you speak to Liz,' he adds. 'Liz knows what she's doing and she's the only decent one there.'

'And the rest are all bastards,' Nige finishes for him.

Liz is it, then. I make a note of her name. Though by the time I get in touch she's moved on to another department, and, true to Horris's prediction, they ask me to do a Fisheries Plan, documenting every species, and how much of them, we would want to catch, for every month of the year. They then decide if her licence is to come to England they would indeed downgrade it to a Cat B and, in addition, would remove any FQAs (which, being over 10 metres, she might well have had).

Neither I nor Nige are prepared to do that. Why devalue a licence someone in Scotland could still make good use of? Because once those rights are lost they will most probably no longer exist; in my opinion, another nail in the coffin of our fishing industry.

The truth is that had I relied upon the resources available to me through internet searches on government websites, then we would for sure still be deliberating over this. As it is, and as it *always* is with Horris, I've learned something.

Transferring *Fairlass*'s licence would not be the best thing we could do, as it's plainly worth more financially in Scotland than in England, so we are decided. We are buying the boat, but not the licence, and make an offer for *Fairlass* that Iain says is acceptable.

Enough of the regs. It seems I'm about to become part-owner of a vessel of the type commonly known as 'a hole in the sea into which one regularly throws money'. But I'm up for it. As Nigel says, we have to think of the future and how the boys and I will make a living once he's hung up his oilskins. So we need to raise money. Some serious money. Which means we need to get back to work.

Chapter 9

'Swallows are a good-luck omen'

These small birds always find their way home.
After completing 5,000 nautical miles sailors will get a single swallow tattoo. They earn a second once they have completed 10,000.

With a figure of somewhere around £40,000 agreed for *Fairlass*, we give Iain a deposit and he agrees we can pay the rest in instalments, which is a real godsend, and so typical of the camaraderie of the fishing community. Iain didn't know us from Adam till we rocked up in the Hebrides, yet he trusts us to make good on the timescale we've agreed (end of the summer), just as we trust him with our deposit, and to honour our commitment to buy the boat. There is nothing in writing; just a 'gentlemen's agreement', the same way it's probably been done for centuries – the simple business of doing business by trusting one another, sadly disappearing from so many aspects of our world.

The deal struck, now it really is time for austerity measures – not that we weren't on a make-do-and-mend attitude anyway, but wages are stripped back and we all take the bare minimum – and I really mean the bare minimum, just enough for us all to survive on and, since this new boat is mostly going to be for them to work, this includes Jack and Kenneth. Happily, they are both highly motivated to go without, since they are so excited about having their own boat to run. Investments are made into new whelk pots as well, to maximise the amount of fishing the four of us can do, and we scrape the money together to bring *Fairlass* home.

For a while it feels as if not a week goes by when there isn't something arriving, or something needing doing ashore, all in the service of getting our new gear to sea. Because the kind of lay-down whelk pots we use are actually repurposed plastic drums (the bottom lined with concrete, and the mesh in place on top), they need their lids nailing on so they can't spin open in the tide and provide an escape route for our precious haul of whelks. They also need their strops to be fitted and to be individually bent on to the main line of rope. It's a dusty job, this one, due to that layer of fresh concrete, but what you might not know is that it's often also quite a pleasant one. The recycled plastic drums come from all kinds of places, most having previously held some kind of liquid, from cleaning products, to shampoo, to culinary ingredients. Andy Mac once had a whole shank that had held peppermint oil in its former life; when Nige used to work with him it was the one he always used to look forward to working because, believe it or not, even after months and months at sea, the minty freshness of those pots never faded.

Probably because of some deal done by our supplier with a local factory at the time, our own pots, in the main, used to contain argan oil. This meant the business of prepping them by the quayside was accompanied by the sort of scent you'd more usually expect to find in a high-end hair salon. A small detail, but it never failed to cheer up my day, as I'd go home and, instead of smelling of dead and rotting fish, I'd be dusty, yes, but also beautifully fragrant.

As well as setting all the new whelk gear, we decide we must also redouble our efforts to catch crab and lobster. Where 80 per cent of our income comes from whelk fishing, crabs and lobsters are the (heavily armoured) icing on the cake.

Up until 1980, no crabs, historically, were being landed at Wells, other than those used for whelk bait. It came about due to a pair of brothers, Andy and Martin Frary (both whelk fishermen, on their boat, the *Black Beauty*), and their idea that it might be commercially viable. At least, something worth giving a go. So they upscaled the crab pots they were using to catch bait, and so began a trend that's still (hashtag) trending today – every single fisherman in Wells still catches crabs.

Fishing for crab isn't that dissimilar to fishing for whelks except that every step in the process is a) more expensive, b) more cerebral, and c) comes with its own set of dangers. This is down to the fact that unlike slothful whelks, crabs are always zipping about on the sea floor.

Crab fishing is done in more or less the same way as whelk fishing, as in anchor, then pot, rope, pot, rope, pot, rope, and so on. The only difference in technique is that with crab you shoot the pots *with* the tide rather than across it, as you do with whelks. You shoot across the tide partly to allow the scent of the bait to travel, which is important when trying to attract whelks. With crab, however (who as I've said, zip about across the sea floor), you not only don't need that tidal advantage, you also want to pin your bulky crab pots as tight to the sea floor as possible, as you don't want them rolling around and into each other, and perhaps even tripping an anchor. Shooting *with* the tide allows you to do just that.

Unlike whelk pots, which are varied but fundamentally just variations on a couple of basic themes, the world of crab pots is, to put it simply, endless. So sure of this am I that I can almost 100 per cent guarantee that someone will be inventing a new crab pot design as I write (probably Horris, even if he has retired). If you think of crab pots as a kind of *Origin of Species*, at the top are the main groups – your three-bows, your creels, your inkwells, and your parlours – you then move down to the subgroups attached to these standards, which are all of the above but with different additional features.

The arch-shaped crab pot (the three-bow, and the parlour) is the one that's most commonly used on our stretch of coast. The parlour version does exactly what it says on the tin. There is a first chamber containing bait – a kind of lobby, if you like – and once they've had their fill, they trundle on into the parlour, a second chamber from which they cannot escape. The three-bow, in contrast, is just a big open space. Both have their benefits, which is why both are in use. The three-bow fishes quicker, but the parlour preserves bait.

Different fishing areas have evolved different kinds of pots. Some prefer creels, and some inkwells, and others use a mixture;

it's really a case of personal preference. The same applies to the additional features; how a pot is rigged is down to personal preference as well, plus the local culture, hence the dizzying amount of options, some of which will including rigging the pots so they attract lobsters as well. (This is actually becoming much more common. Where once a 'hard eye' – a fixed ring opening, as opposed to a 'soft' entrance – was relatively rare, pretty much all crab pots in Wells now contain a hard eye as standard, as it seems lobsters prefer them, and, given their price, why wouldn't anyone want to attract lobsters?)

Crab fishing is expensive mostly because of the cost of the pots, and also of the bait. Where whelks are attracted to dogfish and crab (a box of dog is currently around £12, and shickle is free, as you'll remember), crab are mainly interested in much more expensive bait: salmon heads and frames, gurnard, scad (horse mackerel) and 'butts' – that being a collective term for dabs and flounders. And since nothing is ever wasted in the fishing industry, particularly when it comes to bait, if some haddock frames become available, you can try those as well but, once again, it's a lot more expensive.

Crab fishing is more cerebral because there's more thinking and planning involved. Unlike with whelks, whose life cycle only affects the fishing of them a little, crab (and lobster) fishing is both seasonal and highly life-cycle dependent. The crab goes though the same seasonal changes every year. The mated females (hens) start producing eggs in the autumn and, by November, start 'berrying up' (this being the term for the proliferation of eggs – up to three million – that have migrated from inside the shell to a purse outside their mothers' bodies). They will be fully berried up between December and March and will release their eggs once the sea temperature is warm enough – usually sometime in the spring. Now the hens are ravenous, having eaten very little over the winter, and by June, will have eaten so much that it is time for them to literally burst out of their shells, a process we all know as moulting. Now they are 'soft-shelled', the males (jacks or cocks) will mate with them. The hens' new shells will now start the process of hardening up and by the autumn, when they are full of roe, berrying up once again begins.

The jacks' life cycle is equally important. Jacks moult at the end of the summer, only once they have mated the hens. They will then harden up over the winter, and be fully hard by the spring (sorry; I can't seem to help this), at which point, having been fairly immobile during the cold months, and with the water temperature increasing, they will begin to run about in search of food and sex. What a life, eh? All of this activity, with both sexes, makes for good fishing.

The sea itself obviously changes through the seasons and a summer sea can be a real joy to work. Where, in winter, the North Sea can sometimes look like a bowl of Coco Pops, by late spring the water is starting to clear and such is the clarity that when you're out in deep water, it looks almost black far below. On sunny summer days, when you look across rather than down, it can even look emerald. On days like these you can watch the pots coming up from the depths, and get an idea what you've managed to entice. If Nige's watching I always know if we've managed to snag a lobster, because he hollers 'Bugfish!' or 'Beast!', or, sometimes, when we're not so lucky, an enraged bellow of 'Where's my lobsters?!'

Another Nige quirk, incidentally, which he always does just before we start hauling, is to spit into the water, just to let them know we're here. There's no logic to this – they'll be 12 or 13 fathoms below us, after all – just as there's little logic in many a sea-based superstition, but as it's always worked for Andy Mac (well, allegedly) Nige swears by it. And who am I to roll my eyes? I would never say 'rabbit' on a boat, after all. Feel free to make of that what you will . . .

The pots up, the next step is to empty them and sort the catch, a very different process to riddling whelks. Some shake them out to sort, and some 'scud' them (sorting as you remove them). We do the latter, due to the relatively small size of our boat. Our pots have D doors, which you have to unhook to gain entry. With a three-bow, you have access to the whole open space – as do the crabs, which means I get very wet when sorting them out as, if I'm not fast enough to grab them before they can scuttle away, I have to reach right to the back of the pot to get hold of them. With a parlour pot they are trapped in the business end, the end where I'm standing, ready to deal with the chaos that's about to ensue.

Why are crabs chaotic? Well, because by the very nature of their life cycle, they are different in lots of important ways. Is it big enough? Is it on the cusp? Am I going to have to measure it with my handy little measuring tool? (Which, easy to lose, is affixed to the boat at all times.) Is it hard enough? (Even if it isn't it might appear so at first glance.) Has it got both its claws? If it's a good clean crab, we might take it anyway, but if it's in any other way substandard, we definitely won't, as no one wants to get a reputation for landing shit crab, so straight into the bait box it goes. We also have to look out for 'black jacks' or 'black hearts', ones who've fallen victim to Black Spot Disease. These (almost always jacks) head for the bait box as well. Females which don't make the grade, on the other hand, always go back into the ocean, even if they're ancient and unlikely to breed again. With these elderly grandmas, Nige always tells me to add them to the bait box, but I slyly slip them back over the side; as far as I'm concerned, these old ladies have had a long but tough life (jacks not being noted for either gentleness or chivalry) so I reckon they deserve to enjoy their dotage.

This all probably sounds quite straightforward. In practice, it is anything but. Try to visualise the scene as if you're standing in my Xtra Tufs. The door opens and a jumble of brown crab tumbles out, part of a seafood cocktail which also includes devil fish (which can give you an electric shock), hermit crabs (bait-robbing bastards, essentially), velvet crabs, and even the odd whelk, much of it hidden beneath and within layers of lemon weed and, as Nigel says, we can't sell fucking salad. Our job then, is to sort carefully through this moving tangle, trying to weed out the stuff that's of no use to us commercially, and, crucially, get it back into the sea alive, while avoiding being bitten (pinched) by a crab who has its own ideas about its immediate fate. And you have to be fast. As with whelks, there is a rhythm that must be maintained. It's hard enough that lots of the crabs are clinging onto one another, but when a crab's clinging on for dear life to a crab pot, it will obviously not want to move. And with six legs and two claws, if you try to pull harder, it will double down and cling on to the pot harder too, and you run the risk of ripping its claws off. Sometimes you just have to admit defeat, even if grudgingly, and stack the pot with it still clinging on to the bars of its prison, and accept you'll just have to get it next time.

Fishing for crab holds the same dangers as whelk fishing, in that you have the same risk of accidentally shooting yourself away. There is added danger, however, because the need for human intervention is greater, due to the height factor – a stack of crab pots can be 6 feet high or more – and the fact that you need to manually put each one down on deck, with precise order and accurate timing, ready to be shot away. Plus, as you are shooting away with the tide rather than across it, the whole operation is much faster. (Where it's quick to shoot whelk pots away at 7 knots, we shoot crab away at 8½–9 knots, which feels a *lot* quicker.)

As mentioned, there is an added bonus to fishing for crab, and that is lobster; when the fishing is good, we'll catch about half a boxful, on average, for every three boxes of crab we bring home. We also have a couple of shanks specifically for targeting lobsters, and during the summer months, it's worth checking on them weekly. Though this is where things get a little fun, as what you might not know is that prime fishing spots for 'beasts', as we call them, are often in and around shipwrecks. Lobsters like to climb into crevices and holes, both for protection and for reasons of stealth. And wrecks, of course, give them those things in spades.

What you might also not know is that our patch of the North Sea is home to literally hundreds of wrecks. (This is mostly due, or so I'm told, to it having been one of the most heavily mined stretches of seabed around the UK during the Second World War.) So why does it get fun? Well, let's just say that most of those wrecks are 'occupied', in that pretty much everyone in Wells has their own patch, and if you were ever to shoot anywhere near 'someone else's' wreck, it would be the surest way ever of never seeing those pots ever again. Seriously, it's like Ice Cream Wars out there. (Though with more money involved.)

Aside from their predilection for the dead souls of broken ships, lobsters are fascinating creatures in themselves. They look like aliens, for a start, and hold a mystique unmatched by any other crustacean, and I've yet to meet a fisherman who isn't happy to see one. They feel like such a treat, and not just for commercial reasons. There is also a huge respect. If we happen to catch a really big lobster (lifespan: indefinite, maximum size: indefinite – in theory, they are immortal), it's not just the fact that it would be hard to sell something so expensive, it's also because I feel it's fundamentally wrong to take an animal that has evaded capture for what's probably been a very long life. I know some might but, for us, and lots of others I know, it would feel morally unfair. As Andy Frary says, 'Take what you need and leave enough for the next generation.'

Lobsters are slow growing. Only one in 20,000 (the number of eggs a female usually carries) will make it long enough to reach the sea floor, where it will hide away from predators for two years. It then takes a further five years for it to grow big enough to be landed, and a big lobster, one that's perhaps the size of a small baby, could, incredibly, be several decades old.

Lobsters are highly aggressive. You might be familiar with the sight of them with elastic bands around their claws, and the reason is probably obvious. They love a scrap, and there is nothing more heartbreaking for a fisherman than having a pot come up, one that you can see contains two lobsters, and realising that one of them is very much dead, consisting of little more than body parts and mess. Worse still is when you realise, from the size of those claws, that the big one has been killed by an opponent who is some waspy, undersized female. I mean, go her. Nice to see her standing up for herself. But a commercially painful moment nevertheless.

There is also an art to the dangerous business of banding them. (And this is in addition to the dangerous business of having anything to do with them at all. They are highly unpredictable, and can react to being picked up in all sorts of ways, none of them conducive to friendly relations.) The art consists of great speed, and confidence, and a certain amount of courage, and knowing which claw to band first. Clue: always go for the small one. It holds none of the crushing power of the big one, but it's a hell of a lot faster to give you a good squeeze. (As Nige's left nipple can attest to.)

This, then, is why lobster is so expensive. If you can do so, go and buy your lobster fresh from a fisherman on the quay. It will taste incredible, and cost you a third of the price you'd pay for it in a restaurant.

There is another seafood cocktail I need to mention. The one made up of the common fisheries policy, quotas, privatisation, and the unplanned industrialisation of the under-10-metre fleet ensures that crab fishing has become very lucrative. Everyone is at it and we'd like to do more of it, and right now, with a boat to pay for, every crab and lobster counts. So we work our butts off to catch every last brown crab (*cancer pagurus*) we can, and pay the owner, Iain, off, as promised, bit by bit until at last, in early August the final goal is in sight.

At last we can go and get our boat.

Chapter 10

'Cut neither hair or nails at sea'

These are seen as an offering to Proserpina (wife of Hades), and while in his kingdom they will enrage Neptune.

For a lot of fishermen who buy a new boat the logical and easy thing to do to is to pop your new toy on a lorry and deliver it by road. But, Nige being Nige, he isn't daunted by the dangers of the alternative, which will be a long voyage of some 750 nautical miles, through the Hebrides, the Caledonian Canal, and the North Sea. Which is no surprise to anyone who knows him well. The sea is in his blood, having been exposed to it very young, when his mum and stepdad took him and his brother on a two-year adventure around the Mediterranean, only popping home to St Ives, Cambridgeshire, where they lived, during the darkest months of the year.

It was an audacious thing to do, especially given that this was back in the 1980s, but Nige's mum was – and still is – the kind of woman who, rather than go and state her case to the education authorities, cap in hand, would go and get hold of the school curriculum for their respective year groups, and simply do it. And that's exactly what she did. It's no wonder Nige is as capable and decisive as he is. As it turned out, no one objected to this unusual variant of home-schooling, and, as a result, for those two years, they got a rich and unique education, that went far beyond anything a school syllabus could have taught them.

The boat they had chosen for this epic voyage, *Ros Min*, was a 50-foot wooden ex-trawler, originally from Ireland and built in 1953. With it moored on the river Ouse, which was close to their home, they then spent several years painstakingly renovating it to a live-aboard, taking care to build theirs and the boys' cabins at opposite ends to minimise the kind of flare-ups usually associated with living with young boys, never mind ones in such a minuscule living space.

Having notified the relevant authorities and with the first year's worth of school books packed away in the hold, they set off on a fine July morning in 1979, steaming first along the Ouse, through the fens, to King's Lynn, and then down through the French canal network. Having 'doodled about' in France, as Nige's mum, Elizabeth, puts it, it was late summer by the time they were down in the Med, where the two boys, both strawberry blond and blue eyed (I've found that a curiously large number of fishermen seem to have blue eyes), were a constant source of fascination among the local communities. For the two young boys themselves (Nige and Neil were now thirteen and nine respectively) this was a childhood like no other. Though the mornings were mostly spent wading through all the non-negotiable school work, for the rest of the time they were getting an education that was infinitely broader. Every afternoon, as well as frolicking about in crystal blue waters, as any self-respecting teenager would, they would also become deckhands, apprentice fishermen, navigators, divers, mechanics, and boat engineers.

None of this was happening in isolation, either, as family and friends would often fly down to join them and, travelling round many of the Mediterranean islands that first year, they also became part of a community of like-minded souls. And as something of a novelty, Nige and Neil would often be co-opted by local fishermen, to help them sort catch when they landed, usually paying for their efforts with seafood. They regularly brought back prawns, calamari and other more exotic sealife for their mum to cook – including, one time, an octopus with a body the size of a rugby ball, and which needed to be beaten several times against the rocks to make it edible. And on one occasion, a very excited Nige told his mum he could bring her a whole swordfish, all 6 daunting feet of it. She declined, of course, and they settled for a couple of swordfish steaks, but to this day, Nige still has the sword.

Nige also, to this day, has a journal of his adventure, in which he faithfully recorded important moments on the trip, such as the informative *today Yolaro off the fishing boat behind us gave us some shells, so now we have fifty two shells* and the time when he saved the life of a sea turtle in the sea off Sardinia, recorded in his usual understated style, but which memory still burns very brightly for him.

There is no question that, for Nige, this was the time of his life. The sea is not just in his blood, actually. It is in his heart.

He had always been around boats; his maternal grandparents lived on the riverfront, so he had always spent time mucking about on the water. But this trip, coming at such an influential age for him, saw a childhood pastime turn into a real passion. As a result of the trip, he had come to associate the sea with total freedom, and in boats he had found his passport to being where he felt a happiness he could not achieve anywhere on land.

It's no surprise to me, therefore, that Nigel wants to steam *Fairlass* home. After all, it's the best way to get to know any new boat. It's also the best way to create that bond of trust between skipper and craft, a unique relationship that is essential when two entities must depend on one another so much. And now I'm in the mix, an absolute beginner. Yes, I've been at sea, but I've never been on a voyage, not in the sense of relying on the sea to get me from one place to another. Unlike Nige, I've never done a journey *across* a sea, let alone been integral to the making of that journey, rather than just travelling as a passenger. And I *am* integral to it; this is not a journey to be done alone. Despite knowing that if I suggest this to Nige, he will roll his eyes – of *course* he could do it on his own, the stubborn shit – I know there will be challenges where he *will* need my assistance, and that, though it will undoubtedly be a test for me, it will also be a brilliant baptism of fire. But how do I prepare for a journey like that on a boat we barely know? What do I take with me? How long will it take? How easy or hard will it be? I am about to find out. The hard way.

~

It's 5 a.m. on a warm late July morning, and Wells is looking as beautiful as ever. Everything is bathed in a deep orange light, the boats silhouetted by the first rays of the slowly rising sun. I arrive in my van, and park it down on the quay, where it will stay till we return, whenever that may be. I have that same sense of excitement I feel whenever I'm going on holiday, and even though I know this isn't one and that there are challenges ahead, I don't feel an iota of anxiety or nerves – just this feeling that I am doing something magical.

Nige is already there, and watches as I lug my suitcase from the van, his expression changing as he sees just how big it is.

'Fucking hell, Ash,' he says, as I wheel it towards him. 'We're not going on a cruise!'

I pull a face at him. 'Well, I don't know how long we're fucking going for, do I?'

And it's true. I really don't have a clue how long we'll be away. He's told me that if all goes well it 'might be a week', but I know things can happen. We might get weathered in somewhere, and possibly more than once. And, since I'm the organised one in this partnership (don't tell Nige) I have done the sensible thing and planned for contingencies. In one half of the case are what I deem my essentials: enough clothes for a week, and plenty of toiletries and underwear, since I have no idea if or when I'll be able to do any washing. And I'm not being remotely high maintenance here. As there is nowhere to sleep on the boat, we'll be making port every night and at the very least I want to be clean and presentable.

In the other half of my case is our copy of the 3-inch-thick *Reeds Almanac*, the mariner's bible. First published in 1932, and updated annually, the *Reeds* is a guide to every harbour in Europe, along with tide tables, distance tables, and passage and navigational notes, as well as communications information for when travelling through different countries, and even sunrise and sunset times at different latitudes. I think most seafaring people would agree that it's indispensable when going on any kind of voyage. So though Nige might look at me askance about my voluminous case, it was he who asked me to buy a copy and bring it, so, in fact, I am only following orders.

I have taken my orders to the nth degree, however, as I have spent the last few days poring excitedly over my new acquisition, meticulously labelling all the pages for the destinations I believe we are going to need, with little sticky tab notes. I've also already estimated our likely mileage, and pre-booked both the Mallaig ferry and the B&B in Uist.

I've also packed a notebook, so that I can make a log of our journey – not of the kind Nige wrote in the early 1980s, but more a 'captain's log, stardate whatever' kind of record, albeit encased in a purple sequinned cover, which says 'Shell Yeah!' on the front. (I'm a fisherman. I never said I'm not still a girlie girl.)

The case is also stuffed – take note – with all kinds of essential tools and accessories, including a hammock (very 'days of sail'), for 'just in case' purposes, a socket set, various spanners and screwdrivers, and the extra tools we'll need to fit the new autopilot we have purchased and had delivered to Iain's house. An autopilot is an essential bit of equipment for any fishing boat, being an automated means of keeping it on course. This one cost us over £3,500, but, as a piece of kit, it's worth every penny, as, when you think about it, it's like hiring a third hand. It'll also do far more than we're going to need it for on this trip (mostly we want it to hold the helm for the majority of the time out at sea, to save fuel and to give us both a break) so it's also an investment for the future. We know it will be invaluable for fishing once we've discovered its many programs.

In contrast, Nigel has a Co-op bag for life.

~

Now I'm a fisherman, I'm excited to be going to Scotland again, as it's one of those places in the UK where fishing and the sea are the beating heart of many of its communities. With its thousands of miles of untamed wild coastline and bountiful seas, its commercial fishing legacy goes right back to before 1889, the year official records began.

It is hard to visit any coastal locations without being reminded of their proud fishing heritage. Be it as romantic as the poem engraved in the stone quay in Footdee (pronounced 'Fittie') . . .

> *Keepin the watch on a winters nicht,*
> *Heedin the rin o the sea*
> *See the blinkin o trawler's lichts*
> *Slinkin oot frae the Dee*

. . . or as harrowing as the bronze *Widows and Bairns* sculpture that sits along the harbour wall at Eyemouth, and depicts the anguish and grief of the 78 widows and 128 children who tragically lost husbands and fathers in the Black Friday storm of 1881. Both have an uncanny way of making me, as a fisherman, feel part of something bigger and exclusive; being a fisherman, it just hits different. Just resonates more personally.

Scotland was a key player in the four Cod Wars of the late 1950s which continued until the late seventies, along with boats from our distant-water fleets of Grimsby, Hull and Fleetwood. The Cod Wars, instigated by Iceland, set a precedent for managing boundaries at sea. So what happened? It's no secret that as a nation we bloody love cod: to be precise, we love about 115,000 tonnes of it every year. So catching these beloved demersal dwellers has always been a priority for our fleets.

Our fishermen found good fishing off the coast of Iceland and in the fifties there were no boundaries, meaning we could happily make the long journey to the Icelandic coast to target the cod we were insatiable for. That was until Iceland imposed a 4-mile territorial boundary on the waters surrounding the entire country in 1952. This unilateral move sparked the first Cod War and saw both governments at loggerheads and issuing sanctions upon one another, until political debate concluded that Iceland could indeed claim a 4-mile boundary.

In 1958 Iceland increased its boundary to 12 nautical miles. Round two of the Cod Wars got underway and saw the Royal Navy accompanying our fleet for protection. This war was resolved in 1961 in much the same manner as the previous war. 1972 saw the boundary moved again by Iceland, now to 50 nautical miles, and, despite it being adopted as law, both UK and German fleets continued to fish within it. We were again supported by the Navy as Icelandic vessels rammed the British fleet and would deploy gear to cut away their trawl nets while towing.

It wasn't until NATO waded in that an agreement was put in place in 1973 to allow our vessels to fish in certain locations within the 50-mile limit and round three was, somewhat begrudgingly, resolved. But in 1975, and with the distant-water fleets still coming to terms with their loss, Iceland revealed its intentions to increase its limits to 200 nautical miles and the hardest-fought cod saga got underway. Enraged by losing fishing grounds that had supported many fishermen, their families and wider communities back home, Iceland ramped up its defensive tactics as the Royal Navy continued to protect our fleet. In early 1976 Iceland achieved its aims and a 200-nautical-mile Exclusive Economic Zone (EEZ) was created. This paved the way for other territories to adopt the same strategy.

The EEZ was often hotly debated during Brexit as, thanks to these wars, we (along with many others) now also have an EEZ, which extends up to 200 nautical miles from our shores. It was irrelevant to fishing in our partnership with Europe as common access was granted, but our departure saw us with the power to reclaim the entire zone exclusively. But, like many break-ups, it got messy.

European vessels own the rights to catch fish in our territories (remember those FQAs and the common marketplace from Chapter 8?) and have done so for many years. We also rely heavily on European markets to export the fish we do catch. (Eye-wateringly, 80 per cent of all fish caught by us is exported abroad.) So the UK agreed to continue to allow our European neighbours access, and would issue licences allowing them access to our different zones: 0–6 Nautical Miles, 6–12 Nautical Miles, and External Waters. These licences have been issued at no financial cost to the owners, and, to date, 1,571 vessels hold them, and the right to access our waters for fish. This may sound like a small amount, but if you consider that the UK's *entire active fleet* amounts to just 4,269 vessels (which, by the way, also contains UK-registered boats with foreign ownership – but more on that later), those fifteen-hundred boats represent an additional 37 per cent, also taking fish from our waters.

This, then, is the current state of play, and if there is one thing I can confidently predict in all this, it's that whatever happens next, it's likely to be complicated. I remember hearing once that if you're offered a very simple solution to a very complex problem, whoever is offering it is likely to be talking a load of old bilge. Having made a lengthy voyage round the history, politics and regulation of our fishing industry, I cannot agree wholeheartedly enough. And, be warned, there is still more to come . . .

In the meantime, back with the plans for our own, much more pleasurable voyage. Having made the ten-hour journey north in Nige's car, along with Jack and Kenneth, who are going to drive it home for him, we arrive at Mallaig ferry port at around 4 p.m., and decant both my suitcase and Nigel's carrier bag (already tatty, frankly – how he thinks it'll survive the trip is beyond me) from the car. Having waved the lads off (and clutching the blanket Jack has loaned me – my one packing fail) we then board the ferry to South Uist.

I am no less excited. We have been saving up for this boat all summer, driven to cope with the deprivation – and there's been a lot of deprivation, as we've had to pay ourselves far less than the national minimum wage, and apply a stringent cost-conscious attitude to all aspects of our lives – just by the thrill of knowing not only that she will soon be ours, but by the commitment and leap of faith *Fairlass* represents for me personally. Bringing our boat home is the tangible confirmation that I am now full-time crew on a fishing boat, and part owner of one, to boot.

As I lie in my B&B bedroom that night, staring up out of the Velux window and watching the evening mist descend on the munros that surround us, I realise my holiday butterflies seem to have metamorphosed into something different. I know why, too. Holidays are great, but, invariably, they end. This new relationship – with a piece of beautifully crafted timber – is my passport. To a whole new start.

Chapter 11

'Dolphins swimming with the boat is a good omen'

Because we have an autopilot to install on *Fairlass* before we leave South Uist, we plan to spend the next day and night on the island, so we will be able to make an early start the following morning in the hopes of reaching the mainland before nightfall.

After a full Scottish breakfast at our B&B, Iain picks us up and we head down to the harbour at Lochboisdale. He has the autopilot with him, and has already moved *Fairlass* up there for us, because everything we might need will be closer to hand.

We've only just got everything down onto the boat, however, when Nige's mobile trills at him. It's Carl. (You might remember him. He's the one with the amazing mechanical skills, who loves dogs.)

'Alright Nige?' he says. 'You got a load of whelk pots turning up today?'

'Shouldn't have,' Nige says, 'They're not due till next week.'

'Well, they're sat in the middle of the road, mate. DHL have just dropped them. D'you want me to do anything with them?'

'You're alright mate,' Nige says. 'I'll sort it.'

He puts down the hydraulic hose he's holding and wipes his hands on his trackies. Then calls the supplier, who doesn't answer, then DHL, who don't either. Then, just as he's about to call the harbourmaster to pre-empt the inevitable, the harbourmaster is already calling him.

'You got a load of whelk pots turning up today, Nige?' he asks him. 'Only there's a load of them sat in the middle of the road.'

You wouldn't know it from his voice, but Nigel's face is a picture. 'Yeah, Robert,' he says. 'I know. I'm trying to sort it.'

'You do know it's Carnival?' the harbourmaster continues. (It being Carnival week means the town will be *heaving*, and two 8-foot-high pallets of whelk pots, slap bang in the middle of the main drag, will be about as welcome as a bucket of cold sick.)

'Yeah, Robert,' he says again, face darkening further. 'I'm on it.'

'Well, if you need a hand mate,' Robert tells him. 'Just let me know.'

Realising that he does need help, which is painful, as Nige hates asking favours, he makes his special stress noise, like a high-pitched baby elephant trying to whistle through its trunk, and has a calming fag. He then calls Carl back.

'D'you mind moving them onto the quay for me, mate?' Nige asks him. That done, we get back to fitting the autopilot. These sorts of spanners in the works are pretty commonplace for us – and, I'm sure, many others up and down the coast.

Or, at least, we get back to laying out all the tools and parts in readiness for fitting the autopilot and, speaking of spanners-in-works, we then discover we are probably missing a vital component. Nige puts down the rudder sensor he's currently swinging about, and once again picks up his phone.

Twenty minutes and several to-ings and fro-ings later, we manage to establish that we are *definitely* missing a vital component and Iain and I drive back to his house, just in case it's been left behind. Which it hasn't, and further phone calls establish that though the supplier can send one, it will take three to five days to reach the islands, so we have no choice but to give up, and accept we'll need to do the whole journey by hand-steering. A pretty deflating prospect, which takes the wind out of our sails. (Which, incidentally, is something our new boat does have; unlike *Never Can Tell-A*, *Fairlass* has a mizzen, which, in this setting, i.e. a small fishing boat, can be used to turn the sea state down a notch when hauling gear, as it helps to slow the boat's rolling motion.)

We decide to head to the local café to mull over our misfortune, and leave feeling marginally better. We've got this. It'll be hard, but it's still a first-world problem. They didn't have autopilots back in the old days, did they? We're just agreeing on this when I hear a female shout behind me.

'Hellooo!' the woman is calling. 'You left your handbag in the café!'

Nige rolls his eyes. Not least because inside it is everything important that we need, including my mobile, vital documents, and both our bank cards. I take the bag and thank the woman profusely for heading off that disaster; though, in my defence, I very rarely carry a handbag. Dora the Explorer, as Nige calls it, is only ever deployed during adventures. And this particular adventure is becoming increasingly tedious, as Nige's phone starts ringing yet again.

This time it's Kenneth. 'Dad,' he says, even as I'm thinking, 'What *now*?' 'The boat won't start.'

'Oh for fuck's sake,' says Nige, and I can see his brain whirring as he begins mentally listing what Kenneth has to do.

They need to get it somewhere with power so they can get a jump pack on her, which means moving her from the quay to the pontoon. Having told him what needs doing, Nige leaves him to it and, given this new and frustrating development, we do what first needs to be done, obviously, and go for a beer.

Half an hour later, while we're enjoying the view from the pub garden (it's a beautiful day, so we're grateful for that at least), Kenneth rings again. The alternator's not charging. Nige gives him instructions to check three or four things, and another half an hour later, establishes that the alternator is broken, which means Nige has to make another call, to order a replacement, to be delivered to Wells the next day. Thank god for those bank cards we nearly mislaid.

Having given up on the autopilot, all that's left now is the paperwork, so Iain comes to pick us up to take us back to his, where we deal with all the documents and complete the bill of sale.

Our newly raised spirits, however (Yay! We actually own her!), only last as long as it takes us to establish that we've missed the call for dinner at the local hotel and restaurant – the only place where we can get a hot meal. So forlorn do we look though – we can actually *see* other diners tucking into huge platefuls – that the owner takes pity on us. 'If I can fry it you can have it,' she kindly tells us, and so excited am I when my scampi and chips arrives fifteen minutes later that I even take a photo of it – and back then, I didn't even have Instagram.

Before getting the taxi back to our B&B we walk over to the local Co-op, as we'll be leaving before it opens in the morning, and stock up on all the essentials we're going to need for our first journey, of over 90 nautical miles. It's mostly cider, Rustlers burgers, a couple of hearty ready meals, two premixed spiced rum and cokes (not just to be nautical, by the way; according to my paternal grandmother, I'm distantly related to Captain Morgan), and lots and lots of cigarettes. Because with our luck who knows where (or when, or if) we're going to make landfall?

All probable needs catered for, we finally head to bed. Tomorrow can only be better.

~

The following day dawns as bright and beautiful as the one before. It's only 7 a.m. but I can sense there's heat in the air. We are actually doing this. Our epic adventure now properly begins.

I open my case and pull out my Barbie-pink canvas shorts, imagining Nige in the room next door, rummaging in his carrier bag, and having to choose between two crumpled pairs of trackies. HAH! (Me feeling smug? Never.) Then after another breakfast, the size of which means we won't need to eat again for hours, Iain arrives to drive us down to the harbour, where he's to say goodbye not just to us but to his beloved *Fairlass*, a boat he might only have had for a couple of years but which he has poured so much of his heart and soul into. (I know this because I've seen pictures of the condition of her when he bought her, and the transformation has been incredible. With this boat the glow-up is real.)

We head down the pontoon beside which *Fairlass* is moored, and I notice that numerous grey plastic boxes with integral lids are suspended in the water. About a metre down, they are tied by rope to the cleats at the edge of the pontoons, and have been drilled with multiple holes. Since Ian's still with us, I ask him what they are.

'Lobsters,' he replies. 'This is where we store them while we wait for the collection.'

He goes on to explain that with no holding tanks and a collection that only happens once a week at best, this is the only viable way of keeping them alive until they are picked up by the buyers.

'We wouldn't get away with that in Wells,' Nige remarks. 'This time of year, they'd mostly likely die within a day or two. Either that, or someone would pinch them.'

He's joking about that part, of course, but it's a good point he's making. Down where we are the sand gets very hot in the summer and when the water comes in, it's soon heated up to a temperature the lobsters couldn't withstand. Here, with the cold sea, and the fact that it's not tidal, it's obviously a really clever solution. It's also an example of the way small-scale fishermen constantly need to adapt to stay profitable.

Furthermore, don't let the dozen or so boats at Wells fool you. It's a busy port for shellfish, with lobsters contributing a large amount financially to its own fishy economy. The boats from Wells alone have been known to land anywhere between 20 and 50 tonnes per year, with summer being the prime season to target these elusive beasts who are busy procreating and hunting down food. And, as controversial as this may sound, I have to wonder how many of these ten-footed, navy-dappled, fan-tailed sea bugs should have been thrown back, not just from our coastline, but around the country. Since 2017 it has been illegal to land a 'berried' lobster, i.e. one bearing eggs, to protect the stocks and ensure longevity of the fishery. (It seems odd to me that it took that long to introduce such a restriction.) This rule, however, is sadly abused nationwide.

The abhorrent practice of scrubbing female lobsters of their eggs in order to pretend they are legal to be landed and sold makes my blood boil. All I, and other like-minded people in our community, can do to prevent this problem, is to cut a 'V' notch in the fin tails of every berried female lobster we catch, before sending her back on her way (sometimes with a snack), so that effectively no one can legally land her until the notch has grown out over the next few years. I live in hope that this greedy behaviour is not a massive issue at Wells, and that the mentality of 'well if I don't take it someone else will' doesn't plague our fishermen. However, there will always be people who cannot see beyond the end of their own noses, given the hefty price tag for these fascinating and highly sought-after sea critters.

In my opinion this issue really does need tackling nationally. Surely the MMO and the IFCAs (Inshore Fisheries and Conservation Authorities) should be highlighting and finding solutions to this? (Note to fishermen everywhere: if you do this, please stop! It's not cool. Try harder. Be better.)

As we climb aboard with all our gear, it occurs to me how hard it will be for Iain to wave off this boat he loves so much. It's something I have never had to bear witness to as yet, but I imagine it will be heart-wrenching to watch her sail away without him, especially when I consider that his only reason for selling her is that he cannot find anyone to crew for him.

As Iain gives us one final heave off the pontoon (*Fairlass* is heavy, weighing in at over 10 tons), we wave our goodbyes and I start picking up the fenders, the little brightly coloured plastic balls of air that most will be familiar with, as they dangle from the hull and are used to protect the boat when alongside. They come in lots of shapes – lozenges, sausages, space-hoppers – and it's an automatic action to lift them every time you set off. (You can sort the 'men' from the 'boys', as in the seafarers from the tourists, by whether they are out at sea with their fenders still a-dangle.) I then stand on the deck and just try to drink it all in. We are flanked on three sides by the dramatic, velvety green rocky outcrops of the outer Hebrides, and ahead of us, mirror calm, is our watery route out to sea. We are already spoilt, because our jobs mean we work such in a beautiful environment, and I wouldn't have Wells any other way. But this is different. Where at home we have to

136

share that beauty, almost year-round, with throngs of travellers and tourists, here it's just me, Nige and *Fairlass*, and all that wild, fierce, totally isolated beauty. Within a matter of minutes, not only can we not see another boat. Bar the flora, and a couple of birds flying high above us, we cannot see another living thing.

We are properly on our own now. It's a sobering moment. Not alone in the sea we work almost daily, where we pretty much know where all the other boats are as well, but alone in what, for us, represents uncharted waters.

I join Nige in the wheelhouse, and plop myself down in what will soon come to be known as *my* chair. It's sprung, so it will provide shock absorption in heavy weather, though the springs will definitely not be needed today. As I watch the depth plummet on the echo sounder to some 300 feet, I am in shock. It's something I've never seen before, due to the shallowness of the puddle that is the North Sea, but this is the Sea of the Hebrides, part of the North Atlantic Ocean, and it is already staggeringly deep.

Our goal is to make the 90-mile journey back to the west coast of Scotland by nightfall and find somewhere to lay the boat for the night. I've already done some research, thanks to the trusty almanac, and estimated that this will be possible.

Considering we're steaming through the hotchpotch of islands, both big and small, that make up this scenic and busy stretch of coastline, it's amazing how far we can see. The grey-green bulk of land comes and goes all around us, and we have fun trying to guess what we're seeing without checking. We pass the Isle of Rum, which Nige quips he could definitely set up home on, and the Isle of Muck, which we both agree we wouldn't. We also pass a tiny island called Eigg, pronounced 'egg', which, astoundingly, since it's so tiny, is home to some one hundred people. We spend a while chatting about the reality of living in such isolated places and agree that though the idea always seems idyllic, especially on a day like today, the reality, and its isolation, is definitely not for us.

'Ash! Dolphins!' Nige's voice cuts like a blade through my reverie. I follow his pointing finger, and we hurry out to the port side of the boat, neither of us worrying about that fact that we'll almost certainly drift off course. This is too good a spectacle to miss.

At this time in my life I have only encountered dolphins from a distance. On ferries, on a cruise ship once, in Seaworld in Florida; and I have seen the odd solitary porpoise off the coast of Wells. This school of dolphins, which eagle-eyed Nige has spotted, is equally distant – just an agitation in the water, as they repeatedly break the surface.

Nige has experience of spectacles like this, obviously. 'Keep an eye on them,' he says, turning back to the wheelhouse. 'Let's see if they want to come and play with us.'

He makes a minuscule course correction – 'Just to attract their attention,' he tells me – then, within little more than thirty seconds they are right up at the side of the boat.

'Get up the bow, Ash,' he commands, flapping a hand at me. 'Get up the bow. That's where they'll be.' He is right, and for the next five or ten minutes, dolphins are all I can see. There must be thirty or forty of them, big, small, and everything in between, plus a couple of tiny infants, who stay so close to their mums it's as if they are one entity. And they *do* play. They seem to be revelling in our unexpected visit to their territory, surfacing and diving, all around and underneath *Fairlass*, and treating the bow wave like a fountain in a water park.

I am awestruck. This is the first time I've had the privilege of such an intimate encounter with these beautiful creatures, and best of all, it's all mine: I don't have to share it, or jostle for space with anyone else. I am in their world. They have no concept of what a human is, and I am moved to tears by knowing that they want to come and spend this time with me. Nige is back steering the boat now – and can still see them, because they are everywhere – and though he says it's because we need to press on, I know these few precious moments alone with them are his gift to me.

~

The sea remains silky for the rest of the journey and by 3 p.m. we arrive at the Sound of Mull, which separates Mull from mainland Scotland. It's a kind of shortcut to our destination of Portnacroish. Just as we approach we see another thing of beauty: a fishing boat I recognise, called *Dawn Treader*, which I've read about online, and is one of two wooden vessels that have been maintained so incredibly well that they almost look too perfect to be working fishing boats. The exposed wood also gives them an air of heightened reality, better suited to a seafaring Disney film – I can easily imagine Moana at the bow.

We are soon brought back to actual reality, however, when we see a load of white triangles ahead, all zipping about, and know our route through will now be accompanied. It looks like a regatta of some sort, and our industry term for them is WAFIs, which stands for Wind Assisted Fucking Idiots. It seems harsh but is essentially harmless banter, born out of the colregs that state that steam must always give way to sail. Which is fair enough – if you're wind-powered you have less manoeuvrability – but it does make it difficult to travel in a straight line when you have boats moving in all directions all around you. Nige is good at this, however, and despite there being twenty or so yachts constantly tacking all around us, manages to keep an eye on, and steer a course through, them all. It's things like this, he comments, that keep you sharp.

Sharp being the operative word. A sharpie is not just an indelible pen, it's also a small traditional sailing boat, with a flat bottom and flared sides, and we have a large collection of them at Wells. They can often be seen darting around the harbour on windy weekends, cutting quickly across the channels which can be a hazard if you're not paying attention to who's tacking and where they are heading when making passage through the harbour. It is not out of the ordinary to have one come whizzing past your bow at high speed before making a quick turn and passing you again.

Through the regatta, we take a left to enter the waterway of Loch Linnhe, and it's just a case then of finding a mooring for the night. Tomorrow we are going to take the mother of all short cuts, crossing Scotland via the 60 miles of the Caledonian Canal.

Chapter 12

'Do not sleep with your head towards the bow'

It's around 7.30 p.m. by the time we enter the inland waterways of the west coast of Scotland. Because we're not sure how soon we're going to lose the light, and don't want to steam in the dark on our first day if we can help it, we decide to tie up for the night at a little honesty harbour tucked in just behind Shuna Island, a quick phone call having confirmed they have pontoon space.

Honesty harbours are a first for both of us. The deal is that, having grabbed the codes over the phone to unlock the adjacent showers and toilets, we put £15 into a box bolted to the wall of the facilities cabin, and we're good to go. Or, more accurately, to stay. A few spaces are already taken, but there is no one about so, once again, with empty-looking hillsides all around us, we have a keen sense of solitude. It's another beautiful evening, and I'm grateful that we have found it before nightfall, since the red and green marking buoys that guided us to its entrance seemed little bigger than matchsticks compared to the ones we're used to back in Wells; they stand so proudly in the water, but without a lot of justification. We'd never have spotted them in the dark.

It is not unusual for us to steam or work in the dark, given the restricted daylight hours of the winter months; however, dark summer mornings are seldom dark for long. As a fisherman you are rewarded for those painfully early starts with some of the most fabulous sunrises. They feel so exclusive; given the solitude of your surroundings it's as if they are only meant for you. I am often reminded of the first few lines of the *Walrus and the Carpenter* poem by Lewis Carroll (google it) as I watch the night slowly dissolve in the east, the black darkness melting to a blotted blue, as the pinks, oranges, reds and purples creep up over the horizon, while in the west the night sky still claims the space. You can be on deck baiting a pot and witnessing the colourful birth of a brand-new day, but when you turn to stack said pot the darkness of night is glaring back at you.

We have had some scorching days this summer in Wells. With little to no reprieve from the heat we have at times cooled off by sitting on the frozen boxes of dogfish between each string of pots. With temperatures in the mid- to high thirties so many of the fleet have opted to fish the anti-social tides at night purely to beat the heat, not just on themselves but on the catch too. All shellfish has to be sold live, given that once it is dead harmful bacteria can build up fast. Crabs and lobsters are adaptable, and their gills will convert oxygen from both sea water and the air we breathe, so long as their gills are kept cool and moist. This is much easier to achieve in the cooler night-time temperatures, with damp hessian sacks covering them and methodical rotation of the deck wash hose through the stacks of boxes they are in. Molluscs will simply shut up shop and close their shells to go into 'standby' mode until they are once again submerged in seawater where they can then reopen and filter the oxygen, while whelks keep their own handy saltwater supply inside their shell to help them survive a period of time out of the water. Hot temperatures, however, can evaporate this supply and dry the whelk out, so keeping them damp and cool too is essential.

The guy I called to see if there was space for us to tie up has already pointed us in the direction of the nearest place we'll be able to find some food, which is apparently just five minutes up a track into the woods. So as soon as *Fairlass* is made fast on the pontoon, we waste no time in grabbing Dora and setting off, turning right up the track as directed. Twenty minutes later, and by now really out of puff, since it's been uphill from the get-go, we see a sign with an arrow, which says 'Beer, food, whisky'. This cheers us up no end, and, after a final scrabble up a steep incline, we emerge into a pub beer garden, which has a spectacular view of the long-derelict Castle Stalker, which sits on an island of its own.

In contrast to the seemingly uninhabited little harbour, the pub, The Old Inn, which is 'highland' themed almost to within an inch of pastiche, is absolutely heaving, almost every table filled, and with a warm hubbub of conversation in the air. The welcome is equally warm, and the food is amazing, and we rattle back in the dark with full bellies and a great feeling of satisfaction that we've completed the first leg back to the mainland.

The pub has one downside: there is no room at the inn. No rooms, period, but we're not bothered as the weather's been so lovely that we've already half decided to save a bit of money by spending tonight on our new boat.

This is a first for me. I have slept on a boat before, and on both of Nige's in fact, but only to get a couple of hours' kip if I've had an early start or a poor night's sleep, and there's a couple of hours steaming ahead. But I've never had to bed down for the night on board a boat with no accommodation.

'This should be fun,' I say to Nige, as I survey the expanse of space and consider the options. Given that all we have are the deck itself, the tiny wheelhouse, and the erroneously named for'd 'cabin' (a triangular cubby hole beneath the foredeck that not even the smallest seventeenth-century cruelly press-ganged cabin boy could swing a ship's cat in) the extent of our privations is becoming clear.

He grunts in response, and I can soon hear him shuffling about down for'd. I shine my phone torch in his direction as he clambers his way back up into the wheelhouse. I'm dazzled by reflective tape and red neoprene. 'What ya doin there?' I ask.

'Tryin' to make a friggin' bed, aren't I?'

I can't help but laugh at him as he brandishes a survival suit.

'I don't know what's funny,' he adds, in his best mock serious voice. 'I'm comfy as fuck already.'

I laugh again. It dawns on me now that though my suitcase is packed for any wardrobe requirement, I am totally unprepared for this version of camping.

It's a warm night and we stand on deck looking at our options: two survival suits, one blanket and one hammock. Given the confined nature of the wheelhouse and for'd cabin we decide the deck is going to give us the most space. So with a survival suit each acting as a mattress and with rolled-up jumpers for pillows, Nigel takes the hammock as his duvet and I get the blanket.

I might have been able to appreciate the darkness, or the silence of the highlands that flank us, or the chaotic clusters of stars above me, but I can't. Not with the singing pain of the fucking rock-hard deck, which is digging into my shoulder, ribs and hips. But it's been a long day, one full of excitement and adrenaline so, despite the pain, I eventually feel myself slowly drifting off, just as my phone check shows it's nearly midnight.

'Is that rain?' Nigel's voice stirs me out of my descent into sleep, as fresh spits of cold water land on my face. 'Oi Ash?' he doesn't whisper. 'You asleep?'

'Yeah, it's rain,' I grumble back. I can hear it pattering on the deck now. With the spots now gathering pace, armfuls of our 'bedding' are scooped up, and we make a dash for the wheelhouse.

'You go down the front, Ash,' Nige commands me. 'I'll manage on the floor in here.'

I look down at the wheelhouse floor and back at Nige, and once again consider our options. *Fairlass*'s wheelhouse is around the same size as *Never Can Tell-A*'s, but it doesn't seem so because she's not only better equipped (with all the standard navigation equipment you'd expect to find along with a small hot water boiler and microwave), but also has a big central console, which pretty much divides the wheelhouse in half, apart from half a metre of floor space just inside the wheelhouse door. It's a perfect set-up for skipper and crew, with all the equipment and instruments enveloped around you on the starboard side, but as a sleeping

145

space, it's obviously hopeless, unless you are half a metre by half a metre square. (Nige, for context, is 6 feet tall, so little short of 2 metres, and obviously built as strongly as you'd expect.)

I do as instructed, sitting down on my bum, grabbing the side rails that lead the way down into the port side of the cubby hole, and sliding myself down for'd into the small triangle of space.

Nige, meanwhile, lays out his survival suit on the zigzag bit of floor to the left of the console, which is just about big enough for his head and torso. This means his legs and feet will have to spend the night out on deck, and as the hammock isn't waterproof, he instead chooses to curl up in a foetal position with his legs resting on the door sill instead – which is a slightly inconvenient 20cm higher than the wheelhouse floor. He's now using the *Reeds Almanac* under his jumper as a pillow.

'Still comfy as fuck?' I call up from my oubliette.

'Yeah, babe!' he calls back and though I know he's joking, I also know he isn't – not really. He's never one to be beaten, and we're on our new boat, and we're on an adventure, and he *is* happy. I know it. We've had such an exciting day; plain sailing all the way, with added dolphins. Being bent up in the wheelhouse is just a minor inconvenience, and I know he has slept in *far* worse places.

I'm right. Moments later he's snoring. And, despite being curled up into the tiniest of balls, with my head wedged hard up against the ribs of the hull, I sleep as well. The next thing I hear is the phone alarm I set, and I'm astonished. We have slept right through till 6 a.m.

～

The early morning air is fresh and a bit hazy and across the water the distant hills of Sgurr Dhomhnuill are shrouded in a thick mist. I clean my teeth out on deck while Nige, having unbent himself and sparked a fag, puts the kettle on for coffee, and I can soon hear a familiar sound in the distance. A rhythmic chug-chug-chug, coming closer. It belongs to a little fishing boat, which draws up alongside the pontoon. She's called *Our Catherine*, and is a prawn boat (what Scots fishermen call a langoustine). Her owner tells us that he knows *Fairlass*, and has seen her for sale online. 'She's a fine boat,' he adds. He then tells us a little about his prawn fishing business and how they are struggling – which is pretty standard when fishermen talk among themselves, even if they're actually doing brilliantly. He's here, he tells us, to pick up his crew, and, as if on cue, a young guy in oilskins comes marching down the pontoon, and they chug-chug-chug away shortly after.

Once I've completed my ablutions in the facilities, we set off ourselves, for the hour or so's steam to the basin at Corpach, which marks the entrance to the Caledonian Canal.

Begun in the early years of the nineteenth century, the canal, masterminded by the noted Scottish civil engineer Thomas Telford, was built to provide a shortcut for shipping from Corpach in the west to Inverness in the east (the alternative to using it being to travel over the top of Scotland, where the tide is so fierce that it can really hinder progress, which is probably why they called it Cape Wrath).

Big tides don't just hamper the progress of a boat getting from A to B, they also affect fishing. I can only speak for the fishing we do, as big fast-moving currents may benefit some fishermen, but I have seen from experience that the shellfish we catch certainly seem to be less active, so it makes sense to stay out of the currents: it probably takes a lot of effort to go out and hunt for food or a mate when you're being blasted by strong tidal forces that stir up the sediment on the bottom. It must be like going out to pick up a takeaway at rush hour.

Tides also have an impact on the way in which we work. You'll remember that we work pots facing into the tide, pulling our relatively light boat along on the rope as it comes into the hauler. On a big tide you run the risk of parting the rope, given the amount of opposing forces on it, so the boat has to be put in and out of gear to make your way along the shank. (Big heavy boats will do this all the time.)

There was an occasion earlier this summer when one of our ropes parted mid-shank because of the aggressive flow of the tide. By some stroke of luck, I not only noticed, but also made the quick decision to dart into the wheelhouse and, as Nige held on to the loose end, *à la* stretch Armstrong, was able to steam the boat back up quickly enough so we had sufficient slack to get the rope back in the hauler. Yes, he could have let go, I suppose, and we could have steamed to the other end, but things like that all take up precious time and the whole thing would have been a huge faff. As it was, Nige's arm was probably by now four inches longer, but that's fishing for you.

The tide also affects the way in which we shoot gear back to the seafloor, especially with whelk gear, which you'll remember is shot across the tidal flow. If I want to shoot the gear at a 0-degree angle (so directly north) I do not steer a heading of 0 degrees. In this case I would have to allow for the force of the ebbing tide pushing against the boat at the time, so I may have to steer at 20 degrees (roughly north-north east) to maintain a course overground of 0 degrees (north).

~

No tides to worry about today though. One third of the canal is manmade, then it takes in three lochs: Lochy, Oich, and Ness. It has twenty-nine locks, including Neptune's Staircase, the longest continuous staircase lock in Scotland, and which raises the canal a whopping 19 metres.

It's with this staircase of locks that we are going to begin our trip along the canal, but first we have to wait in a holding basin until the tides coincide with the lock operation, which today is going to be 1 p.m. Though our plan was to chill on deck as soon as the sun burned the clouds off, as we enter the basin Nige notices that the engine is barking. Nige has a sixth sense when it comes to the sound of Ford engines, and I've come to realise that even if I can't hear anything, if Nige can, there is definitely something up. We then also notice that the temperature gauge is beginning to creep up. Only by a smidge, but it's enough for him to know something is wrong.

Once we've tied up, further investigation reveals that part of the sea water cooling system is blocked; the end cap and pipe are gummed up with debris. And, unfortunately, because it's not been taken off for several years now, the only way Nige has been able to investigate what's wrong is by cutting a section of pipe.

So instead of a morning spent sunbathing on deck, I am tasked with a mission: to somehow get hold of a length of inch-and-a-quarter diameter heat-proof flexible hose and, to fix it in place, some jubilee clips.

By the time we have managed to establish all of this, it's getting on for 10.30. And, inconveniently, we are in the middle of nowhere, and, with no harbours or marinas around, are highly unlikely to be anywhere near a boatyard. So while Nige chain smokes and stresses, I am now on a quest.

I grab Dora and the cut-off length of hose as my reference, then set off out of the empty car park, but see nothing bar a moderately busy road, which I assume is the main one into Fort William. And a bout of googling while I walk ('exhaust places near me' seeming the obvious best bet) pulls up almost nothing. Which is no surprise, as no sooner have I started walking along the road than it becomes clear that there is nothing for miles. I then revisit the idea of boatyards, which we'd previously dismissed, and googling that brings up a big online chandlery, which has a base just over a mile away, and seems also to a have a boat building yard. It's definitely worth a try, so, with the clock ticking, I up my pace down the hill, and walk through the front gates just after 11.

It takes me ages to find a human, finally tracking down a bloke in a giant hangar, where he is busy building a boat. 'I think I've got some of that somewhere out the back,' he says, when I thrust my bit of hose in front of him. This is music to my ears, because the size of pipe I need would be a big thing for a car garage, but is actually a very small thing for a builder of big boats. I go with the man into a series of side rooms, where he rummages in several cupboards and drawers. And eventually comes up with a foot of the correct rubber piping, plus a couple of jubilee clips to hold it in place – hurrah! By this time, however, Nige is blowing up my phone, as they want to move him to the staircase to get ready. He has already temporarily patched things up as best he can, so we can at least limp up the staircase, but needs me back because he obviously can't set off without me – on his own he cannot get through the locks.

Luckily, the woman in the boatyard office, who I'm busy paying, overhears us, and very kindly offers to drive me back in her car. Five minutes later I'm in place at the top of the first lock in the staircase, proudly brandishing my new pipe. Mission accomplished! I feel smug. When it comes to a side quest from Nige, Ash *always* delivers the goods.

First hurdle down, but still a *long* way to go.

Chapter 12 plus 1

'Never say "thirteen" on a boat; instead, always say
"twelve plus one"'

If the Caledonian Canal is a feat of engineering (it really is; if you ever get a chance to go though it by boat, do – you will not regret it) then Neptune's Staircase is the jewel in its crown. I google it while waiting for Nige to get into the first lock, but can't find anything about why it's called that. But I have this nice little theory that Neptune wanted to visit mainland Scotland but the land was too high for him to reach. So he waved his trident around a bit (or whatever Roman gods did to get things done), and fashioned a staircase for his convenience.

At any rate, standing at the bottom and looking up, I have such respect for the engineers who designed and built this, not least because my research also tells me that the whole idea of the Caledonian Canal was conceived to help the fragile fishing and agricultural communities of the western islands to survive, and to halt emigration to the mainland.

As we ascend the staircase, lock by lock, I have a great sense of privilege to be doing this. It gives me such pride that we are bringing this beautiful boat home to Wells with us – and she is, without doubt, the most striking vessel making the passage today. It's also fun, and at the same time a little nerve-wracking, admittedly, to be the focus of attention of all the gongoozlers who are milling about, and apparently, given all the pointing and picture-taking, watching our every move.

With *Fairlass* through the first lock, we then get into a rhythm, with me holding her head rope while the locks fill with water, and then Nige steaming her through into the chamber. I stay on the towpath while this is happening and keep hold of the head rope so between locks it's like I'm walking a very large blue dog.

It takes two hours in total, by which time we are a well-oiled machine, then it's time to tie up and roll our sleeves up, as if we try to go further we could easily cook the engine, and we still have sufficient time to effect the repair on the cooling system before dark. With limited tools to hand, it's a long, tedious, fiddly kind of job, but at least not a complicated one, so by 5.30 p.m. we're ready to clean up in the adjacent shower block, and go in search of a pub.

Once again, Scotland delivers on the food front. The nearest pub is called The Lochy, and since they have haggis as a starter, we get some, as neither of us has ever tried it. It's so nice that we finish it and order it again, creating a kind of highland tapas-style vibe, washed down with draught Tennants and Scottish G and Ts. Once we're completely stuffed with food we stumble back to the boat, where we happily opt to spend a second night aboard and, in our slightly inebriated state, take our chances with the weather and sleep out on deck.

As I slip into sleep (no marvelling at the wonders of the heavens tonight – I'm too adrift to even make a proper bed up, let alone count stars), I don't have a care in the world. I'm fast asleep in seconds.

Chapter 14

'Green is an unlucky colour when it comes to boats'

Green is the colour of the land, so it was believed that painting a boat
green would cause the vessel to run aground. Similarly, take nothing
green aboard.

I'm woken at 5.30 a.m. by an insistent urge to pee, and my first
thought is where the fuck am I? I'm flat on my back and as soon
as I open my eyes, I have to shut them again, as I'm blinded by
the light. I'm also cold, proper cold – with the kind of whole-
body shiver that means the freezing air has permeated my very
bones. I gingerly try opening my eyes again – just a tentative little
peep – and now it's marginally more bearable. I'm able to take in
the underside of the wheelhouse canopy, and, when I sit up, an
expanse of still ochre water; what I'm looking at is the canal, seen
through the hole in the transom, and the hull of the luxury motor
cruiser that moored behind us last night. I have, I realise, just
spent my first whole night out of doors, as in *really* out of doors,
without even a tent. Without any shelter whatsoever.

My first thought after that one is that I really need to do my wee, but with the toilets all the way over the other side of the canal I'm going to have to do what I usually do and go on deck. Except sitting here in this canal, without any seawater sloshing up through the scuppers, bopping down on the deck doesn't feel right. So I hop up on and sit on the wire mesh of the cat catcher instead. Sod the boat behind us. I doubt they're awake anyway.

While I'm peeing I realise that the mountain that almost fills my vision to the right is Ben Nevis. I don't absolutely know this; but at the same time I do. We saw signs for it yesterday so I already knew it was somewhere in the vicinity, and there is something so huge and majestic about it – the way it looms so omnipotently and magnificently above me – that it simply cannot be anything else. It's a bright but hazy morning, with lots of low-level cloud, but all I can see, gazing at it, is a tapestry of velvet, as if stitched together out of mother nature's favourite colour palette. I also have this strong sense that the mountain is gazing back at me, in judgement that this bedraggled, puffy-faced, wild-haired human has the audacity to stick her arse out in its presence.

I hop down off the cat catcher and nudge Nige with my foot. He's been sleeping properly out on deck too, without even the canopy to keep the wind off, but then he's a proper seafarer and, for him, this isn't any kind of hardship, even with the frigid nature of the early morning air. He fakes stirring, even though I know he's already awake – he was just being a gentleman while I did what I needed to – and I tell him I'm going to go and flick the hot water on for coffee. I feel a whoosh of excitement about the

60 miles that lie ahead, which I imagine, given the chill vibe this whole place is giving me, will be nothing short of blissful.

Coffee-d up, we take a long meandering walk to the local Co-op, some twenty minutes away. The canal doesn't open till 8 a.m., and we need to stock back up on essentials. Well, most essentials, at any rate, because, when we get there, it turns out that due to some annoying law in Scotland, they're not allowed to sell alcohol till 10 a.m., scuppering Nige's fond imaginings of elegantly sipping on a cider while cruising serenely through the canal. Heading back, and fully committed to breaking at least one Scottish law (that there must be strictly no traffic on the canal before 8 a.m.), we fire up the engine and slip the ropes, keen to beat the inevitable bottleneck.

We start our journey surrounded by a natural beauty the like of which I've never seen before. The wild landscape is so vast and we are so small in comparison, that if a giant came galumphing into view he would not look out of place. And, with every blind curve the canal takes us round, the view gets even better. My senses are overwhelmed by the sheer scale of everything, as we pass under bridges that look like they should be guarded by trolls, and chug by small lazy waterfalls.

By 9 a.m. we reach the lock that marks the entrance to Loch Lochy. (There is a limerick in there somewhere, I'm sure.) Like all the other locks we've encountered up here, the system works on hydraulics, so there's no need to faff about with a windlass, and we're soon entering the loch itself which, after the last hour steaming through what felt like an enchanted Middle Earth forest, is almost like emerging into the sea. Or at least a massive lake, which, as Nige points out, is exactly what it is. And a very deep one. A glance over the side immediately confirms this. The almost opaque water we've been travelling through so far is now crystal clear to a depth of many metres, so much so that it looks almost black.

We cover the 9 or so miles of the loch in just under two hours, after which we have another lock to negotiate, which, with its enormous metal gates reminds me of Jurassic Park, which automatically makes me start doody-dooing out the theme tune at the top of my voice. Once she's let us through, the lovely loch keeper lady squats down on the towpath and wags her finger at me.

'Thanks for that,' she says cheerfully. 'I can't unhear that now, can I? Every single time I press that wee button there from now on!'

She's winding me up, surely. Has no one done that before?

I ask her. She shakes her head. So apparently not.

'Sorry,' I say, even though I'm not. It's hilarious. She's still shaking her head as we chug on by.

The scenery continues to be stunning as we recommence our journey, and the heat – which is growing fierce now – makes me sleepy. We pass through Loch Oich, which, rather than locks, has swing bridges to mark its entrance and exit, though as I'm now fast asleep on the black rubber deck mats, Nige has to manoeuvre through the latter by himself. It's only when we come up to the next obstacle, the lock at Cullochy, that he wakes me up with an ear-splitting 'Ash!!!!!'

Our journey is brought to a halt in Fort Augustus, where the five-lock staircase lies between us (and everybody else) and Loch

Ness. It's due to a mechanical fault with the hydraulics, rather than any mythical serpent mischief – well, allegedly. The sheer number of international tourists wearing 'I love Nessie' badges and 'monster hunter' T-shirts makes me a little bit proud that if she *is* in there somewhere, she's our own; one of the United Kingdom's greatest and most enduring treasures. Either way we don't much mind the enforced break. After all, there are worse places to be stopped; everything here is chocolate-box, model-village, cricket-on-the-green twee; as if we've arrived on the set of the CBeebies kids' show *Balamory*. The grass is so green it makes both of us wonder if someone creeps in overnight and sprays it with paint.

With the weather being so nice, we don't worry too much about finding accommodation for the night, though I will still try, as I'm desperate for a shower. But that's all; we're fully invested in the nautical nomad lifestyle by now and things like beds, duvets and pillows, not to mention phone chargers and flushing toilets, are luxuries we have happily forsaken in our quest to steam *Fairlass* home rather than ship her on a lorry.

Going with the touristy flow, we get drinks in one of the busy lochside bars, and spend the next couple of hours people-watching like everyone else, while I make a couple of calls to B&Bs I find on Google. To my surprise, I strike lucky pretty quickly, though Nige points out that the majority of the visitors buzzing around us have come just for a day out, on coaches.

Having both showered, we head off to find dinner, and strike lucky once again, as we find an amazing restaurant right on the shores of Loch Ness, before trundling back up the road to the local pub, which has the kind of live music that we'd expect to find in a hipster pub in Norwich rather than this genteel, highly manicured setting. As soon as we make our way to the smoking area out the back, we are accosted by a woman who is clearly a few drinks in and keen to engage us in conversation.

She immediately picks up that we don't have Scottish accents and demands to know who we are and why we're there. She's stuck there because the ferry she works on has been held up, a job she tells us she has decided to quit, due to working crazy hours and rarely getting a day off. Her name is Sue and she is fascinated by everything about us, wanting to know all about our 700-mile voyage. She's particularly aghast to hear that we've spent most nights roughing it on deck, with only a small blanket and a hammock.

'God,' she says. '*God*. I have *so* much respect for you! You fisherman are *so* tough!' She pores excitedly over the pictures we show her of *Never Can Tell-A* and *Fairlass*, and we twitter on companionably till our cigarettes are all smoked.

After we head off, we think little more of it. It's just one of those pleasant encounters that can be seen and heard in pub smoking areas everywhere.

The next morning, refreshed after a night in one of those beds we've been so busy eschewing, we are back on the boat early (again, keen to beat the rush) to find an enormous, and slightly ominous-looking, bin bag slung on the deck. It seems we were wrong. I gingerly open the bag, to find a note sitting on top of the contents, which are two pillows, a duvet, and a huge thick blue blanket. The note says '*Helloo! Hey, if you two are the guys from*

The Richmond, lobster-potters, you two are my kind of people. Yes, I've had too much wine. Good talk! Hope no more sleeping on the deck in cold. Want me to find you a blanket!!! I quit! So off Sunday. Sue. PS If wrong boat, sorry! Regards Sue.'

It takes a while to decipher the words as they are scrawled all over both sides of the scrap of paper, but the thought – that lovely thoughtfulness, that random act of human kindness – couldn't be clearer.

Nige grins. 'It's like winning the lottery, this is,' he says, wrapping the blanket around me. And I have this sudden image – of this lovely, thoughtful, self-confessed drunk woman, out on a side quest to help us, for no other reason than because she liked us, plundering bedding in the dark from her employer's ferry.

What a star. Forever grateful to you, Sue.

Chapter 15

'Do not step aboard a boat left foot first'

Always put your right foot forward. Failure to do so could mean
being asked to reverse your steps, swap your shoes, and start the
whole process again.

Loch Ness, without question, delivers. For starters, since we're a
commercial boat, we apparently qualify to get priority, so are one
of the first vessels to make our way down the lock flight. Which
is fortunate as, after the hold-up yesterday, there is a plethora of
different vessels all trying to make passage into Nessie's lair at the
same time as us. Once the swing bridge opens and we turn left
into the main channel, however, we realise just how big Loch Ness
is. I'm used to seeing, and working in, endless bodies of water, but
here, where it's inland and runs between hillsides, the fact that
I can't see the end of it feels really strange. It's calm too – like a
piece of polished glass. The sort of conditions that are a rare and
special treat when at sea. (And when it *is* like that at sea I tend

to find myself whispering, almost unconsciously, so I don't risk disturbing the sleeping beast.)

Speaking of beasts, I can't stop myself keeping my eye out. 'Turn the echo sounder on!' I command Nige immediately. And he does, saying nothing – far less admitting that he believes a word of it, or is doing anything other than patiently indulging my silliness. But I know he does. I won't press him on it, but I just *know* it. Because if he didn't then he wouldn't put the echo sounder on.

We don't spot Nessie, but even so it's a magical kind of day; despite the number of boats all travelling through it, such is the scale here that it soon feels as if we have the whole loch to ourselves, and the sense of privilege at just being here, in this iconic setting, this place of myth and legend, is profound. It feels a world away from the grit and grind of the day job, and as we steam along, Nige in the wheelhouse and me out on deck, watching the miles disappear behind us from my perch on the hauling table, my mind can't help but compare and contrast – not least, given the natural beauty here, the peace, and the easy companionship we're enjoying on this trip, to a day not so long back that keeps niggling into my thoughts.

We've spent most of the summer fishing quite a way offshore; the weather having been more settled gives us the opportunity to work further afield, and to give the inshore grounds a reprieve. The distances involved have meant that the days have been long, leaving on the first incoming tide and returning some twelve to fourteen hours later. Leaving me feeling, up to the point where we escaped to buy a new boat, as though I've been doing more miles at sea than by road. It's been good though; having put so many long challenging days in this summer, I know my knowledge, experience and ability have grown no-end. I don't think Nige sees me as fragile any longer either; nor does he hold back if I do something wrong. I always knew that a skipper's word on a boat is absolute. You don't question it. If they ask for something, you do it, and you most certainly do not answer back.

Hence the insistent nature of that niggle. Just a few weeks back, I broke that cardinal rule, and *did* answer back, and that niggle is my conscience, which won't let me forget it.

We'd been hauling our whelk gear, me at my bait station as normal when Nige suddenly stopped the hauler, having heaved up a giant mass of tangled rope and pots, which looked like a complete clusterfuck; our gear had obviously become entangled in another fisherman's anchor and the resultant muddle – think giant spaghetti and meatballs – would take a good deal of sorting out. First though, with the weight of two shanks trying to pull themselves back down, we needed to lighten the load, not only to have any hope of untangling everything, but because with the boat already drifting back in the tide, the tension on the leading tow was getting bigger.

'Quick, Ash!' Nige yelled. 'Get me a bit of rope!'

Having spare bits of rope a few fathoms long nearby are essential when trying to sort out these kind of messes. By tying on to the leading tow that comes after the mess (and which is leading down to the remaining pots) you can make it fast somewhere on the boat which will give you time to try and clear the mess without the added danger of all that weight.

Trouble was, I couldn't find a length of rope. 'Quick as ya like, Ash,' Nige said, while I cast around vainly. In the empty boxes, under my bait, in our so-called 'junk basket'. I simply could not find any.

Nige, meanwhile, was still gripping the nearest pot in the muddle, his tone now as dark as the sea underneath us.

'Fuck *sake*, Ashhh,' he said.

I was still searching around wildly. 'I can't *find* one!'

'KNIFE!' he demanded then. Quick, decisive and angry. Abandoning my search, I grabbed my knife from the dogfish swill in my box of bait, and passed it to his free hand handle first.

He made a quick cut, and the tangled heap disappeared back where it came from and, to add insult to injury, he had no choice but to let go of the pot he was holding as well, collateral damage in an emergency situation. With nothing now in the hauler and everything sunk back to the seafloor, I could see he was fuming.

'When I ask for a piece of rope,' he growled, 'you *get* me a piece of rope. Not in five minutes' time. When I *ask* for it.'

I was stunned. He had *never* spoken to me with so much anger before. I also knew we would now have to steam to the other end of the string and retrieve the rest of the shank from there, and *still* clear that bundle. So his mood was unlikely to improve.

Still, I couldn't help myself. 'Alright,' I fired back, now similarly narked. 'There's no need to talk to me like a c**t over losing a £10 pot!'

As soon as the words had left my mouth, I thought, 'Fuck'. I'm not confrontational at all, and I know better than to back-chat my skipper, and I was immediately filled with shame and dread.

I was right to be. 'It's not about the pot,' he replied, firmly but even-toned now. 'That was nearly my hand that got caught in with those ropes. If I hadn't cut the pot off I could have lost it. Or, worse, have been pulled over with it.'

Since the ground wasn't available to swallow me up, I had no choice but to stand there and take it. We steamed up to the other end and cleared the mess mostly in silence, using just the bare essentials to communicate. I knew – and still know – that Nigel didn't hold a grudge, but it was a period of self-reflection on my part. There is a reason why the skipper's word has to be absolute; all the responsibility for everyone's safety is on their shoulders alone. From that day on I made it my business to ensure I knew where every single thing on the boat was, no matter how seemingly insignificant, from a piece of rope to a 13mm spanner, or a knife. Because it was an important lesson for me to learn; you never know what you might need quickly to prevent serious injury or save a life.

And you never, ever back-chat your skipper. I look across at Nige now, and still feel a twinge of guilt. What possessed me to speak to him like that? Who the fuck did I think I was? I head into the wheelhouse and flick the switch on the hot water boiler.

'You want a coffee?' I ask him.

~

On leaving the Caledonian Canal at around 5 p.m., at the Clachnaharry Sea Lock, we are spat out into the fury of the Moray Firth. The tide as we arrive is screaming out of the harbour, and the wind is fresh north-east: on this coastline a nor-easter is coming straight off the sea, with nothing to stop it and no way of sheltering from it.

The wind isn't howling but it is fresh enough to be a nuisance. And with the tide in the near opposite direction to the wind it's always going to add that little bit more chip as the two opposing forces meet, and we're speeding along at something approaching 12 knots, in a boat whose top engine speed is normally around 7. Which is fine, because we are keen to make some progress, having already decided to make the most of the remaining daylight hours and steam a little way east to find a place to tie up for the night. I've been charged by Nige with having a look in the almanac and finding a harbour that will be able to take us. Sounds simple enough, right?

It's worth mentioning at this point that not every harbour is suitable for an 11-metre boat that has a draught of around 5 foot. For example, we wouldn't want to leave her against a quay wall where the rise and fall of the tide is unknown, for fear of not leaving enough slack on the ropes or leaving too much. Neither would we want her to dry out, as a very tidal harbour may mean a later-than-wanted departure the following morning. This leaves us with very few options.

After a call to Burghead harbour, to tell them our approximate ETA, I quickly learn that due to silting of the harbour entrance (the reason being that it's not been recently dredged) there will not be enough water for us to gain access at the time we would be there. Unfortunately, I hear the same story from the other harbours in the Moray Firth that I contact.

One fella I speak to, though, has better news for us. 'Give Lossiemouth a shout,' he says. 'They should be able to take you.' So I read the almanac on Lossiemouth and to my relief it says the same, though just to check, I call the harbour, who confirm it. So onwards to Lossiemouth we go, but now it's less than ideal, as our ETA is now around 11 p.m. We have little choice though.

After a couple of hours constantly punching the weather on our port bow, we finally arrive, and, with the darkness of night now upon us and a fine mizzle in the air, we cautiously approach the harbour entrance. Ahead of us, we can both see a fair amount of white water, normally a tell-tale sign that it's quite shallow. So Nige checks our chart plotter and the entrance is shaded green, which indicates that it dries, or, as is already our concern, that it *is* extremely shallow.

'Let me see that almanac again,' Nige says. And, having pored over it for a while, is confident that we should still be able to get in.

It's worth mentioning that *Fairlass*, at this time, doesn't have a big spotlight, as I don't think she's been worked much in darkness. But she does, at least, have outside controls, which gives us the ability to knock her ahead, i.e. we can put her in gear and steer her. With visibility difficult and no obvious red or green lights we make our way to the entrance as per the almanac's direction, and the faint suggestion of a red light in the distance. Nige puts me in the skipper's position in the wheelhouse then goes out on the deck by the hauler to steer her, as it's much easier to see from that vantage point. He leaves me with very clear instructions.

'Ash, watch that sounder,' he tells me, 'and shout me the depth.' So I get into place to do exactly that, anxiously looking down at the sounder as we edge closer to the surf.

'Eighteen foot,' I shout.

'Righto!'

'Twelve foot!' Then, 'Nine!'

Because it's the job Nige has given me, my eyes don't leave that sounder, and as I call out 'Six feet!' I can only hear, rather than see, the sea now breaking around us, and my ears are full of the crash and pull of moving water. This is not an unfamiliar position for me to be in, as the sea over the bar at Wells can react in similar ways. It's obviously shallow here – the sounder's only confirming what the almanac has already told us – but if this is the way in, then so be it. It's the way. Six feet beneath the hull is doable, theoretically, at least. (After all, if she's floating, she's floating.)

But then the sounder suddenly reads 'XXXX'. *Fuck,* I think, and shout over my shoulder to Nige, '*No depth!*' In that same instant, I feel the boat behave differently. She's not going forward any more. It's like she's being pushed.

I look out into the darkness behind me and see the foaming white teeth of a wave come barrelling through the shooting door cut out of the transom. It barges its way up the entire length of the 8-metre deck, hitting the bottom of the wheelhouse, and changing its direction back astern, heaving its way back and out of the scuppers. I then hear an almighty bang, and the thud of the keel hitting the bottom travels up through my body like the reverberations of a ringing bell.

I'm snapped back into the moment by the sound of Nige shouting. 'Ash!' he yells, 'STEAMING SPEED, NOW!'

I don't panic. I just do. I immediately push the throttle controls forward and down, applying as much speed to the old girl as I can, as Nige brings her round hard to port to get us out of there before it's too late, and we are beached. Or worse, so much worse, smashed to pieces.

BANG! She makes contact with the bottom a second time, and Nige now re-enters the wheelhouse. I dart out of the way so he has enough space, and now I'm out on deck I can feel the power of the waves as we lie broadside into the weather, while Nige turns *Fairlass*'s head round to get us out of there. I look over to my right, out the starboard side, and see Lossiemouth's hard-faced pierhead walls no more than 20 feet away. We are too close. We have come in *much* too close.

As *Fairlass* turns her head around, I can sense, in the darkness, that the waves are now in front of us and I feel a great whoosh of relief to know we are getting out of there at last – clear, blessedly clear, of the shallow water.

Nige shouts out again. 'Ash, I'm turning on the bilge pump! Count for how long it runs!'

He means till it automatically cuts out, and I know why he wants to know. He's worried we might have damaged the hull seriously enough that it's been breached. I start counting. One, two, three, four . . . All the way to fifteen seconds. I shout him the number and he replies with a reassuring 'Good! That means we're not taking on water!'

That blessing now established (well, at least for now), we head back out to deeper water, and my heart rate begins to slow a little. We're okay, and more importantly the boat is okay – this boat we've only owned for *three days*.

I exhale heavily. Though it's only been a matter of minutes, those minutes have stretched to feel like half a lifetime, the serenity of Loch Ness now feeling as historic as the legend itself.

'Pass me that fucking book,' Nige says. I can tell he's angry with himself. I give him the book and he checks it for several long seconds. Then he flings it back at me again, his expression stony. 'Fucking thing. I should have trusted my gut the minute I saw the harbour entrance. My gut and my instruments. I know better than that bloody thing. Where's the next harbour?'

It's now past 11.30. Soon it'll be midnight. Back to the cursed book I go.

'Buckie,' I tell him.

'How far?'

''Bout ten mile.'

Which means another two-hour steam in the dark. Nige sets the course, before telling me to call the harbour at Buckie, to see if anyone's there, and to check – and double check – that we can get in.

Thankfully, despite the hour, my call is answered immediately. And yes, of course they have a berth, and yes of course we can get in. And – music to my ears – at any state of tide.

We steam on, phoning Nige's boys to tell them what's happened, but after that the two hours pass mostly in silence, as, after all the drama, and the 'what ifs', we're all out of chit chat, and the only sound is the incessant squeaking of our respective sprung seats in the wheelhouse. All our focus now is on steaming along that straight line to Buckie.

It's such a dark night that there is nothing, literally nothing, to be seen. No other boats. No flashing lights. No twinkling evidence of life ashore. Just us and the heavy night, as if we're in our own bubble of blackness.

I don't know if there are any stars even, as we remain in the wheelhouse for the entirety of the journey, both smoking. It's all we can do. We've nothing to eat. Not so much as a biscuit between us, and, apart from water, all we have to drink are two cans of cider, which are obviously verboten till we're safely tied up.

We see the red and green lights of Buckie's wide and calm harbour entrance from half a mile away. It's like seeing the arms of your own mother, welcoming you in for a reassuring embrace after a hard day. Though it's now 2 a.m., there's a young lad there to meet us on the quay, who gives us a choice of places to lie for what's left of the night. He cuts quite a dash, in his voluminous – and luminous – hi-viz jacket, waving his arms around to indicate a choice of two berths, as if shepherding in a Boeing 747. And when I go over to his office to do the paperwork, he even shares his pizza with me.

When I get back to the boat Nige and I crack open a can of cider each. I don't even like cider, but we've been in this thing together, and I need us to have that moment of quiet contemplation together too. We just sit for half an hour, in the dark and the quiet, coming down after the adrenaline high. Much as we love it, the sea is not a natural environment for a human being. And human beings are fallible. We had two sources of information to help us into that harbour: the *Reeds Almanac* and our plotter. And with those giving us conflicting information, Nige had to use his experience to make the call, then his quick wits to save us from smashing the boat to pieces and potentially losing our lives. Those quick wits of his did save our lives, no question, and though Nige was, in the moment, fully confident and in control, it's only now sinking in just how close we could have come to being claimed by nature. I can tell how hard it's hitting him now; his lack of words speaks volumes.

Tiredness soon creeps over us, however, so we quickly make our beds up; the small triangular space down forward for me, and, once again, the wheelhouse floor for Nige. Though, thanks to the kindness of Sue, back in Fort Augustus, at least our humble quarters are a little more warm and cosy.

~

Waking up at Buckie is a shock to the system. Mine particularly, as, once again, I'm in urgent need of a wee, but we're right in the middle of everything, and there are so many people around, it's difficult to go. There just isn't a single place on the deck where no one would see me.

In the end I have no choice but to repeat what I did yesterday morning and whip down my trackie bottoms and squat, reasoning that none of these people are likely to see me again anyway. Plus we belong to the sea now, and it's a case of needs must.

Once I've brushed my teeth, swilling my toothbrush in a cup, I open my suitcase, fearing the worst. Given its size, it's had no choice but to spend the whole journey out on deck, and, as I already guessed, given the size of that wave which came barging up the deck uninvited, most of the contents are now damp. And, since we're back in the open sea now, also salty. So I get down to a bit of housekeeping, sorting and tidying, and hanging what I can around the deck, while Nige sits on the gunwale with a coffee and a fag.

After the jaw-dropping beauty we have spent the last few days steaming through, Buckie, for all that we're grateful to be there, just feels angular and cold and dark and sad. The harbour is square. All the buildings are square. The all-pervading colour is a depressing shade of brown. The buildings are high, too, and so densely packed together that they block out any view of the countryside beyond them. The whole place gives a sense of having once been the hub of industrial fishing here, all of which is obviously now long gone. It feels forlorn. Once a thriving fishing port and home to the largest steam drifter fleet in Scotland, Buckie suffered badly after the Common Fisheries Policy came into force in 1972, and fishing by big, non-domiciled boats caused herring stocks to be decimated. The subsequent ban on herring fishing was something they could simply not recover from. Once the fishing industry dies, the infrastructure that it supports simply dies along with it. For the people of Buckie, as with ports up and down the North Sea, it was a disaster, and still feels like an open wound today. The bounty of the North Sea had brought wealth to this community. But it brings it no more.

It looks like it would be such a mission to go off and get any supplies here that we don't bother. My housekeeping efforts have unearthed two packets of Quavers and, since we still have a few cigarettes between us, that'll do. We do dip the tank, but though it confirms we'll need diesel, we can't get any here anyway, it being a Sunday, so we head off and continue steaming south. And as we leave, as I still have a good signal on my phone, I make a quick call to my sister, Camilla, who I've not touched base with for a couple of days.

Millie's nothing like me. We could not be more different. We're like the city mouse and the country mouse. I'm the chalk to her cheese. She's in resource management for one of the big firms of accountants in London, and I've always thought she was, well, pretty courageous. She's always been so brave and so focused. Where I spent my childhood full of dreams but with no single clear career plan, my little sister – ruled very much by head rather than heart – took herself off to uni, one many, many miles distant, then started a career and a life in a completely unknown town and, for a while, in a completely different country. All things I could never have done in a million years.

Millie's also my very best friend. It's good to hear her voice and tell her about our dicey time at Lossiemouth, finishing up, as is often the case these days, with 'Don't tell Mum!'

'Weren't you scared?' she wants to know, and I tell her I wasn't. But after we finish chatting, that lack of fear gives me pause for thought. Because it's not just bravado. I know it's true. I was entirely aware of the potential danger in the situation, of course. But there's something else at play, which stops fear getting a look in. A dynamic that's so natural now I realise I never really give it thought any more, and that's the trust between the skipper and the crew.

To a crew, and this is always true, the skipper's word is final. Their judgement is never, ever questioned. Every single decision made on a boat falls to the skipper, not least because, as a fisherman once told me on the quay, the only ship that does not work at sea is a partnership. One person, and one person only, must be in command.

I know that *the* most important thing to Nige is keeping his crew safe. It's his job to get everybody on the boat safely home and it's a duty he does not enter into lightly. And this doesn't just apply to Nige. It is true of skippers everywhere, and if it's not, then they aren't very good skippers.

I know when we're at sea that Nigel's word is ultimate, and that if a situation presents itself, then I need to be alert and ready, so I can immediately react as he needs me to. I trust in his ability, his wisdom, his long, long years of experience, and that he will always prioritise keeping us all safe (because the boat is very much included).

Looking back now, as we steam away from Buckie, I realise Nige's decision to bring *Fairlass* home the 'hard' way (and there's no question 700 nautical miles of hand-steaming constitutes a hard way, given that she could equally have been loaded onto a lorry) wasn't him being contrary. It actually makes a lot of sense. It's an opportunity to test out the new boat, establish what she's capable of, and to lay the foundations (and how!) for his relationship with her in the future.

It's also a chance for any skipper to top up their own skills. When you come into the same harbour every single day and your rope is always waiting for you, exactly where you left it, there are few opportunities to test your mettle. In an unfamiliar harbour, on the other hand, you don't know what the tide and wind are doing, or how to use both to your advantage, and performing on the hop, when you have to do things differently than you're used to, is what keeps you sharp.

It tests you to go into unfamiliar places, and believe me when I say that every fisherman in that harbour is watching, silently judging; the fishing community isn't that big and it loves a gossip. If you fuck up, your colleagues in your home port will know before you do.

It's also good to test yourself as a crew. There's no question that being placed in such unfamiliar situations has taught me one hell of a lot too. Even more than that, though, it tests us, and how we perform as a team under pressure. And that includes *Fairlass*, because our boat is as much a part of the team as we are. More than that. A boat – any boat – is always going to be better performing in a crisis than any human can hope to be. They are designed for that environment. We are not.

So *Fairlass* herself is key. And now we've got to know her so well, in good times and bad, our trust in her is absolute.

Never Can Tell A high and dry

Men at work aboard *Never Can Tell A*

Jack, being chased down by a flock of hungry gulls on *Fairlass*

Whelks

Brown Crab

A deck full of whelk pots on *Saoirse*

Us at work on *Fairlass*

A rare moment of sunbathing between strings
of pots aboard *Never Can Tell A*

Me and
a jack crab

Lovely
lobsters

'Sisters' *Fairlass* and *Saoirse* together

Myself and *Saoirse* on the slipway waiting for some tide

Saoirse at rest in her new home after her long trip from Kilkeel

Nigel, looking like a Pokemon (adrift somewhere off Hartlepool) ready to go and remove the rope from the propellor

Chapter 16

*'Do not set sail on the second Monday in August, as this was the day
Sodom and Gomorrah were destroyed'*

We pass back out through the loving pierheads of Buckie harbour,
and settle in for our onward journey to the largest fishing port in
the UK, Peterhead (PeterHEID – sorry to all the lovely Doric
folk). The sheltered sanctuary of the inland waterways of the canal
feels like a lifetime ago. Back now to the North Sea where short
sharp waves are a familiar friend. It's a grey mizzly day so I spend
most of it tucked up in the wheelhouse, still in my trackies and
snuggled under the blanket, rationing my cigarettes and Quavers.

Compared to the last leg, which felt interminable, the seven-
hour steam seems to fly by quickly as we round Scotland's
triangular headland, finally passing Fraserburgh, where the busy
port is evidenced by the quantity of trawlers' masts just visible
behind the harbour wall. It's just another couple of hours, then,
before the behemoth that is the floating city of Peterhead comes
into view.

Nige puts on his best VHF radio voice as he calls to request permission to enter the harbour – something I will continue to take the piss out of today, because it's like your phone voice, except the language feels much more formal.

'Peterhead harbour Peterhead harbour – *Fairlass Fairlass.*'

Silence.

'*Fairlass* – Peterhead harbour, go aheid.'

Crackle, more silence.

Connection established, a painfully stunted bout of 'conversation' then ensues, the crackling Scottish accent coming in fits and starts through the static being mostly unintelligible to Nige's ears. (VHF communications are fuzzy at best but combined with 'spikkin broad', I am being given many a blank look from my skipper.) I translate as best I can, but it's a tortuous business, full of frustrated gurning (on Nige's part), but impeccable politeness (ditto) – all 'Yes sirs' and 'No sirs', and 'Thank you, sirs', and 'Three bags full, sirs' as the particulars of *Fairlass* and potential mooring locations are discussed.

As we round the pierheads, I have to do a double take and get out of my nest to stand out on deck and gaze up in awe. The fishing boats, resting peacefully at various stone-walled docks, are the size of multi-storey car parks. My wonderment is quickly snuffed as the noise of that thick Doric accent chitters in the wheelhouse once more and I know I'm back on translating duties. We are guided through the labyrinthine deep-water harbour by the voice that sits omnipotent, somewhere in a lofty tower. Eventually we find our way to a large basin with many fishing boats of similar size to us, and make *Fairlass* fast alongside the tyre-cladded wall. The VHF crackles once more.

'*Fairlass* – Peterheid harbour.'

'Peterhead harbour – *Fairlass* – go ahead.'

'Ye'll nae wint tae leave 'er ere the nicht if yer plannin gaun intae toon ... move 'er ower the ither side o the hairbour mou', it's a forty meenit walk aroon the hairbour fae there, but ten fae the ither side.'

Silence.

More silence. (I'm busy translating.)

Finally, 'Peterhead harbour – *Fairlass* , thank you, sir.'

Peterhead harbour team, thank *you*, I think. For saving us that forty-minute walk. And if that doesn't illustrate perfectly the size of this gargantuan harbour, I can't help you.

Because the rise and fall of the water here is unknown to us we decide it is best to stay aboard *Fairlass* tonight so that we can adjust her ropes if need be. I arrange a fuel tanker delivery for 7 a.m. and we make a quick pass round the town. After stocking up on supplies, we decide to sample a couple of the local pubs, including one very much of the 'drink up and fuck off quick' variety, not least because one of the well-oiled characters in there takes a bit of an unwelcome shine to me. So much so that Nige is anxious about leaving me even to go for a quick pee.

We do drink up. I'm not generally intimidated by men (I'm 5'11" – and a half, in my Xtra Tufs), and not exactly a waif, but drunks, male *or* female, do make me uncomfortable, so I'm more than happy to make a swift exit.

It's only a short walk back to *Fairlass*, where we order a Chinese takeaway. Once it arrives, we devour it sat on the deck, watching a film on my phone while being eyeballed by seagulls who are even more intimidating than my admirer back at the pub.

As it's turned into a warm August night we decide to attempt al fresco sleeping on the deck tonight and with full bellies, and after our late, adrenaline-fuelled night yesterday, it doesn't take either of us long to drift off, swaddled in Sue's blankets, duvets and pillows. Over the next hours, the steady din of fishing boats coming and going from the harbour stirs us frequently, as *Fairlass* gently jostles and laps in their wake. As I'm sure any fisherman will attest, however, that gentle rocking, which is exclusive to sleeping on a boat, is one of the most soothing and relaxing feelings there is, so any disturbance is quickly remedied.

A swift nudge in my side wakes me properly, however. It's Nige, gently kicking me with his foot. No trace of the VHF phone voice now. 'Get up and get inside – it's pissing it down!' he grunts. It really is too; I can see a screen of fine persistent sideways rain, back-lit by the orange harbour floodlights. I grab my phone: 2 a.m. Nice.

Back down the front I go, wrapped in my duvet, and it's the wheelhouse floor once again for Nige.

~

By 7.30 we have fuelled up and pushed off from the quay, making our way back through the maze of Peterhead. We leave the harbour and head south. We want to crunch some miles today and get as far down the east coast of the country as we can. I've not washed since the hold-up in Fort Augustus, which feels like a lifetime ago, and by now, needs must. *Fairlass* is well equipped with a microwave and a hot water boiler. I flick the water heater on and hunt round on deck to find a bucket. Luckily the centre console allows me enough privacy for a strip wash in the wheelhouse and, having tracked down some clean underwear and clothes, I definitely feel less grubby. I settle back in my seat under a blanket and reheat what's left of our Chinese for breakfast, as we continue to trundle our way south. While Nige keeps us on course, I spend much of the day perusing the almanac for a suitable harbour and, given our previous escapade, I want to find somewhere that isn't tidal. I make many phone calls to many harbour authorities, with slim pickings down this stretch of coastline. Pitenweem is a potential option, but its location is a little off course, and we want to make as much progress as we can. By late afternoon, we have pretty much concluded that Eyemouth is the best port of call. Like Buckie, it used to be a significant herring post, and also like Buckie its fortunes have changed. First the herring stocks collapsed, then the white fish they switched to, and, like many North Sea ports, they are now highly dependent on shellfish. Luckily, when I call them, they can take us for the night.

The hundred-mile passage has taken us all day and evening, and it's 10 p.m. by the time our approach to Eyemouth is imminent. We suddenly feel very small. As well as the red, green and white lights which are standard for all, fishing boats also display certain light patterns mounted high up the mast, so that other vessels know who's who, and ultimately who has 'right of way'. A boat engaged in fishing of static gear (pots and gill nets) has a red over white, and has right of way over a craft which isn't fishing. A trawler, which has right of way over a boat static fishing, displays green over white. (It's largely academic, this, as, for obvious reasons, you'd almost never find boats trawling where others are static fishing.)

At this time we are just a boat making passage, so we have no rights at all. And as I gaze out over the expanse of sea still between us and Eyemouth, it's clear we are little more than a fly in a bowl of trawler soup.

Trawlers are big, heavy, distinctive looking boats. And seeing them in Wells, or should I say just outside of Wells' harbour limits, is a sure sign that winter is around the corner. The iconic green and blue boats from King's Lynn – *Jolene*, *Lucky Luke*, *Tessa*, *The Lynn Princess* and *Jaleto*, to name a few – will be familiar names on our doorstep once more. Sea temperature cooling brings the shrimping fleet from King's Lynn who will start to pop up in Holkham Bay, their boats normally flanked by throngs of hungry seagulls bobbing patiently, waiting for a meal as they cook their catch onboard. Cooking the shrimp quickly prevents them going mushy and ensures that their vibrant flavour is locked in.

There are often times at the end of the day, when steaming home from our fishing grounds, when we will play spot the shrimper. Yes of course we have radar to help, but often you can see their lights emerging out of the darkness before the radar has picked them up. Nige and I count them aloud to each other: how many we can see on the horizon as they pick their way through the darkness to target these tasty nocturnal treats. No, it's not the most thrilling game in the world but, hey, we don't have a TV.

Where there are high stocks of fish, there will always be trawlers, and we are now clearly over grounds where there are plenty of fish, because all of a sudden they are *everywhere*. These are all stern trawlers, and they are towing their nets in every direction ahead of us. People often talk about the scourge of abandoned fishing nets, but this is unfair. These nets are enormous and very, very costly, some running to tens of thousands of pounds. They are therefore precious and the truer picture, perhaps, is the one of the fisherman on the quay busy mending them. No one discards a fishing net unless they absolutely have to because the boat, and therefore life, is at risk – another of those quick, life-or-death decisions that skippers occasionally have to make, as a net that's come fast on an obstruction on the seabed can turn over a vessel in a matter of seconds.

We pick our way carefully through, having to keep adjusting our course – no mean feat at night, especially without radar – and it's thankfully not long until we can see the more reassuring red and green lights of Eyemouth pierheads.

The entrance looks narrow and, as we've seen on the chart plotter, it has a dog leg. Nige puts me on deck; I'm now his eyes out there. My role is now to tell him (or rather yell at him) whether he needs to come to port or starboard in order to stay in the middle of the narrow channel, which will avoid scraping the boat down the stone walls that guide the way to the harbour basin. This harbour has access at all states of tide, but there isn't a lot of water when we arrive. Two fishermen, suitably lubricated and fascinated by the fact I'm a woman *and* a fisherman (here we go again, I think), are on the quay wall where we are looking to tie up. They are really helpful, however, grabbing a rope for us, and helping us make *Fairlass* fast. (If anybody knows them, please pass on my thanks as I'm sure they probably will not remember!)

A bloody long climb up to the top of the wall (the tide being out, of course) reveals that there's not a single shop or pub open, so we scavenge our way through our remaining pack-up (mostly sweets and cider) and retire once again to our on-board accommodation for the night.

~

For the second night running, I am woken in the wee hours. This time not by rain but by an almighty BANG, and the sound of water sloshing against wood. I immediately hear another sound – Nige exclaiming 'WHAT THE FUCK!'

I scrabble up from down the front to see him silhouetted in the beam of a blinding spotlight. He's standing in the rain on deck, hollering 'Where'd ya hit!?'

I can hear angry shouting coming from the wheelhouse of the boat behind, which it seems has run into us on making its departure from the quay.

'Where'd ya hit!?' Nige is demanding. By fuck is he cross. 'Might wanna take ya fuckin head rope off before leaving the quay!' He then adds, 'Ya twat!' for good measure.

The *Bella B* (that's her name) slopes off out of the harbour, having not even acknowledged us. But that's probably because the guy on the bow, who had been charged with removing the rope under Nige's frosty scowl, is most likely still having his arse chewed by the skipper in the wheelhouse.

A quick inspection reveals that, thankfully, there is no major damage done. Just a bent support on the cat catcher. Nige and I trudge back into the wheelhouse ourselves. 'I got fuckin wet socks now,' he complains. And fair enough, he probably only has the one pair. But at least we're on the home stretch. When we wake up again, this time at a more respectable 7 a.m., I work out that we've been away for seven nights now, five of which we've spent on board the boat. This is our last stop in Scotland, so we take the opportunity to restock and take a moment of harrowing silence at the Black Friday memorial, the anguish in the bronze faces of the families of those 189 lost fishermen resonating deeply with both of us.

Our passage continues with a plan to push as far south as we can, the coastline changing as Scotland turns to England and the land smooths out on our right-hand side. It's a calm day and we make great progress and, with the tide working with us (at least for now) we start predicting how far we can get today.

I'm just putting this idea to Nige – 'Maybe we can make Whitby?' – when we are interrupted by an almighty shake, and what sounds like the rattling of every metal component on the boat.

'FUCK!' Nige says, immediately snatching *Fairlass* out of gear. The rattling instantly stops. He's clearly worked out what's happened, though, for me, it takes a little longer for the penny to drop. He darts down to the stern and pokes his head out of the stern door. I follow. Rope. We see rope. And the fact that we can see it means there's a good bunch of it wrapped round our screw.

Nigel, now back in the wheelhouse, puts *Fairlass* back in gear, to see if he can clear it using the action of the propeller itself. But it clearly hasn't worked because *Fairlass* is still shaking like a shitting dog. Then she stalls.

'FUCKKKKK!' Nige says again. (It's a bigger fuck this time.) Because we're clearly going to have to do it by hand; it's obviously wound itself round the prop and the shaft pretty tightly. Nige gets to work, first lashing a knife to a wooden stick and, while I sit on his legs, hangs out of the stern door and starts cutting away at the rope. Balls of the stuff soon start coming up in his right hand, which I grab and chuck on the deck. Far too distracted by the chart plotter and our onward journey, it looks as if we've run over someone's dhan tow.

It's not long before I have a very significant heap, and we hope it's going to be enough – which it is. At least for now. When Nige puts *Fairlass* in gear again I can still feel a wobble above where the shaft comes through the hull, but it is minor in comparison to what it was. We will need to give it a better look the next time we stop.

Trundling onward past the industrialisation of the busy Tees, we both notice that the 'steel river' certainly lives up to its name. As we steam by, the river's entrance is choked with maritime traffic; mostly cargo ships coming and going from Teesport with goods to support the numerous metal and chemical industries that rely on them. In previous years the banks of the estuary boasted British steel and coal manufacturing. Now, though Teesport is still, arguably, the third largest port in Britain, business has changed somewhat. No question, however, that it's still booming.

Incidentally, I can't reference the Tees here without mentioning the mass crab die-off that happened in 2021, when thousands of dead crabs and lobsters washed up on the shores of Seaton Carew, Redcar and Seaham. Around that same time, fishermen started reporting empty pots or pots with dead crabs in. Fishing is never a guaranteed pay cheque, but after a while you get to know roughly what to expect in your catch and when something's wrong. The lads working from these ports took a huge hit. There were no warning signs, and no time to prepare – from productive to barren almost overnight. Imagine their horror. Imagine turning up to work one day and finding that you are going to be given a pay cut of 95 per cent but you still have to do the same amount of work. How would you feed your family? Pay your bills? Keep the wolf from the door? Despite fishermen being a secretive breed, it wasn't long before they got together and the folks at the Environment Agency and DEFRA were called in to investigate. Samples of water, sediment and the dead crustacea were taken and sent to CEFAS – the government's Centre for Environment, Fisheries and Aquaculture Science. Their conclusion? Algal bloom. Which is essentially an abundance of algae that has grown in the right conditions, some of which can be toxic to sea life. As a fisherman, you have a pretty intimate relationship with the sea, noting her colour, texture and mood. Fishermen hadn't noticed any kind of bloom, so it really wasn't long before they called bullshit on that conclusion and got together to conduct their own science. With the help of numerous scientists from various universities, a new theory was emerging. Samples of dead crab and lobsters exhibited signs of a chemical called pyridine, a toxic compound found in coal tar. That infamous 'steel river', home to so much manufacturing since the mid-eighteenth century, needed to expand, bigger, deeper and wider, to facilitate more import and export. So the river had to be dredged to meet that expansion. Could pyridine disturbed from beneath the seabed as a result be the cause? The fishermen, backed by their own scientific findings, seemed to think so. DEFRA, however, would not accept this conclusion, sticking with their algal bloom theory, so with more work on expanding the Teesport continuing, more marine life died.

In 2022 Parliamentary-level investigations were held, which scrutinised the results of CEFAS, and looked into the dredging theory that had been put forward by the fishermen and the scientists who had helped them. Meanwhile, fishermen themselves were – and still are – struggling to make ends meet. Expansion of the port, however, is still going ahead. After all, what has greater value to the economy? A thriving fishing fleet or a thriving shipping port?

I give credit to all the fishermen on the North-East coast for coming together and fighting this, and I hope they do not give up their quest for the truth, and the chance to be fully involved in finding both the cause and a resolution to this desperate conundrum – one that does not only destroy lives and livelihoods, but also our centuries-old, precious fishing heritage. At the very least, I hope they are fully compensated for their loss of earnings. However, no amount of compensation or corrective action can take away their sleepless nights of worry, as the prospect of losing everything they've loved and worked for is still a clear and present danger. I mean, think about it – how would *you* feel?

Meanwhile, leaving the Tees in our wake, and keen to get into a harbour while we still have some daylight, I contact Seaham Harbour Authority. They wouldn't usually take a fishing boat of our size in their small marina but given that we potentially still have rope around the prop, they graciously allow us in on this occasion.

Unable to clear any more rope, but happy enough that she's running, we get underway again by 10.15 a.m., feeling clean and well rested, having had the time and good sense to get a B&B. The finish line is finally, and now literally, in sight. All being well, we can probably make Scarborough by early evening, where Nigel's lads – who have been on our cases the entire way home, and have driven up to meet us – cannot wait to see her.

The journey to Scarborough is mostly hassle free until *Fairlass* starts shaking again, ominously. As suspected, there is clearly still some rope round the propeller, which has obviously moved.

'Ash?' Nige asks. 'Where are them survival suits?'

'Why?'

'I'm going in.'

Within minutes and with *Fairlass* drifting quietly in the tide, Nigel is standing on deck looking like a giant red Pokémon with a knife in his hand. He gets busy again, tying a rope to the cat catcher so he has something to hang on from, then shuffles himself out of the shooting door while holding the rope, till he's sitting with his legs dangling over the edge. But not before looking over his shoulder at me. 'If the boat rolls on my head, it'll knock me out, so be ready to haul me back in if you need to.'

Plop.

Great, so it's just me now, drifting helplessly somewhere north of Hartlepool. Before I can freak myself out too much I see a hand chucking some rope up through the door followed by a very bedraggled-looking Nige, who heaves himself back on deck.

Starting the engine again reveals that there is no more shaking, and we are able to make Scarborough harbour without further incident – well, apart from the spectacle of two fully grown men jumping about like a pair of spring lambs in their haste to clamber over the seaweed farm boat that lies between us.

Love 'em, but after all the drama, the tranquillity, the awe-inspiring scenery, the beauty, the quiet, the challenges, the teamwork, the al-fresco sleeping, the confinement, the bonding of skipper, crew and craft, and the starry, starry nights . . .

All peace, every bit of it, is shattered.

Chapter 17

'Do not say the word rabbit at sea'

Rabbits kept aboard to feed the crew were believed to tempt fate as they would often be the sole survivors of a wreck, floating ashore in their crates.

Back in Wells, we are soon back to reality. Since Nige and I drove back, to allow the boys to get their first taste of handling *Fairlass*, the following afternoon it's our turn to be standing on a quayside, waiting excitedly for their arrival.

The excitement, however, is necessarily short-lived because however enjoyable it is to show her off to the community, there isn't a lot we can do with *Fairlass* yet; without a licence she is mothballed, unable to do the job she was bought to do, and getting her that licence involves many hoops to be jumped through and much red tape to be untangled, most of which will be done via a lot of frustrating and lengthy phone calls. We need another key thing that's in short supply too: money. Licences themselves do not come cheap, but neither do the multitude of smaller non-negotiable things that we need to get in place before we can even apply for one.

We therefore have two main objectives. One is to work both ourselves and *Never Can Tell-A* to the bone. And with autumn in the air it's time to home in on the beloved sea snails that form the bread and butter of our income. The water has started to cool and the crabs we've been targeting over the summer are beginning to slow down for the winter months. Which means the whelks, who've been previously lying dormant, safe from predation, start popping out of the sea floor.

Autumn also means competing with the local seals – something we'll be doing all the way now through to spring, some of our fishing grounds being territory for the colony at nearby Blakeney Point. They don't want the whelks. They have no interest in them whatsoever. But they definitely are interested in the dogfish we use as bait, and have worked out how to open a whelk pot and remove it. Sometimes they will go through an entire shank.

Blakeney Point, which in the late 1990s was entirely devoid of pinnipeds, is now home to 7,000 of these grey seals, the largest seal population in England. The reasons for this massive population explosion are multi-factorial, but a key one is that they have no natural predators. It's good that a marine mammal like this is thriving, of course, but there are obviously implications not only for our whelk pots, but also for fish stocks, something that's of great concern to fisherman in the area, and with a further 3,000 seals being born annually, leaves us wondering how much more population growth the North Sea can sustain.

Right now, however, sustaining ourselves is the order of the day, which means *Fairlass* needs to be taken out of the water. She's safer there, as well as out of the way, and perfectly placed to undergo all the work we are going to have to do on her. We know she needs a new shaft and the propeller needs rebalancing, along with replacing anodes and anti-fouling. She also needs a radar, a more compact echo sounder, a screen for the CCTV and for the autopilot to *finally* be fitted.

With a licence to find and earn the money for, we again must get to work and set ourselves some targets. If we don't get a licence on *Fairlass* within six months she will be struck off the Fishing Register, and I can't get her licensed without a safety certificate. So we must knuckle down to some Boat Admin (or BADmin as I affectionately refer to it, given that, in my opinion, it is exactly that: bad, complicated and clunky).

A great place to start is to ask: what sets a fishing boat apart from any other boat? And who is responsible, administratively speaking, for managing all the different types of boats and how? The answer to the latter question is the MCA (Maritime and Coastguard Agency), who are an executive agency of the government, charged with implementing maritime safety and law. They use His Majesty's Coastguard to coordinate search and rescue operations, develop international policy standards for shipping, and administrate port and flag state control of commercial sea-going craft.

Every fishing boat in the United Kingdom has what is known as a PLN (port, letters and numbers). Think of it a little like a registration plate on a car. Every PLN on every boat is unique. And in a lot of cases it will tell you where that boat's administrative fishing port is; for example, Wells does not have its own prefix but Lowestoft, King's Lynn and Great Yarmouth do. All PLNs start with identifying letters for the port which, in the cases above, are LT, LN, and YH respectively. The number sequence that follows these letters is then chosen at random or by the individual boat owners, who, in a lot of cases, choose a sequence of numbers that reference something personal or important to them. If a fishing boat changes hands the seller can choose to retain the PLN to put on a new vessel for themselves, or it can go with the boat without the need to be changed, like a personalised car number plate. For example, we have a boat in Wells with an EX (Exeter) PLN and *Never-Can-Tell A*'s is WY (Whitby). However, vessels moving from England to Scotland, Wales, or Northern Ireland, and vice versa, fall under the devolved administrations of the country they are moving to, and therefore must be changed. *Fairlass* displays a CY (Castlebay – Scottish) registration, so therefore we must re-register her in England, using LN as her prefix.

If you are buying a fishing boat that is already active you must fill out a bill of sale and send it to the MCA to update the ownership and, in our case, as above, also request a change of PLN. You must then request a date for an MCA Small Vessel Safety Inspection in which you must now jump through that series of hoops. Some are logical, sensible and practical – the kind of things that do save lives – whereas others are tiresome, difficult and contradictory. Passing this inspection means you will be issued a certificate of registry, detailing the boat's particulars and ownership information and that all-important safety certificate, without which a licence cannot be issued.

If I don't get this inspection booked within six months of the change of ownership *Fairlass* could, as I've said, be struck off the Fishing Register, and re-entry to that register becomes even harder. As the safety inspection is carried out using a set of guidelines that are relevant to your boat and its build year, exceed that six months and the rules change: your boat will be inspected using the most current regulations, i.e. as if your boat was brand new and just floated out of the builder's yard. For a boat of nearly fifty years old this would be practically impossible unless I had infinite time, money and expertise. And I mean that. We are talking scrutiny down to every last piece of mechanical equipment, valve and design, and their associated hallmarks.

September blurs into October and while the clock is still ticking to get *Fairlass* up and running and we are working like stink to raise funds for a licence, a conference in London, advertised on Twitter, catches my eye. I can make out from the 280 characters or less that with Brexit on the horizon, Seafish (our industry's quango organisation) are hosting a forum to discuss the challenges faced by fishermen, and practical recommendations for our sector's management in a new Europe-less landscape. This inaugural 'Future of Inshore Fisheries' conference is open to be attended by all relevant stakeholders to our industry, of which there are so many, from marine biologists, merchants and economists, to quota managers at government level, and POs from around the country. There's also DEFRA; the MMO; IFCAs from various sectors and regions; and NGOs that take the form of multiple charities and trusts that are involved with fisheries and the marine environment. Oh, and fishermen.

Having seen and heard first-hand the way this industry has chewed up and spat out some of the most hardworking fishermen, thanks to our ties with Europe and knee-jerk reactions to fisheries 'management', I am of course eager to attend. This is my future now. What could be in store for it?

Nige and I decide to make a mini-break of it. We take the train to King's Cross and make our way via the tube to the swanky conference hotel, near London Bridge, where we meet up with an already disgruntled Horris. (No surprise there, then.)

The conference room is rammed; there must be something approaching two hundred people present, already filling up tables that have been pre-allocated, so that each holds a cross-section of those present. Among all the suits and polished brogues the fishermen are easily identified, not only from the look of scepticism in their eyes and tell-tale signs in their gait, but also by their appearance, which differs markedly from everyone else's; most are dressed informally, in jeans, and maybe a shirt. I love that about fishermen; their absolute confidence in who they are. No airs, no graces, no need to hide behind a suit, no need to conform to 'business dress'. The only business attire that matters to them is a set of oilies (preferably ones that don't leak) and a decent pair of wellies. I am proud to say that, with a corporate lifestyle happily now somewhere in my rear view mirror, it's jeans for me too.

At a guess, looking around the room, fishermen make up just over 30 per cent of the attendees, which is a high turnout considering that most of us believe that all decisions made by those on high are already, in fact, a done deal. For many fishermen, meetings like this feel like lip-service, as if they are just ticking the box for industry engagement.

Personally, though I feel similarly, I have come here to learn. Unlike Horris, whose experiences give him every right to feel bitter, I am all about making things better for our industry, which means listening – coming to scope out the field. You can't influence the future without first understanding the past, and I'm here on a mission to work out what the fuck is really going on, and being among this lot should help. Well, in theory . . . In truth, I don't know what to expect from this conference, in either its context or its format, only that I'm determined to go into it with an open mind and equally determined to contribute to it where I can.

The first day sees guest speakers talking about the history of the inshore fleet and its management models, including a fisherman from Canada who discusses their 'co-management' model and its creation. He makes it sound as if it could be a universal cure-all, but, despite his cheery tone, I'm deeply sceptical; this is exactly the sort of thing that *won't* work in the UK, because why should fishermen trust the people with whom they should 'co-manage' after so many decades of being shafted and lied to? Yes, it could work, if fisheries management were willing to concede a few things, not least to accept that fishermen know their work, know the fishing, know our seafood, know our waters, and have given blood, sweat and tears to amass that knowledge. Instead, the feeling is generally that any 'discussion' with fishermen is a contradiction in terms. We are rarely properly consulted in things that affect us directly, and such consultation is often offered in a way that, while 'efficient', is only efficient for someone who's sat in an office, with a computer, an internet connection, and a salary – i.e. they are paid to gather information that we are requested to supply for free. While this works for a few (the young, digital natives, those with time on their hands and who feel there might be some benefit in getting involved), most fishermen work long hours at sea, and, after a fifteen-hour day, aren't highly motivated to get involved in initiatives where, most likely, we fear it will be to our detriment (because it usually is), and that a decision has already been earmarked in any case, before we've had a chance to digest what it's about. For co-management to work, we fishermen need to be recompensed for our contribution, and for the whole process to be more transparent. If we are asked to provide data for any fisheries stake-holder, then it should be clarified both what our data will be used for, and for us to be fully involved at every stage, from designing the study to drawing the conclusions which result, *and* in implementing any subsequent measures. This is after all, our livelihood.

In two days, I learn so much about the recent history of our fishing sector that by the time I'm on the train headed back to Norfolk, not only does my brain hurt, but my heart is hurting too, for the loss of our rights to fish for our own seafood in our own waters, and the appalling affect it's had on real people's lives. And it's our *own* successive governments that have let this happen, too. I've always thought of our fishing industry as a kind of inverted triangle, with the people who do the actual job of catching fish, and caring for the sustainability of our oceans, propping up the increasingly fatter cats above them.

It seems incredible that I even have to pose the question, but why don't people understand that we fishermen are the guardians of our fish stocks *precisely* because if we don't care for our oceans we will, inevitably, reap what we sow, and destroy our own, and our children's and grandchildren's, livelihoods?

One fisherman (easily identified by his jeans and his shirt) who is both well-known and well-versed in the UK's fishing industry, stands up mid-discussion during the close of the event, walks up to the front, and politely takes control of the mic. Not to mention the whole room. He's seen his moment and he's taken it, and we are a shoal he's fishing: he is now standing in front of his fellow fishermen, fisheries managers, scientists, economists, processors, and spokespeople from NGOs, and he now casts his net to catch as many of us as he can.

'Our fishing industry,' he tells everyone, 'is in a poor state, because of the power of the offshore industry. This division we keep making between the under-10s and over-10s – we're *all* fishermen, and it's in *all* our interests that our environment is fished sustainably. We've all got to work together on this. We have the ideal opportunity to throw everything we have been doing away and start again. Brexit is the chance for us to have the world's *best* fishing industry. To rewrite all the rules and start again.'

Right across the media, particularly in the run-up to the 2016 referendum, the fishing industry was the 'poster child' for Brexit. Is it too much to hope that we weren't just a cynical PR tactic for the Leave campaign? Could real change actually happen?

Chapter 18

'Do not stir your tea with a knife, as this is sure to bring
trouble and strife'

In pursuit of raising the funds for *Fairlass*'s licence we have been back to straight turnarounds with the lads on *Never Can Tell-A* for weeks now. And as the days begin shortening and the sea temperature drops, there's no doubt about it; we're in for a long laborious winter. Despite that – and winter fishing is a damp, filthy business – we couldn't be happier. The whelks, relishing the cooler water (not to mention the smell of our lovely shickle) have virtual free rein, as they're not competing with the crabs, and come marching hungrily into our waiting pots. It's a time of digging out favourite jumpers, of buying new oilskins, and of sun-induced freckles giving way to mud ones. Of not just gritted teeth, but of finding *actual* grit in your teeth when you get home after a long day or night at sea.

This, for me, is one of the great joys of fishing. It doesn't matter how shit the weather is; when the fishing's thick and the whelks are 'on', as we call it, you wish your shanks were a million pots long. It's just the sheer exhilaration of knowing that you are not just doing your job, but that the ratio is right. You are working hard for fair reward, getting out what you're putting in. There are few noises as satisfying as the ding-ding-ding-ding of loads of fat whelks hitting that riddle. Like a win out on a slot machine or a fairground penny falls. That's exactly how it feels. You head home salty-lipped, knackered, but so satisfied.

You always know it's going well when Nige starts dicking about on the hauler, chucking starfish at me, quipping 'You're a star!', and hurling comical abuse at random seagulls. If there is a barometer for good fishing, he is it. However, as suspected, it isn't long before *Never Can Tell-A* starts calling the shots again. On the way out of the harbour one early November morning Nigel notices the oil pressure gauge drop like a stone. Having not left the harbour entrance yet, we spin her round and bring her back along the quayside to investigate. Nigel dips the oil and even I can see what's wrong. The tell-tale milky grey colour on the dipstick means there is water or fuel in your oil. Either way, it's contaminated.

As we have recently replaced various components that could cause this, we know the problem is most likely internal. Which means the engine is a write-off. Luckily, Nigel had the good sense a year prior to send the last engine for refurbishment. So, though we're now going to have to pay for that, which will be a touch painful, this is definitely not the end of the world as we can pick it up and put it in this knackered one's place. It's a like for like swap, and this shiny new refurb has been in her before, so,

214

though both engines weigh three quarters of a ton, requiring us to carefully orchestrate the lifting out/lifting in process, it's actually a comparatively minor job.

We are back up and running by mid-November and very keen to start earning again, having just parted with a few thousand on the engine. We're feeling quite chipper now; we have two boats and an achievable target to work towards, but little do I realise that by the end of the week our prospects are going to take a nose-dive.

Which starts on Sunday evening, heralded by the interruption of my mobile, just as I'm settling down into a nice hot bath. It's Kenneth.

'Where's Dad?' he barks at me. 'I'm sinking!'

I'm bolt upright in the bath I just climbed into. Blindsided. Speechless.

'Where are you?' I manage.

'In the channel, over the bar, I've taken on a lot of water, I still am. Bilge pumps can't keep up.'

I'm dressed, out of the house and in my car in a matter of moments. I need to get hold of Nige but call after call goes unanswered.

Meanwhile, I'm still in constant touch with Kenneth. *Never Can Tell-A* is so heavy by now that he's struggling to move her.

'Kenneth, have you tried reversing the deck wash to use it as an additional pump?'

'I can't get to it,' he says. 'It's under water!'

'Right, I'm on my way,' I say, 'and I'll keep trying your dad. I'll call you back,' I add, and feel a strong need to reassure him. 'But

Kenneth,' I tell him, 'you're the skipper, you're in charge, and if you need to call on the boat, then so be it.'

I mean the lifeboat, of course. And totally appreciate that it's a very big decision. You don't call out the lifeboat unless you really need to.

Meanwhile, call after call after call to Nigel still goes unanswered ... *Come on Nige, where the fuck are you?!*

I call Kenneth back. 'I can't get your dad, but I'm on the dry road now. Where are you?' (The dry road being so called because there aren't any pubs on it, so no point hoping to find Nige there.)

'I'm coming alongside the beach,' he says. 'Fuck she's heavy, Ash – I can barely move her.'

I've arrived in Wells now. It's late in the day for Nige to be out and about but I drive past all his usual haunts anyway – without success – then I head straight for the outer harbour, praying that Kenneth has managed to drag *Never Can Tell-A* alongside the pontoon. Abandoning my car, I dart up and over the bank and when I see her tied up against the pontoon, let out a huge sigh of relief. Though she doesn't sit there plucky and arrogant, the thing I love her for. She's a sorry-looking shadow of the boat I know.

I race down the gangway to the pontoon, the angle of which is still fairly severe, confirming what I initially thought – that there's no tide here yet. It's at least four hours before the water. What has happened here? As I approach ever closer I can see her scuppers are only just teetering above the water line and I am horrified when I jump on and peer into the open engine hatch. The water inside her is probably only three quarters of a metre below deck

216

level, and the engine and gearbox are now submerged up to the level of the engine's fuel filters.

I turn to Kenneth, who is white-faced in the squally rain.

'Fucking hell,' I say to him. It seems the only thing *to* say.

'You got a fag, Ash?' he says.

I toss him the packet. He won't have been able to make a rollup yet, I realise. He definitely needs one more than I do.

I see the electric submersible pump we have has been plugged into the power on the pontoons and is heaving water out through a green hose hung over the rails. But it isn't taking any water out – all it's doing is holding the current level. *Still* unable to get hold of Nige, I ring Carl in the hope he might have a petrol salvage pump. After a brief explanation of the situation he says he doesn't but that the harbour will. A call to Robert, the harbourmaster, and within ten minutes I have driven to the harbour storage shed, frantically loaded my car up with pumps and hoses, and am racing back to the boat. I dump both on the pontoon and with great thanks to Robert (who we soak in the process), we get the pump running and at last *Never Can Tell-A* starts to empty.

So the with the situation finally under some semblance of control, I *have* to find Nige. I decide he must be in Langham, where he's been staying since looking for a house, so I drive there and find my hunch is correct. I get to his room, finding, luckily, that the door is unlocked, and see he's asleep in bed, blissfully unaware of the events unfolding, and what's happened to his pride and joy in Wells.

I pause, knowing that waking him is about to cause him so much hurt. I really want to turn straight around and walk back out of the door, wishing this whole situation would just go away. But he stirs. My entrance has disturbed his sleep, and he sits up.

He looks confused. Astonished to see me there, my face flickering in the light of the muted television, which is playing to itself.

'What are you doing here?' He swings his legs over the edge of the bed and I kneel down and put my hands on his knees. Despite the light from the telly, his face is shrouded in shadow. He falls silent now. Uncharacteristically silent. Does he know something's wrong? Can he see it in my face?

As soon as I open my mouth to speak, I realise I've been rehearsing this entire conversation. I know *exactly* how much that boat means to him. Christ – I know what she means to *me*, but the connection between them goes even deeper – *so* much deeper. So I start with the positive. 'Nige, your boat's in the outer harbour. She's taken on a lot of water. We've got pumps on her now. I don't know the details but Kenneth is down there pumping her out.'

My horrible news delivered, I brace myself for a rapid fire of questions. What? Why? How? When? But they do not come. He is calm and still silent as he pushes his feet into his old DMs and shrugs on his coat. Maybe it hasn't sunk in yet?

Within minutes we're in my car and headed back to Wells, and I update him on all I know so far. Again, he says little, almost nothing, bar nodding and acknowledging what I'm telling him – which is, of course, very little. Till we're on the road between Stiffkey and Langham, when he says, very firmly, 'Ash, slow down. Better we get there than not at all.'

By the time we're back in Wells, Nige has silently smoked about four cigarettes, and I can feel his composure beginning to calm me as well, as we return to where *Never Can Tell-A* is still tied up against the pontoons. She is now empty of water and the loud reverberating din of the petrol salvage pump has been turned off, as the electric pump is holding the incoming water level steady. I'm glad Nige didn't have to see her how I saw her barely an hour before. He still doesn't say much. I don't think he has even asked Kenneth how we've all come to find ourselves in this position.

There is a switch then – like Nige is clicking into gear. He's in boss mode now and doling out instructions to all of us. Kenneth is charged with starting Andy and Martin Frary's skiff and bringing it alongside, as there are around fifteen boxes of whelks aboard and they need to come off. (We know they'll be only too happy for us to appropriate their little skiff given the urgency of the situation we're in.)

The whelks might sound like an odd priority, but I think Nige just wants to give Kenneth something to occupy him while he focuses on what exactly needs to happen next. We know she can't stay here the night – she needs lifting out of the water as soon as possible, and Robert has already told us he will of course lift us out on the following morning's tide. We just need to get her to the slipway where at least she can dry out overnight, once the tide falls.

At some point in my absence the boat's engine has been stopped, maybe for fear of water getting into it and causing terminal damage. Either way, Nige wants to start her up and,

219

with a salvage pump running, steam her the mile up to the town and put her on the slipway. However with every power-hungry deck light and bilge pump running, the batteries now don't have enough juice to turn the engine over, the old Ford making slower and slower attempts at spinning itself into life. Fuck.

From where I'm standing on the pontoon, I see a familiar light sequence glide past the outer harbour. Mac must be away tonight then, I think. It's a pretty dank night and it's started to freshen from the north, not that time, weather or conditions matter to him. He is one of the most dedicated fishermen I know, and because of this he is the most successful one too. He does the job for the love of it, not the money.

I watch Kenneth buzz away with the whelks on Andy and Martin's skiff, and just as Mac's lights vanish into the distance, Nige calls to me from *Never Can Tell-A*. They have been talking on WhatsApp and it seems Mac is turning around again, due to a leaky wheelhouse roof, and has offered to hip us up for a tow. Though Mac being Mac, I can't believe a leaky wheelhouse roof would stop him going out. I'm already feeling emotional, so this act of what *I* believe to be nothing to do with his wheelhouse – just an act of selfless human kindness – is enough to almost tip me over the edge tonight.

But I can't stay mushy for long as we need to turn the boat around. The way she's facing, he can't pick us up. There's also the question of the tow itself. We'll need to keep the pump running for the whole mile he's going to tow us, which means we're going to need extra petrol just in case. So my next job is to jump back in my car, get a petrol can off Carl, then drive to the petrol station to get some.

That done, I head straight back to find Nige has already got the noisy salvage pump running, and Mac, who's now back, is in position, ready to take the ropes. Nige will stay aboard *Never Can Tell-A* but I'm to drive down and meet them on the slipway.

'What about Kenneth?' I ask Nige. 'Is he on his way back yet?'

He shakes his head. 'No,' he says, 'I've sent him home.'

I have no idea what, if anything, has been discussed between them, but if I were Kenneth right now, I know how I'd feel, whatever the cause of the breach. Nige's expression, however, tells me nothing – he's focused on the task at hand. The post-mortem can wait till the morning.

Once I'm at the slipway, I walk out onto the north-facing staging behind the harbour's storage shed. I hear footsteps crunch on gravel and a powerful torch beam coming from behind me. A torch that powerful? It must be Carl.

'Alright Ash.' He knows the headlines of the evening so far, as I briefly appraised him on the phone earlier when I rang him about the pump, and then visited him to borrow a petrol can. But this is a greeting, not a question.

'Shit night, innit?' I mumble back. (That's what we do when we have nothing else to say, isn't it? Talk about the weather.) 'How come this kind of stuff always happens on filthy nights like this?' And it is a filthy night; I feel the wind pushing directly against me, and a torrent of stinging rain starts to pour and lash directly at my face. I left the house in such a blur, I don't even have a coat.

221

'Where's he got to?' Carl asks. In the distance, I've already spotted Mac's boat, *Two Brothers*, coming down the beach bank, the dark silhouette of *Never Can Tell-A* beside her.

'Just there,' I say, pointing in the general direction.

I see him following my finger. 'Oh yeah,' he replies, eventually spotting it. Carl's eyesight isn't the best because he lost one of his eyes after a chisel fell in it. Although you'd never notice, not without really looking, that one of his eyes is, in fact, glass. 'Do ya need a hand?' he asks.

I shake my head. 'Nah, mate. Should be alright now. We'll get her pulled up the slipway as far as we can tonight and see what's what in the morning.'

'Well if you need anything,' he kindly offers, 'you just let me know.'

Carl really is the best. Ditto the Frarys. All exemplars of that rare and precious breed; people who will step up and offer help whenever it's needed – doesn't matter how inconvenient the time or how filthy the weather. You never need to ask. They just know you'd do the same for them. That feeling of solidarity is, I think, something you find particularly in endangered communities such as ours, not just because we do dangerous work – it's also because we know we have to stick together.

I watch Carl crunch his way back across the gravel, and make my way down the wooden ladder to the pontoons by the slip. I see the red and white lights start to converge on *Two Brothers* as she makes her turn in the quay to approach the east end. In the orange streetlights that flank the water side I can see the inky black outline of two boats side by side, and a pulsating arc of seawater spewing from the pump, back-lit by the amber glow. I stand ready to catch a rope as Mac inches closer, and positions *Never Can Tell-A* close enough to the pontoon for Nige to chuck me a rope and make her fast. With her tied-off he darts back to the other side of the boat where he and Scratcher (Mac's crew) untie the tow rope and *Two Brothers* gracefully spins around to make her way back up to Mac's berth on the quay.

Nige has by now stopped the racket of the salvage pump and at some point in this boat ballet I realise Robert, the harbourmaster, has appeared again to lend a hand. He helps us move her along and around the right-angled turn of the pontoon, and pull her alongside the sanctuary of the wall.

We do at least still have the tide in our favour (just), so it's not long before *Never Can Tell-A* is floating above the concrete slope of the slipway. We pull her up as far as we can before her keel gently grazes the concrete below. This is as far as we can get her tonight. Nige hops back on board and once again fires the pump up.

As we say our goodbyes to Robert, both thanking him profusely, I reflect that he, as much as any of our fellow fishermen, is a dear and precious friend. We are so lucky to have a harbourmaster who really gets it the way he does, and who is not only always ready to step in and help us out, but who also always stands up for us as a community.

Robert tells us he'll lift *Never Can Tell-A* out as soon as there's enough tide in the morning, then he's on his way, none of us in the mood for hanging around to chat. Nige and I then retreat to my car, to find some refuge from the damp and bitter cold, and

223

sit watching the life support machine that is the salvage pump grumbling on, keeping *Never Can Tell-A* clear of water until the tide turns and the water creeps away inch by inch from her penetrated hull.

As the first hour ticks by, we take stock of what we are looking at and how we have come to be in this predicament. I break the silence. Knowing Nige as I do, I know he likes to be in control of what's going on and often does not want to involve other people or ask for help unnecessarily.

'I'm sorry I rang Carl and Robert,' I say. 'I had to get a bigger pump.'

'Don't worry about that,' he replies gently, 'You did the right thing, Ash.'

I hesitate before asking, 'Did Kenneth tell you what happened?'

He answers immediately. 'Reckons he read the tide book wrong and came over the end too early.' He pauses then, and I don't interrupt him. 'Must have been a bit of lift there and maybe she's hit the bottom hard?' he goes on. He's surmising now, but come to think of it even I could hear the dull crashing of waves in the distance when I raced down that gangway hours earlier. And that sand on the bar *is* as hard as rock in places. But I know Nige doesn't want to chat about it – he's just thinking out loud. So I just nod, and we continue our silent vigil.

The tide is now steadily making its way out of the harbour and with Nige satisfied that *Never Can Tell-A* can be left for a bit we turn off the pump, evaluate the time and decide that the only place we might get a beer at 10.45 p.m. is the Eddie. At the bar is Mac, accompanied by Ben, who is a local boat builder, and has already been brought up to speed on the night's events. We discuss things, and Ben is hopeful that repairs can be made quickly – quickly enough that we could even be back afloat again on this set of tides, which luckily are still putting in, and are at least big enough for the harbour's hoist to lift boats in and out.

After a couple of beers for Nige, and a shandy for me, we know all we can do is make sure she dries out and takes the ground okay tonight. We will not know any more until the cold light of the day. The night for both of us is spent, sleepless, sat in the car, watching and waiting, punctuated by short miserable exchanges; despite Ben's reassuring words, for which we're grateful, we won't know what we're dealing with until the morning.

~

Daylight breaks bright and cold, and we both have the same thought. Before we do anything else we have to deal with the whelks Kenneth's left on the skiff. We make short work of zipping it round to the quay wall but, with the water still low, it's a job and a half to bump three quarters of a ton of whelks up onto the quay. Then it's much-needed coffee and back to *Never Can Tell-A*.

I follow Nige down the slipway. The tide hasn't started properly yet and as he walks along the length of her, there is no obvious damage to the hull below the waterline. As Nige walks round her stern I jump down onto the pontoon she's lying in front of. We both arrive at her back end at the same time, and we both see it. Her name board, which usually proudly emblazons across the

225

entire transom, is missing a whole section. It now reads '*Never C – l-A*'. She must have hit the bottom hard to snap that, I think.

Nigel lays a hand gently on her, and I only just catch his whispered words. 'He's hurt you real bad, baby.'

In that moment the connection between them feels so strong. It's like the rest of the world doesn't exist. In that private moment – and it really does feel private – it's just *them*, and I'm a spectator. Every hair on my body stands on end and my throat begins to close. I have to swallow back tears.

The intensity is broken by reality as the tide starts edging its way up to *Never Can Tell-A*, so Nige turns the pump back on and in the background I can hear Robert starting up the hoist. As she is lifted up and out of the water, I can instantly see the problem. Water is cascading out of her, mainly on the starboard side, coming from four sprung planks where the keel meets the first clinked plank, right at her stern.

'Get a video, Ash,' Nige says, but I'm already on it, my phone camera following her as she rises up out of the drink, the water continuing to gush from where she's breached, like she's wounded and the bleeding just won't stop.

Now I cry.

Chapter 19

'Start no new endeavours on a Friday'

Due to many bad omens associated with Fridays, do not start a fishing
trip on a Friday, or lay the keel of a new boat.

By late morning *Never Can Tell-A* is safely out of the water on the
hard, with stands underneath her hull and blocks underneath her
keel. There is still water pouring in a steady stream from where
she was breached, and we can now get a better look at the extent
of the damage. Looking at the sprung planks, we both agree that
Nige's theory about her hitting the sandbar is probably correct
and when Ben comes down to join us an hour or so later, he
agrees. He also tells us the kind of nails we'll need to make her
seaworthy again – the kind of in-depth nautical knowledge
few have, and which is sadly dying out, so it makes Ben highly
sought-after on this stretch of coastline. Luckily he also has some,
so he gives us a handful. We also need to get a new sign for her,
anti-foul her hull, and replace her sacrificial anodes. Not right
away though. We're not just emotionally tired, we're physically

knackered, so before we do anything we both need to head home and get some sleep.

The following morning, we reconvene in identical moods. A decent night's rest has given us both a much-needed boost, and we set about repairing *Never Can Tell-A* with our sleeves rolled up, both actually and metaphorically, determined not to dwell on our misfortune, or be broken by this setback. It helps that right there, in the periphery of our vision, is our big, blue and beautiful *Fairlass*. Just knowing we have her is sufficient to keep our spirits up and our motivation strong; after all, *Never Can Tell-A* is our means to get *Fairlass* licensed, and the clock is still very much ticking. In fact, so determined do we feel that while we wait for the sign we've ordered, we use the golden opportunity of her being out of the water to also repaint her hull.

Ben's advice has been to nail the planks back up tight into the deadwood above the keel, so on Thursday, having fitted the new nameplate and pressure-washed and anti-fouled her, we make our first attempt to get *Never Can Tell-A* watertight again. This turns out not to be a success. Nige has his head down one of the hatches, watching proceedings, and the minute Robert lifts us back into the water, out he pops again, shaking his head at me and wearing a disheartened expression. From where I'm watching, however, as she is once again lifted out, I at least have a good view of the affected area, and can get a sense of where more nails are needed.

Later that day, while we're in the pub, Nige gets an odd phone call, from a number he doesn't know (so he naturally doesn't answer), immediately followed a by a voicemail. It turns out to be the MCA. 'What the fuck do they want?' he says – though the question is rhetorical. All we do know is that calls from the MCA are rarely good news. As there's very little signal in the pub, he goes outside to do the call back and returns five minutes later, if that.

'So what did they want?' I ask him.

Turns out it was answers to some questions. Had she sunk? And when Nige told them no, what had happened? They also said they'd had reports that there were five people on board, when she's only supposed to have a maximum of three.

'So I told them no, obviously,' Nige says. 'And where the fuck have they got that from?'

I'm as bemused as he is. 'Well, someone's obviously made a call to them,' I say. I'm not going to waste my energy on shit stirrers. So I tell Nige exactly that.

He nods in acknowledgement. 'Fuck 'em. It's nearly Christmas.'

And at least the call seems to have ended on a more positive note. He goes on to tell me that the inspector said that if Nige is happy with the repairs, and considers her to be seaworthy, then he has no further concerns. So we put the whole thing out of our minds.

We go to work adding more nails the following morning and when we try *Never Can Tell-A* again the next day, having had to wait for the tides, she is, thankfully, no longer leaking, but we leave her against slipway for two more days, so Nige can recheck the hull after she's had a couple of tides afloat. It also gives him a chance to properly check that there's been no damage to the (expensive, newly refurbished) engine and gearbox, and, again, all seems to be okay, so finally, on the last day of November, we take her back where she belongs, to her home on the quay.

She's not going to stay there for long, however, as the annual Christmas Tide Festival is imminent. A seasonal event in Wells since 2004, the Christmas Tide Festival is pretty unique, in that Santa makes his entrance not on a sleigh drawn by reindeer but on a boat, accompanied by a flotilla. (In fact, the first year he came in on water skis, but I suspect they might have changed it on 'elf and safety' grounds.) This is made up of fishing boats, angling boats and small pleasure craft, all of them fairy-lit, and when they all make their entrance into the quay, Santa's arrival is cheered by thousands of people on the quayside, while from over on the marsh, there is a spectacular firework display. Best of all, it's completely free, which I think is amazing; it happens because all sorts of local charities and organisations chip in to make it the spectacle it is. The crowds for it are *huge*; people come to it from many miles distant, and it's the day on which Christmas really begins for Wells. I don't need to tell you how much fun it is being part of the flotilla, which we did on *Never Can Tell-A* last year, and I have a pang of FOMO that this year we won't be able to join in. Instead, we have to load her up with our whelk pots, which are cluttering up the quayside, and move her to the outer harbour as they obviously need that space to be clear.

We duly relocate *Never Can Tell-A* later and have just headed back into town when Nige gets a very strange heads-up. The MCA are apparently on their way down to Wells, to inspect *Never-Can-Tell-A* over a discrepancy on the boat's safety certificate. Once again, Nige is confused. What on earth do they want to see? But there's no time to speculate – we're better employed taking action. So we drive back to the outer harbour, trying to second guess the sort of things they might inspect, which includes expiry dates on life jackets, flares, our life raft and so on, and any other life-saving equipment we have on board.

Nige is highly stressed; the MCA have the power to put fishermen out of business with just a single stroke of the pen and, not wanting me to say anything stupid (which, fair play, I might), he tells me to head off to the pub and let him deal with it.

I obviously do as my skipper says, and sit in the Fleece, phone in hand – if he wants or needs anything, I'll be immediately good to go. As it is, half an hour passes before I hear from him. Or, rather, see him. He arrives in the pub brandishing a slip of yellow paper, his head hanging worryingly low.

He hands me the piece of paper. Detention Order. 'Unless I can produce a valid safety certificate, Ash, we can't go to sea.'

I read the words on the slip again as if they might miraculously change before my eyes. 'What do you mean a *valid* safety certificate?' I ask him. I do a quick think back. MCA inspections happen every five years, and I'm pretty sure *Never Can Tell-A*'s last was in 2016. Which means she's still got eighteen months or so, must have.

I say so to Nige. But he immediately corrects me. 'No, Ash,' he says. 'Apparently she has *never* had a certificate.'

Now I gape at him. 'Well then, how did you get a licence issued? How have you been fishing all this time without one?'

We head back out to the van, to sit and have a ponder, and bump into Mac. Nige hands him the yellow slip. 'But I remember you having your MCA inspection when you first got her,' he says, echoing my own thoughts. 'The inspector wanted you to change the fuel injector pipes and I remember seeing you with them. You emailed a picture to the inspector to show you'd done them!'

But a call to the MCA to explain all this falls on deaf ears, not least because, frustratingly, we don't have anything other than verbal evidence of this. And they say they can't find any record of it – oh, and that the inspector who signed it off has retired now. Which means we've essentially been fishing all this time without a valid safety certificate. Nige had had a temporary one issued until remedial action had been taken, but when it had been, no five-year certificate was ever issued. So an admin error, and on *their* part. Why has this not been flagged up before? It matters little though. We don't have a leg to stand on.

I remember saying to Nigel, on that horrible night when we thought she might be sunk, that we'd probably need to sell the licence on *Never Can Tell-A*, and use the funds to license *Fairlass* instead. Now we think *Never Can Tell-A* is probably seaworthy again, that, tragically, looks like being our only option.

In reality, we had always planned to retire *Never Can Tell-A* once the safety certificate (which she doesn't apparently have) ran out in eighteen months' time. She was already getting tired, and we'd worked out that over the year and a half we had left on her ticket we could earn enough to trade her in for something newer, and transfer her licence to that. But now isn't the right time, not least because we're skint and, despite the glories of individual fishing days being so good, those days will soon be much fewer in number, as we will soon be in our leanest fishing period.

In short, no amount of *joie de vivre* at those bumper November hauls can make up for the fact that the coming months are now going to be fucking bleak. The only light at the end of this dark, miserable tunnel is that we have a licence that's worth a bit of money to sell. All that stands between us and getting back out to the North Sea is finding a licence for *Fairlass* (a time-consuming and complicated business) and getting her through her own safety inspection, after which her certificate will never leave my sight.

If she passes, that is. I email the MCA constantly, explaining our situation and begging them to give us priority, and eventually get given a date just before Christmas, 17th December. Now the real work begins. We have a checklist that includes everything from VHF radios (which all have to be programmed with your MMSI number and call sign), EPIRB, fire extinguishers, lifebuoys and flares, to a life raft, bilge level alarm, radar reflector, waterproof torch (plus spare batteries), fog horn, and lifejackets. And so on, and so on. (Though no cuddly toy.) Which at least sounds straightforward, except there's another layer of stress as most of these items are required to be 'in date', as the majority of them have a shelf life. And though *Fairlass* came with many of these things already in place, some are out of date, and some missing entirely, so there's a hefty shopping list too. There's also the paperwork side, which is similarly massive, as lots of things need to be registered, and sometimes licensed, and risk assessments also need to be in place for all operations that are carried out on the boat, plus evidence of all the compulsory courses we are required to complete. And because we had to change *Fairlass*'s PLN, I had to get new signage for her too.

Somehow though, by the date of the inspection, we've done it. Probably gone overboard on crossing i's and dotting t's, in fact, as we are both highly sceptical that our boat is going to get a fair hearing. That *any* boat would. I totally get that the MCA wants to make a dangerous profession as safe as possible – who wouldn't? – but their big stick policies, which might well work with freight and shipping, cannot, to my mind, be applied in the same way to small fishing boats. And that's also because every boat is different. It doesn't matter that they are all doing the same job – each is unique, like their skippers and crews. So it's impossible to standardise, have a 'one rule fits all' way of working. What's best for one boat doesn't necessarily work on another. And it's a cause of seething rage in many harbours that with the MCA there is no room for discussion or debate. We're also anxious, despite being in the happy place of having passed, that there are rumours that things are going to be tightened up even further in the coming years.

The MCA didn't always exist, by the way. A 'child' of its parent organisation, the Department of Transport, it came to being in 1998. And though inspections for boats have been around since the early 1990s, it wasn't until around 2007 that the full-on safety inspections we know and (don't) love came into being. And it doesn't stop there. The breadth and complexity of inspections are both increasing in an aggressive and unrealistic way. Many other commercial sectors are given the option of being inspected by neutral third parties, and most sectors, obviously, do this. That this is not the case for the fishing industry is an obvious anomaly. Is this de-commissioning via the back door? I'm afraid to say the cynic in me thinks so.

For now, though, things are finally looking up again. We sell *Never Can Tell-A*'s licence via a broker a few days after we pass our inspection, and have the money in the bank by 24th December. Ditto our precious MCA safety certificate, and *Fairlass*'s Certificate of Registry.

Which means we get to enjoy Christmas, and, four months after bringing her home, we can finally license our Lass Fair. Another step closer, then, to being able to fish again.

Chapter 20

'Do not whistle at sea'

. . .or you'll whistle up the wind.

'Nige! Look,' I shout out, as I pull up on the near-deserted quayside. 'I have the actual papers in my actual hand!'

It's an early February morning and the sun is just rising, creating an aura around the frost that's clinging to all the mooring ropes, and sprinkling diamonds over the treacherous-looking pavements. I hate driving on ice and, in my battered old van, the journey to Wells has been pretty sketchy. I don't care. We've got *Fairlass*'s licence entitlement papers, so we're off to Lowestoft today, whatever the weather. Nige has already got the coffees in, so, after a *very* careful totter from the van to the wheelhouse, we clink our cups together in celebration.

And we definitely should celebrate. Despite being currently on the bones of our asses, we have achieved a great deal in the last six weeks. In fact, not being able to go out fishing, coupled with selling *Never Can Tell-A*'s licence, has actually made the process of getting *Fairlass* fit for purpose a little easier. And to get the precious papers that I currently have stashed about my person, she did need to be made fit for *our* purpose. Yes, she passed her MCA inspection, but in order to work as a potting boat for us, in these waters, she still needed a few modifications.

So. We have replaced the elderly GPS plotter with a new one, taken the riddle off *Never Can Tell-A* and made adjustments to it so it'll work on *Fairlass*, and we have *finally* got the poxy autopilot working. We have also relieved *Never Can Tell-A* of her radar, and fitted that too, plus we have fitted the new hydraulic tank that Phillip at Marine Weld has fabricated for us. Not going to lie – it's been hard sometimes. As we toiled away all January, watching friends come and go from the harbour with decks filled with catch made me yearn to be back at sea again.

That yearning wasn't – *isn't* – just a whimsical desire to be out bobbing on the waves; if you work on the sea – if spending most days out there is your version of normal – being away from it for an extended period isn't great for your mental health, and the last few weeks have made me reflective. I've thought back lots to what kept pulling me back to Wells in those early days, and I now realise just how strong the relationship between the sea and me really is. It's not enough to say I miss it. I *need* it. And it's the same for almost every fisherman, I think. Certainly, all of us – me, Nige, Jack and Kenneth – get irritable and snappy with one another if we're forced to stay on land for too long.

One of the great taboos in the fishing sector is being honest about poor mental health. Just as in farming, well known for its high rates of depression and suicide, the fishing industry is full of the kind of strong, silent older men who struggle to admit when they are not okay. And I can understand why they might not be okay. Fishing is a precarious way to make a living, and with increased regulation and changes in policy, it never gets any easier, either. It might feel a bit trite to mention inspirational quotes in this context, but the common play on words, 'vitamin sea', accompanied by a pretty picture, is familiar because it's true. Just as people often feel their stress reduce when they head out into nature, the sea heals those who make their living from it in a way no medicine ever could, being the only place, it sometimes feels, where seafarers feel in control, despite its predictably unpredictable nature. Head out to sea – as I know, because I feel that way now too – and all your worries are left at the quayside. Perhaps fishing really is in a person's blood because being away from it really does raise our blood pressure.

Equally likely to raise Nige's and my blood pressure has been the business of licensing *Fairlass*, which is not a simple process. The MMO are often dubbed the mismanagement organisation. (By other fishermen, I hasten to add, not me. Hashtag don't sue me.) Their remit covers any activity in or on the marine environment, in short, anything that happens at sea, and isn't about safety – which is the role, as we know, of the MCA. If it was a food chain, there would be DEFRA at the top, in overall charge of the environment in and around Great Britain, then the MMO, in charge of sea stuff (though only in England and Scotland, Northern Ireland and Wales have their own bodies). Finally comes IFCA (more on them later).

The MMO are responsible for managing our fish stocks, and the commercial fishing activity that goes with that. Many people will remember a period in our recent history when it was widely reported that fishermen were unintentionally catching fish that were not their target species, only to be told that they were not allowed to land them, because they either didn't have quota for them, or they weren't on their licence, or because they were undersized, and that they would have to throw them – dead – back into the sea. Bear in mind that these fish could have been sold to be eaten, or, in the case of undersized fish, sold for bait, cosmetics, and pet food, but because of the various licence and quota headaches, those who caught them basically had no choice but to waste them. It took years of lobbying, and the intervention of a celebrity chef before the MMO finally opened their eyes to the ridiculousness of this practice, and the rules were finally changed. The long-term effects of this change will be unknown for some time yet, and it may not be a solution that fits all, but what strikes me is why did it take a campaign by a celebrity chef to get that change made in the first place?

To me, the MMO frequently give the impression that all the fish stocks around Britain belong to them. Yes, they are the body charged with managing our fish stocks, but the point is in the 'our'; I prefer to think that the fish around this island actually belong to every person who lives on it, i.e. all of us, all of *you*, and that the fisherman have the privilege of catching them, sustainably, on behalf of all of us, not them. Instead, it often seems as though we have to go cap in hand to the MMO, to beg for the right to bring *your* fish home.

I imagine the MMO would say that's perfectly reasonable, as they are charged with ensuring the long-term health of the various stocks, and to make sure fish is 'responsibly sourced', as it says on the tuna cans. However, the grand plan for our oceans, to maintain healthy stocks and clean seas, is spoilt in its execution by myriad little annoyances (the issues around submitting logs of catches, for instance, and the introduction of IVMS and the digital catch app, will both be familiar recent thorns in the side of countless fishermen). I could rant about all this till the seas run dry, frankly, because there are so many instances of inexplicable regulations, others that seem to contradict one another, demands made on fishermen which are unachievable at best, and prosecutable at worst; particularly ones related to digitisation. Plus punitive systems which take no account of a fisherman's working life, and seem, at least to me, solely designed to trip up honest hard-working folk. But perhaps I should explain myself better.

Take the IVMS mentioned above. (No, please *do* take the IVMS.) IVMS stands for Inshore Vessel Monitoring System – a well-described piece of useful kit, right? Wrong. The purpose of requiring that any boat, from any country, operating in British waters, should install an IVMS unit is to track every boat's movements, all the time. This allows the MMO to know where everybody is and what everyone is doing, information they can marry up with their digital catch app, and add to their ever-growing store of data.

You might argue that there is nothing wrong with collecting useful data, especially when it comes to our precious fish stocks.

(In fact, they already had this, albeit in paper form, and slightly less accurately, as the only requirement was to give a grid reference.) But two things have conspired to make this deeply unpopular. One is that fishermen have spent a lifetime learning the cycles and productivity of their patch of ocean and while they are happy to share their knowledge, there have been too many instances in the past where that knowledge has been used against them for purposes of 'fisheries management' that never seem to benefit fishermen. No wonder they aren't comfortable sharing such data. The other is that the rolling out of the IVMS has been a shambles. Profiteering has been allowed to happen (in my opinion by fly-by-night companies), with units which could be bought for £60 and fitted yourself being sold for over £600, and required to be fitted by MMO-appointed installers. These units were financed by the MMO, so fishermen weren't out of pocket (except for the installation, which they did have to pay £150 for, and could have done themselves), but this is taxpayers' money being wasted. And I've learned that they have recently pulled two of the 'approved' devices from their list, as these now appear *not* to meet the specifications the MMO initially called for. Thousands upon thousands of pounds have been wasted (from both taxpayers' and fishermen's pockets).

This hardly inspires confidence, but the main issue is trust. Something that is hard won and easily lost. Another big area of concern among many in the sector is that a senior MMO figure now helps run a fishing company that is not only part foreign-owned, but also holds the biggest chunk of FQAs in England.

A scenario like this is known as a 'flagship', and to the untrained eye, seems to be a UK-registered company, that owns a UK-registered boat, with its own UK licence and subsequent fixed quota. It looks very much like one of our own, but a little digging through the FQA register (see here: https://www. fqaregister.service.gov.uk/browse#tabs=0) and cross-referencing with Companies House data will show you just how British these businesses actually aren't. They are also under no obligation to land their 'British' fish here, so that our economy may see at least some return on its own resource. Especially when you consider that for every one person on a boat, eight to ten jobs are generated on land. I cannot think of a time when any other British resource has been allowed to be targeted and taken for free, with such ease, by any other country, can you? At least leasing the seabed to the offshore wind giants from other nations pays billions to the UK for the privilege.

It's no wonder, therefore, that small, struggling fishermen feel anxious and resentful about sharing their hard-earned data, and bemused about how something like that could happen. And this is just *one* of the things we get upset about.

I never anticipated (and if I'm honest, still don't) quite how bamboozling getting a licence on a boat really was until we reached that point. Despite having approached Ocean Blue, who are a quota and licence broker, straight after Christmas so, in theory, being able to leave most of it to them, I still wanted to know what exactly was going on. There were large sums of money changing hands and ultimately both Nige and myself needed reassurance that the entitlements we were buying could be turned into a licence that would enable *Fairlass* to fish.

In early January the brokers had found us enough kilowatts and tonnage to fit *Fairlass*, buying the majority of it (all the KW, but only 4 of the 10 tonnes we needed) from one boat, that had a fairly basic non-sector, non-quota licence, and the rest of the tonnage from another boat.

Having agreed to go ahead with the purchase, an eye-watering £36K (which really is a chunk of change in the fishing licence biz, and a complete travesty considering that these were, as I've mentioned, originally given out by the MMO for *free*) was transferred to the broker in mid-January, triggering emails to fly back and forth with various attachments that need printing, filling out in BLOCK CAPITALS, and signing.

We then hit a hurdle with the tonnage top-up licence, however, due to an administrative snafu. Marine Scotland, where the top-up licence was coming from, calculate their tonnage a little differently to the MMO (don't ask me why, it makes no sense to me!). So the top-up wasn't going to work, as we would need a lot more of it to make up for that 'exchange rate', and obviously the seller wasn't going to make up the shortfall, as it would put them some £70K out of pocket in lost tonnage. (I *know*. I am confused all over again just writing that.)

Some alternative tonnage needed to be found, and was, from a seller in Wales. (Whose system, thankfully, matches that of the MMO.) Which meant that, in theory, at least (we still needed those two very expensive pieces of paper to prove it) we had the right to ask the MMO to turn them into a licence for *Fairlass*. The MMO, who have an office in Lowestoft.

~

The journey to Lowestoft will, we reckon, take just over an hour, and hand-delivering the vital papers is, of course, a no-brainer. It's not like we've got anything better to be doing, after all – we're not allowed to go out fishing, are we? So, coffees drunk, and fuelled up (in both senses), we head off in the van. And though the early sun soon gives way to some dull February clouds, as we drive up the A146 there is still sun in our hearts, as the end is finally in sight.

Once in Lowestoft, which, like Buckie, is a shadow of its former glory days, it takes a while to find the MMO office. It almost seems as if they are keen to discourage passing trade. It's a feeling that's reinforced as we rock up at the front desk with no appointment or prior notice. They don't seem to even want us in the building, let alone to converse with us. But, hell, we need our licence as soon as possible, so needs must. And in fact Alison, who I've swapped emails with, is actually really helpful.

With everything now signed and in their hands, we head back to Wells. Where we wait. And we wait. And we wait.

Nige and I are getting sick to the back teeth of what feels like the entire community now asking, 'Have you got your licence yet?', when they pass by us on the quay. I know they mainly ask because they care but, believe me, if we had, they wouldn't be seeing us for a wake, we'd be speeding away so bloody fast from the solace of the quay wall.

Not that either of us has been idle. Nigel can always find something to keep him busy, particularly if it's of a twiddling and tinkering variety, and a new boat gives him the perfect opportunity to indulge his passion for finding out how absolutely everything is put together. He could probably set up his own YouTube channel, called 'Nigel's Boat hacks', or something. I genuinely think it would do well.

Meanwhile, I've been busy on social media myself, having set up an Instagram account last October, in order to reach out to other fishermen and compare notes, especially when it came to fisheries management. I started out small, just connecting with like-minded souls, but bit by bit, I began being followed more widely, and by more influential people. This led to invitations to write pieces about the issues I'd highlighted, so I'm now using the free time to put pen to paper, and bang on about the fear I have for the future of our industry. Having spoken to so many fishermen around the country by now, it's great to have a voice I can put to good use. No, I don't have all the answers, or even most of the answers, but I do have ideas and it feels so good to be making myself useful like this. I am doing it everywhere – in the wheelhouse, in the café, in the van, on the sofa; I'm basically typing my thoughts wherever I go. I have yet to find out that this little Instagram account of mine will be the porthole of opportunity that will go on to allow me to write the book you are reading right now, but it's so soothing to articulate how I feel about it all, as, so often it feels as if no one on high cares. Plus – BIG bonus this – it turns out that building a profile on social media can get you free oilskins and boots. Who knew? And who doesn't love freebies?

While we wait, I also call IFCA. The Inshore Fisheries and Conservation Authority is charged with overseeing the management of all waters inside 6 nautical miles and I like to think of them as the MMO's subservient lap dog (remember they are at the bottom of that food chain). To fish for whelks inside 'their' zone you must purchase an annual permit which runs from March to March and comes with its own set of hoops to jump through. For example, each pot must have two escape holes, no smaller than 24mm, to allow juvenile whelks to easily escape, but, as Jack so often points out to me, if they're being fed they're not exactly going to leave of their own volition, are they? Your riddle will need to be measured by an IFCA officer to ensure that the bars are also spaced a minimum of 24mm apart. This will apparently ensure that very few undersized whelks will be taken, as they will fall through the gaps. The legal landing size for our local IFCA district is also higher, at 55mm, as opposed to the 45mm limit outside the district.

You must also not use edible brown crab for bait if fishing inside the 6-mile limit, and this includes lovely, free shickle. This one I find extremely frustrating, as it makes absolutely no sense to me; I can't understand the justification for it, and when I have questioned it – and I have, multiple times – I never get an answer that makes sense. When DEFRA's own policy on waste is 'reduce, reuse, recycle', why is this not being applied? Instead they would rather you killed a green crab, or as we call it, a Gilly (you know, the feisty little green or red ones that you tempt out of their homes with strips of bacon when crabbing from a quayside or pier), or buy them in at £1 a kilo.

There are various other administrative conditions too. But the last I shall mention here is that every pot *must* be individually tagged, at 50p per tag, with a maximum of five hundred available to each permit holder. This tag holds a number that is unique to your boat, and if you want to use another boat to haul them, you must get permission from IFCA. Hence the phone call I now need to make.

The phone is answered and I'm soon put through to an officer who can help me with my current situation. I explain that *Never Can Tell-A* is no longer an active fishing vessel (they of course already know this; news travels fast, and I've seen a few of the officers around in the last couple of months), and that very soon I will need to haul my whelk gear – gear that is permitted in her name, but now needs to be affiliated with a new vessel. Silence.

'Okay,' says the officer eventually. 'You can just buy five hundred more tags.' He pauses. Then adds, 'It's only £250.'

Remember what I said earlier about how time away from sea can make you tetchy? (And dare I say it, skint?) 'Only £250? ONLY £250! *ONLY* £250?!' I splutter down the phone. I can almost hear the steam issuing from my ears. 'Oh, that's okay then,' I go on, 'if it's *only £250.*' I pause for breath, to let my sarcasm sink in. '£250 might not be a lot of money to *you*,' I add, 'but I've had no income for *three months.*'

He tries to say something, but I don't hear him as I am too enraged to let him speak. 'You want me to buy five hundred new tags? That will, by the way, in any case expire at the end of next month?'

'Okay,' a timid voice replies. 'I'll have a chat with our senior team and get them to give you a call.'

'I think you'd better,' I finish, my tone razor-sharp. (Since I'm now on a roll.)

A few hours later, I *do* get a call, and I explain the situation again. By now I've cooled down enough to be able to calmly quote the permit conditions back to the senior officer, and in the end he agrees to allow *Fairlass* to haul *Never Can Tell-A*'s gear. Everything is at least moving in the right direction, even if I do have to kick up a stink to make that happen.

On Valentine's day I get an email from the MMO to tell me that the licence has been issued by their central team and is snail-mailing its way to me. That's good enough for me. I don't need anything more. It's *finally* time to dust off our oilskins and go and see what gear we have left after three months at the mercy of tide, wind and weather.

We duly go and find out.

~

Jack, Nige and I make our way through the twisting turns of the channel. Despite us having done this commute many times before, this is a new experience for *Fairlass*. I imagine her a vision of bright blue as she proudly passes the beach, which is empty save for a few local dog walkers. We make our way out past the Number 1 buoy and head straight for the fairway, full of anticipation. It's a tad fresh, which will make for a rolly day. So what? I'm just so happy to be out here.

Our gear has been at the mercy of Davy Jones for three months, so it's to be expected that there will likely be no end-marking cans left on the whelk shanks. In three months of winter storms and big tides I imagine anchors have tripped too, pulling the dhan tows down with them. And, as a consequence, the pots will have no doubt found their freedom – and celebrated by rolling around and tangling with each other. I don't care. I'm as free as the seagull that's hovering overhead, keeping speed with the boat so it can pick the ideal moment to dive down and steal some of the dogfish I have cut ready.

It's a short steam out today – no more than twenty minutes. On a longer trip, on a rolly day like this, I'd be busy trying to make myself a nest in the wheelhouse about now, so I'd be wedged in, with everything I'd want to hand. As it is, I reach straight for my oilies.

It's fairly traditional for fishermen to keep their oilies in the wheelhouse when not in use, rolled down over their boots, Fireman Sam-style, so they are ready for action. I wriggle into mine now (they've already been in use for all the dirty shore jobs), with that obligatory jump-and-shimmy manoeuvre that's the most efficient way to pull them up. I then slide my arm under the shoulder strap I always leave done up, and struggle (again, as always) to find the one that's still hanging down at the back. With it clicked in securely, I then turn around to grab Nige's. He can never quite reach it, and it's something I do on autopilot – just a little thing to help make his life easier. (He would, of course, argue that he's perfectly capable, and he is, but I like doing it for him, so that's that.)

Now we're ready for action, I head out on deck to spot what cans might or might not *be* there to spot. Jack won't get dressed till the last minute. That's Jack. You can be gaffing the marker can outside and he will still be in the wheelhouse, making a sandwich, having a drink, or making a rollup. Crazes the tits off Nige, but his predictability never fails to make me giggle.

As we approach the place where the plotter tells us the first whelk shank should be, Nige eases *Fairlass* back and we are on deck scanning the water all around us. The autopilot is charged with keeping us on course as *Fairlass* slowly edges onwards, with no sign of the can, and as we head to the other end of the string, there's nothing there either. Ditto the second, ditto the third ... you get the picture.

'I'll get the grapple, then,' I say to Nige. I would usually say this through a grimace, but not today. Jack bounds his way out of the wheelhouse and down the deck, now dressed, and comes to give me a hand in lunking the long rusty, spiky piece of metal that we call a grapple (but many others call a creep), from its home on the cat catcher. Jack walks it up the deck to the hauling table as I make sure the rope that's tied to it isn't in a tangle, having sat redundant for three months.

Nige spins *Fairlass* round gracefully and places her facing into the tide, in front of where the end of the whelk shank should be. With a quick blast astern he makes *Fairlass* steadier in the water. 'Yeah yeah,' he hollers out from the wheelhouse, and on his signal (Nige uses 'Yeah yeah' to mean 'Do it now' in multiple situations, but we always know exactly what 'it' he's referring to) Jack launches the grapple over the side with an almighty splosh. Fathoms of rope pay out behind it as it descends the depths, on its way to drag along the muddy bottom to hunt for and snatch at our whelk gear. Meanwhile, *Fairlass* drops back over the top of the shank in the tide, with Nige in the wheelhouse, keeping her at the correct angle. This is very important because, if you don't, you could end up with your grapple rope round your prop. (And we all know what rope round the prop means, don't we, dear reader?)

It all sounds simple but, believe me, with certain tide and weather combinations, this can be an arse. Plus *Fairlass* is a good bit heavier than *Never Can Tell-A*. As I wait on deck she is having a good roll about and I come to terms with finding my sea legs once more, learning how she reacts in the short sharp waves of the North Sea.

Our connection – mental, if not quite physical – is interrupted.

'Yep!' Jack shouts in to his dad, meaning the grapple has done its job, one of its spiky barbs having snagged the rope. Nige reaches to clutch in the hydraulic hauler, which crunches into life, with the sound of metal on metal, as it spins the sacrificial tins that grip the rope (imagine a yo-yo) and brings the shank of pots back to the surface.

I am about to be faced with a disgusting mess of sludge, seaweed, dead whelks, hermit crabs, rotten bait, and a stink so bad you'd think it came from the bowels of hell. I couldn't care less. We are fishing again!

Chapter 21

'Pay the fish in silver'

Tossing a coin into the sea to pay for your catch has often been used as a bargaining tool when fishing is slow.

For months we have been at the mercy of other people's priorities. Feeling useless and cut off from the sea, and from the job that gets so deeply ingrained into us that it becomes part of our personality, has been very hard on all of us. So, however tough it'll be to get back on track, this means everything to us.

And it is tough. After a couple of halcyon days, my enthusiasm dips. The days are long and almost all of our precious time at sea is being used to fish for gear rather than whelks. This is because it involves grappling for lost shanks and then struggling to persuade miles of tangled pots and rope aboard, as it hangs limp and really heavy in a clusterfuck alongside the hull. It's held by the hauler, but fighting and persuading it aboard takes real effort as not only is it all full of sea shit, it's also potentially being held by its anchor, or another big ball of anchor *and* tangled pots. This would be hard enough on a mill pond, let alone when being thrown around by the forces of the sea. We then have to painstakingly untangle each tow, before scraping out an obscene amount of black sticky mud that has been compacted into the bottom of the pots. Every day, however, does constitute an achievement; another shank returned, instead of being lost to pollute our precious marine environment.

On which note, first up, I apologise unreservedly for all the lost gear, and hold my hands up; the fishing industry isn't perfect. What industry is? But I will say that we're never complacent. Lost gear doesn't just pollute, it also loses us money, because it's expensive to replace – the cost of a shank of whelk pots is upwards of £500.

It's also true that a lot of what is lost is also found. Whelk fishing is a very methodical business. You don't fish the same bit of seabed twice, so it's odds on that at some point, if lost pots are down there, someone will have it tangled up with their own whelk gear sooner or later. It's also easy to spot, as it will look exactly as you'd expect; liberally encrusted with pungent marine growth, like the crew of the *Flying Dutchman* from *Pirates of The Caribbean*. It's then fairly easy to reunite it with its owner. You get to know whose stuff is whose in a small community like ours, and it's the work of moments to mark its location in the plotter for them.

Some lost fishing gear, of course, does get washed up, but thanks to recent recycling initiatives, these days it can actually be sustainably repurposed, in the form of sunglasses and swimwear, skateboards and phone cases, backpacks and all kinds of other things. Which is great; not only is the material recycled, it's another bit of ocean rubbish removed.

There is more, so much more, we can still do, but in the meantime, every day one of our own shanks is found and straightened is a day that will make us money on the seabed. Our first few days of fishing see us bring back barely enough boxes of whelks to cover our running costs, but slowly we get back to normality; twenty-, thirty-, forty-box days. Nige, the lads and I are so much happier, and not just because we can take a wage again. Even in the beginning, when we were operating at a loss, we *were* being productive – it was under *our* control.

And our fortunes begin to change. Our perseverance starts paying off, as the whelks begin spiralling out of the muddy substrate 8 fathoms beneath our keel in ever-increasing numbers. Getting out to them, however, is no picnic. By now, the sea is truculent often, and sometimes still angry, so much so that we're forced to prepare. We need to tie down our bait, and ditto our catch, every time a stack of boxes of whelks reaches the level of the gunwales, as shifting weight on any boat has the potential to become extremely dangerous.

It's prime whelk season right now, so we push as much weather in *Fairlass* as we dare, steaming out every day in darkness and, most days, also coming home in darkness, In between, the boat and our oilskins are the only pops of bright colour, in a seascape that is a washed-out version of its glorious summer self. (Well, us and the inevitable dozens of starfish, that make cheerful orange arcs as they are returned to their watery homes.)

We are now really putting *Fairlass* through her paces. At forty-seven years old, I don't think she's grateful to us for this, and she is sure to remind us every so often, when a running repair conveniently keeps her in port for a day or so. We forgive her (we always will) because although annoying, these impromptu repairs are to be expected with any working fishing boat.

Spring is in our peripheral vision now, so we need to make the most of the most productive whelk season as they will soon start to slow down and retreat into the safety of the muddy sea floor, as thousands of crabs will soon start to energise as the water warms. These trailblazers will be hen crabs, looking to gorge themselves, as they scavenge for any scrap of food available, amassing energy and filling their shells to bulging point. This will continue till the optimum point in the summer, when they will pop out of their old shell, looking like a perfect crab-shaped Haribo jelly sweet. (Not gonna lie – I'm kind of envious that a crab's sole mission in life is to eat as much as possible, to bursting point, then pop out of their armour, shiny, new, fabulous and frisky.)

You get no warning when exactly the crustacean horde are coming – you're on mother nature's calendar and she consults with nobody, not even Nige. But she will at least do you the courtesy of sending little hints now and then: a whelk pot, devoid of all gastropod life, although there is a token brown crab.

It's liberating being back at sea, my life slotted around the tide again, the familiar aches and pains of physical work returning like a childhood friend. Relying on the strength of my arms, hands, shoulders and legs, really living in my physical body, rather than being limited to the doldrums of my mind, to complete a task, is such a freeing thing. Being cut off from humanity and civilisation and the drama that trails along with it. Free to sing at the top of my lungs to whatever cheesy playlist I have chosen (poor Nige).

To stand on a boat and not be judged by societal norms. To look, act and behave exactly as I choose. Yes, life is back to the very best of normal, and we are once again on an even keel.

~

I should have realised. Every silver lining has a cloud, doesn't it? Because China enters the chat. Wuhan. A killer virus. National lockdowns, closed borders, hospitality suspended. What now?

What now? We've only just started back up. What does this mean for us? Will our borders stay open to allow the export that the entire fishing industry relies so heavily upon? And even if they do, will the nations overseas not be in the same predicament? This could be devastating, as 80 per cent of our own beautiful fish is sent abroad. We are in no position to stop working. As the national crisis that is Covid-19 unfolds, the entire nation is glued to Boris's nightly address, and to the coronavirus tracker on the government website. Thankfully, because it's a lifeline on so many levels, we are lucky enough to be deemed key workers, so we can at least continue to fish and produce food.

But at what cost? I guess, like everyone else, it'll be a while before we find out.

Meanwhile, with no school to go to back home in Cambridge-shire, Nigel's fourteen-year-old daughter, Ellie, is getting bored, so he suggests she spend some days out fishing with us. I've known Ellie since she was a tot and, as a very inquisitive four-year-old, she would sometimes join us on the angling boat. I remember showing her and Nige's other daughter how to gut a mackerel.

Despite an initial grimace from both of them, they soon got their hands dirty and were very proud to go running up the deck, right through the middle of the customers, to show their dad in the wheelhouse what they had just achieved. All of Nigel's five children share traits with their father, not just physically in their fair hair and piercing blue eyes but in their personalities too; in their determination to try anything and not be beaten. (Otherwise known as stubbornness, but we'll let that one go. It's not always a bad thing, after all.)

Although Ellie may look cherubic, do not let this fool you. Ellie does not turn her nose up at the prospect of sloppy dogfish guts, filthy, muddy whelks or having to rough it when it comes to the limited facilities aboard. Just like me, she too finds the passion for being out at sea. Unlike me, however, perhaps because it's already lurking somewhere in her genes, the seafaring life, and fishing, comes naturally to her. Everything she does looks, to me, effortless. I show her the knots we use to secure fenders, I teach her the routine of setting the deck up on the way out, I introduce her to little 'hacks' that will make her life easier. I show her these things once, and it's mastered – just like that, as if she's been doing it for years. I would be embarrassed to tell you how long it took *me* to learn to tie a bowline knot.

I should perhaps mention knots more generally at this juncture, by the way, since they are such an integral part of what we do. There are a dizzying number of knots and bends used in seafaring, but Nige and I, along with most of our commercial pot-fishing comrades, regularly rely on around eight. These include the clove hitch (any inferior variation of which Nige will call a 'cow hitch' – as in 'What kind of a fucking cow hitch is *that*?'), the rolling hitch, the half-hitch and the cleat hitch, all of which are for fastening lines to rings or poles. Then there's the sheet bend and the reef knot, both used for joining two lines, the difference between them being that bends are usually easy to undo whereas reef knots pull tight, so are more permanent). Then there is the bowline, which is the great nautical all-rounder, because it doesn't matter how much weight you put on it; it will always release. Lastly there is the magnificently named stevedore stopper, a knot that is bigger than the hole in the spinner on the strops of our pots – and good luck getting your tongue around that one ... (Finally, there is also the 'any-knot-will-do' knot, usually deployed by me when in a knot-choosing kerfuffle, when Nige says 'Ash! Put a knot in this quick!'

Ellie starts her lockdown fishing training as I did, riddling whelks, and it's not long before I'm teaching her how to bait and stack a pot. Which is great because it means that Nigel lets me loose on the hauler. Sometimes, we even relegate him to riddling whelks. So it's no surprise to either of us, that, just like me ten years or so ago, he now cannot get rid of her. Although technically, Ellie shouldn't even be here, as vessels engaged in commercial fishing operations must only be manned by those with at the very least a sea survival certificate. And that's even if they're only observing.

There are loopholes in all this, when it comes to people like media personnel, as you can get around the need for that certificate if you (as the boat owner) complete risk assessments, do safety briefings, and share certificates for life-saving equipment and insurances. For everyone else, however, without a sea survival certificate, you can't engage in commercial fishing activity, even if all you want to do is stand on deck and watch.

The maritime environment is obviously still very much operational throughout the pandemic, and, to cope with the huge backlog created by furlough etc., dispensations on the sea survival course have been issued from the MCA, which is great. However, at the age of fourteen Ellie isn't allowed to do the course in the first place – she'll need to wait till she's sixteen, so there's actually no legal way she can come out and fish with us, even if we wrap her in bubble wrap and three life jackets.

Fair enough I guess, in theory, because it is a dangerous job, but I refuse to believe that the time she's spending with us at sea is anything other than a brilliant bit of education, especially at a time when kids are mostly locked indoors, doom-scrolling on their phones. Plus how is anyone supposed to inspire the next generation of fishermen if kids can't learn from their (by the way, highly experienced, responsible, and capable) parents? I've thought about this a lot and I genuinely think the fishing industry needs some kind of formal programme of education for young people. After all, if you can do a degree in the psychology of fashion, then surely there could be room for a recognised fishing apprenticeship? After all, not everyone has access to parents like Nige's, do they? (In this, at least, I recently heard rumours that something of that sort is finally starting up . . .)

That's only half the story, obviously. The industry struggles with both recruitment and retention. Recruitment often stalls because of what's above, obviously, and also because it's often seen as a drop-out job, the sort of industry where all the naughty kids end up, and not all fishing families' children want to follow in their parents' footsteps.

To deal with the problem, many of the big boats have been employing overseas labour, something that's not traditionally been common in the sector. However, this has become difficult as recent changes in the law mean they can no longer employ foreign nationals on transit visas; if they do so within the 12-mile limit they are acting illegally. As I write, steps are being taken to try and make the process easier, but with everything still in limbo, it makes for very uncertain times.

For our own would-be new recruits, there is also the issue of the sea survival course costing £200 – which is a lot to fork out, given that almost none will have ever set foot in the environment, so cannot know if it's for them or not. Could there not be a managed programme of work experience placements, such as are done in countless other industries, and boats certified up and down the country to deliver it? (Nudge nudge, MCA . . .)

Retention is an issue currently because of the volatility of the industry right now; many experienced fishermen are at the end of their tether about the relentless march of regulation and the fact that no significant investments are being made in places that will ensure the future of the sector, such as restoring some of the infrastructure and logistics that would make it easier for small artisanal fishing businesses to sell their catch. I know there is no magic bullet to this problem, but a) it isn't rocket science, and b) we used to have independent fishmongers on every high street; as with (sourdough) loaves, can it not be with fishes? We buy fairtrade coffee, fairtrade bananas (not for boating purposes, obviously), fairtrade chocolate and so on. How about fairtrade fish? Could we not at least put the discussion on the agenda? Because once a significant number of fishermen are gone, those skills and vast knowledge are both lost forever, and our food security is in even more turmoil.

Lost already is the ability of most people who work in the industry (particularly in the prettier coastal towns and villages – which, by the way, were built on the fishing industry), to be able to buy a home where they live and work. And when you are priced out so far that to do the job is completely impractical (if you own a boat it's essential that you live close to it) then you will sooner or later make a different career choice.

I can't tell you just how frustrating I find all this. So if you take just one thing away from this book, please let it be that you scrutinise the fish you're buying. If it's being sold to you by a seller who can tell you its provenance then it's more than likely come from a small independent fishing business, so not only will you be able to guarantee its freshness, you will also be supporting not just the people you've met in this story, but their counterparts across the country, who are, in some cases, struggling for survival.

~

Talking of survival, the global impact of the pandemic, meanwhile, soon sees the whelk price begin to plummet from a steady £1.45 per kilo, tumbling to £1.20, then £1.10, until it flatlines at £1. (Three years on and that price has not recovered, let alone risen with inflation.) South Korea (our main clients) are still buying, though demand is significantly down. And with the hospitality sector also on its knees, crab markets are small, so many do not entertain switching over to the spring crab run, which means that everyone stays whelking, leading to a shortage of bait. This is serious – and more so than it needed to have been. If we didn't rely so heavily on exporting we would not now be in such deep water.

People so often step up, though, in times of hardship and crisis, and in some parts of the country a real desire to help is displayed, by people buying fish on the quay directly from fishermen. As a result of that, many new artisanal businesses are launched. (And, due to the new interest in buying small, buying natural and buying local, most are still thriving as I write.) Sadly, we have few whelk-loving Koreans in Wells, so that isn't an option for us, but, even so, we can work and earn a living – and a living out at sea where for, hours at a stretch, we can forget the pandemic is even happening.

As the first lockdown eases and some semblance of normality returns, we realise we should be counting our blessings. And we do, because we've been the lucky ones.

Chapter 22

'Do not set sail on a Thursday'

Also known as Thor's-Day, after Thor, the god of storms.

It's around 8 a.m. on a beautiful May day, and I'm waiting on the empty quayside, rope in hand, and two freshly bought coffees beside me on the ground. The boys have been out on *Fairlass* all night and, having turned her in the quay, they're now bringing her alongside the quay wall, after which it will be a quick turnaround before Nige and I take her out again and the boys head home to bed.

Jack jumps up onto the bow – which means he's had a good night – and as he shouts incomprehensibly at me I chuck him the bow rope. No rest, I think, for our poor old Lass Fair. Which was never the plan. It's a situation obviously forced on us by the loss of *Never Can Tell-A*, which, after much deliberation, is currently sitting at the east end of the quay, and, having been given away in exchange for a donation to charity, is bound for renovation in Fleetwood. It's been a massively hard decision for Nige to have to make, but, all things considered, we're all agreed it's the right one.

Our next step, following the decision to say goodbye to *Never Can Tell-A*, is something Nige and I have been kicking around between us for a week now, and he's suggested I'm the one to share our thoughts with Jack and Kenneth, because 'they never listen to him', at least allegedly. In reality I think it's because I'm more likely to get a straight answer than he is, being their dad. And perhaps because this is my financial investment too. (And it will be. We're thinking of buying another boat.)

I'm not sure Nige is right about his lads – they are a law unto themselves, and boys will, I guess, be boys – but I see where he's coming from, in that if they don't want to commit to it, they'll probably open up to me more honestly, because there's no aspect of not wanting to let their dad down.

Once *Fairlass* is grabbing a much-needed moment of peace, I tempt the boys over with my coffees, and explain to them that their dad has seen a boat for sale in Ireland, but that there's no point in us going to look at her unless we know they're still committed to the four of us working two boats again. It's not a given after all, as the pandemic has changed so much.

'So, are you?' I ask them.

Jack seems genuinely excited at the prospect, which is good to see. '*Really?*' he asks.

'Yes, really,' I tell him. 'Though a lot will depend on whether the seller is prepared to do a deal with us. Similar to what we did with Iain, kind of thing. But in principle yes, if you're both up for it.'

Kenneth always plays it cooler. 'That was always the plan, wasn't it?' But his body language speaks volumes and I know he wasn't expecting this; because the offer in itself speaks forgiveness. It's taken Nige a while, and there have been some arguments and disagreements, but ultimately he knew it was one silly mistake and restoring trust in his son was an important step – not just for Nige, either. For both of them. Actually, perhaps that's why Nige is in the truck, smoking. Because this conversation could be too freighted with emotion.

I tell Kenneth yes, because, actually it *was* always the plan, and now he's all ears, wanting to see the advert, so I pull it up on – you guessed it! – FindaFishingBoat.com.

He screws his eyes up as he's reading. 'What's that?' he says, zooming in on the picture of her. 'Is that her *name*?'

I tell him yes, it is her name. 'She's called *Saoirse*.'

'She's called *saucer*?'

'No, I don't think that's how you pronounce it. I think it's 'say-orsee' – something like that.'

'Say-*o*rsee?' he says, nearly spitting out his coffee. 'What the fuck kind of name is that?!'

Jack's chiming in now. 'Maybe it's 'say-or-*ears*' or something. Or maybe it's sea horse in Irish? I mean, look at that other one he's selling. That one's called *Silver Fin*, so maybe they're both named after fish?'

'Well, I guess the only way we'll find out is if your dad and I go and look at her. So do we?' I look at both of them.

'When you going?' Kenneth says. (Jack's still trying to find a noise that matches what he's reading.)

'As soon as I can get a key-worker's certificate,' I tell him. 'And then I have to get your dad on a plane ...'

'Good luck with that,' Kenneth scoffs.

~

A week later, and Nige and I are in a place called Kilkeel, the most southerly town in Northern Ireland and also home to its largest fishing fleet. As a consequence it has a massive commercial harbour, the quay lined with anything a seafarer could ever want, from a hydrostatic release to a whole new boat (from Gerry Smyth, who is lovely, so deserves a mention here) and pretty much everything in between.

Nige has just about recovered from the horrendous, nerve-shredding experience of being up in the air and not in charge of the engine, and is now happily taking in the sounds, sights and smells of Kilkeel harbour, which are coming at us from all directions. This really is a world away from Wells. There are forklifts buzzing about everywhere, transferring fish boxes back and forth, to the various fish merchants and processors whose units line the harbourside. Over at the end of the quay, three massive steel boats, having been hauled up the slipway, are in the middle of being repainted with giant spray guns – a far cry from me and my little roller. There are no tourists here; just a fisherman's café that really looks like what it is, with a steady stream of men in rigger boots heading in and out of the doors.

'Look,' I say to Nige, 'there's even a car wash for boats!' More than any fishing port I've been to, this one really does feel like a serious working hub. No frills. Just full-on fishy business.

The owner we're here to see, Bob (not his real name – I've changed it to to protect the innocent), has two boats for sale. *Silver Fin* and *Saoirse* are both practically the same, except *Silver Fin* has only got a three-quarter keel. *Saoirse's* full keel definitely makes her our preference, as a full keel gives more stability in rough seas and messy water. She also has the correct licence to allow us to fish for shellfish and access the under-10-metre non-sector pool, once she is under English administration, which would be, if we buy her, our ultimate goal, as it will allow us to diversify in what we catch.

The under-10-metre non-sector pool, which is in itself quite a mouthful, refers to all the species of quota fish available for under-10-metre boats to catch that aren't in a PO, and are managed by way of a monthly allowance. Lots of under-10 boat owners don't own the right to any quota, so this is the official list of what they can fish for. As I write this, we can catch cod in the North Sea (3 tons per boat per month max), cod in area ICES rectangle VIID – which means the eastern half of the English Channel (one ton per month), plus some twenty other species in various other areas, including megrim, saithe, nephrops and 'lemons and witches'; two kinds of sole which can be found chilling a thousand metres deep. This is good news. Though we don't have access to all these species, due to the habitats around Wells, it does mean that we can start diversifying, something I am very keen to do as I'd like to sell more seafood that people feel more comfortable preparing; some people are put off crab and lobster for that reason, and whelks have few buyers in the UK. Diversifying is also a great way to take pressure off the stocks that are regularly targeted, and it helps to keep our fish local.

Saoirse is fairly basic, but what she lacks in luxury she makes up for in practicality and price. We take her out for a sea trial and she feels like a bath toy in comparison to the great wooden lump that is *Fairlass*, but she's a Cygnus Cyclone – light and nimble, and modern by comparison.

The Cygnus Cyclone was THE boat of choice for fishermen from the late eighties, right through to early this century, boasting speed, agility, stability, and big working deck spaces. We make an offer on her, which Bob accepts, so we plunder our savings to pull together a deposit.

Tying up the sale is a particularly welcome distraction today, as it's also the day *Never Can Tell-A* is to be loaded onto a lorry and taken away to her new home in Fleetwood. When it happens Robert the harbourmaster sends a couple of pictures, but Nige doesn't even want to look at them. I do, but I totally get why he can't. I know part of his soul is going with her.

Our plan to get *Saoirse* is to work like stink (again), and save as much as we can, and to bring her back to Wells by the end of the summer. We don't take it as a given, since we doubt if we can raise the whole price in that time, but Bob immediately agrees that we can take her back whatever, and pay off the remaining balance as and when.

'Ach,' he says. 'We've got that many people against us in this job already, that if we can't help each other it'll be a sorry state of affairs.'

We're so grateful. This really is the mark of the man. He's both trusting us as fellow fishermen, and also understands that we need to get her back to Wells before autumn sets in, with the days getting shorter and the seas that much nastier.

Because we will, obviously, do it the hard way.

Chapter 23

'Never change the name of a boat'

It is believed that, among other things, Poseidon keeps a register of all vessels. When a boat is renamed his log will no longer tally, so he will claim the vessel in order to balance his books.

'It's pronounced 'sirsha,' Bob says. 'As in *sir*, and then *sha*. Will ye be changing her name, then?'

'God no,' I tell him. 'So, sor-sha?'

'No, *sir*-sha.'

'Sor-sha?' He speaks so fast that I can't quite make it out.

'*Sir*-sha.' Then he grins. 'But that's close enough. It's Gaelic. It's a girl's name. It means freedom.'

Boat names are a deal breaker for me. If a boat has an ugly name I don't want to buy it. But sorsha, or sirsha – for some reason I can't seem to pronounce sirsha the way Bob does – has a really lovely ring to it, especially with an Irish lilt, and now I know what it means, it feels like it's fate talking. It's for freedom, after all, that I've given up so much.

After a long trip to Liverpool docks and an equally long ferry ride to Belfast (in my case, weighed down as per – autopilot, almanac etc., plus, this time, a beanbag – and Nige with his same old same old bag for life) we're back in Kilkeel, where the immediate impression is of a plethora of different boats, all set up to access different fisheries, from tiny potting boats to enormous stern trawlers. It's one of those late summer mornings, when winter seems a very long way off, and there is a tang in the air that, back home in King's Lynn, the locals might say hails the start of brown shrimp season. My nose isn't acute enough to ratify that, and probably never will be, to be fair, since I'm not allowed to catch it, and I doubt I ever will be, but this is no time to get cross about IFCA's bye-laws. We're going to buy a boat, and we're both very excited.

Bob's borrowed a bit of space in nearby Gerry Smyth's boat yard, as he knows we have a few jobs we need to do before taking her on our journey of some 600 nautical miles. Though this time we'll be crossing the Irish Sea and heading south, travelling to Wells via Cornwall.

We now need a few days to get her ready. We have a new autopilot to fit and a spotlight to mount, but it soon becomes clear that there are a multitude of other little jobs to attend to before we set off, so we book into a little B&B a mile or so up the road, one of very few, given Covid, that are taking visitors.

The hours fly by in a relentless job-based blur, and, with everything we want almost literally on our doorstep, the days are long, productive and dirty. At the end of the fourth, however, we are done with all the jobs we can do before starting *Saoirse* up, which we can't do until she is reacquainted with the water.

It's here that we get a lesson in ingenuity, as though Bob has hired a crane to lift her back into the quay, the yard where she is currently is some 400 metres away and his technique for getting her from the one place to the other is, to say the least, unusual. We've certainly never seen anything like it before.

The route from yard to quay is, thankfully, downhill, so at least no one has to push her up any hills. But as she emerges from the yard, still on the tiny metal trolley she's been resting on while we've been working on her (think shopping trolley wheels here), it becomes clear that this is also to be her transport, as Bob now attaches her via a big strop to the towbar on his van. To deal with the opposite problem – that being on a downhill journey, she might run into the back of the van (or, indeed, just run away, period) – he deploys his chief engineer, Shay, to use his forklift to act as the brake, again with a big strop lashing the trolley to the front of his forklift truck. (Which, by the way, he's not taken the fairly important step of removing the tines from.)

With absolutely zero nods to health and safety (think more 'speed and potential catastrophe') this weird and wobbling convoy then sets off through the harbour, without a moment's reflection about whether it's a good idea or not (not). All week, Nige and I have been hearing people referring to Bob sarcastically as 'the snail' (or, phonetically, the 'sneel') and now the penny drops about what they've meant. We've already seen evidence of him doing most things both on impulse and at top speed, and this boat transport logistics 'solution' encompasses both. As van, boat, and forklift rattle their way out of Gerry's yard, it's hard to believe what we are seeing. Which is essentially a whole 8-metre boat, which weighs nearly 4 tons, perched on top of a rickety and rusting trolley, which is lashed precariously between two definitely not-for-purpose vehicles. If you are interested in monitoring breaches in health and safety you won't be disappointed. As soon as they set off – Nige holding tight to one of the reins, so to speak – it's clear *Saoirse* has her own ideas about where she'd like to go, so some extra manpower is needed to keep her on course. No one actually asks for help, but people start appearing from nowhere, having obviously spotted the procession through their various windows. By the time she's travelled the full 400 metres, there are some eight or nine people clustered around *Saoirse*, all knackered from having spent the last thirty minutes trying to prevent tons of wilful boat from careening off her teeny makeshift platform.

At this point I breathe out, only to breathe in again, as the next step – lifting her by crane – is one that already makes me wince; boats shouldn't fly, and I have a profound unease (get an actual knot in the pit of my stomach) about seeing any boat in the air. Thankfully, however, this process takes a mere three minutes, and, almost before we know it, she is back where she belongs.

That brief excitement turns out to be the highlight of a full week's stay in Kilkeel, as it then takes a further three days for us to complete the remaining jobs. And then, just for a change, the autopilot won't work – what *is* it with us and autopilots? We can't fix it, so we have to leave without it working (hurrah – more hand-steering!), but not before having sent the faulty component back to the manufacturer and arranging for a replacement to be sent to my friend Jessie in Cornwall, ready for whenever we get there.

Still, it's a fine morning when we finally set off for our first stop, which is Wicklow, some 80 miles south.

~

Ireland obviously likes us because it's gloriously sunny the day we leave, and as we make our way out of the built-up environs of Kilkeel, the waves, of which there are a few, but only small undemanding ones, rock *Saoirse* gently from side to side. To starboard, the fuzzy-felt Mourne mountains fade away prettily, the landscape beneath them every bit as green as all the Visit Ireland tourist posters usually promise.

Saoirse feels very different to *Fairlass*. She handles differently, is so much lighter and nimbler, but the biggest difference, and one we both notice immediately, is that she sounds different as well. I'm so familiar with the sound of the sea thudding against the wooden hulls of *Fairlass* and *Never Can Tell-A*, that I've forgotten what a fibreglass boat sounds like. It's a very different sound, this – less deadened, and definitely sloshier – and creates a different kind of connection to what's going on below. I have a much stronger sense of how the boat is responding to the water. It's like the difference, I suppose, between driving around in a Range Rover and something like a Peugeot 206. One wafts along regardless, seeming to rise above all the knocks. The other is much more slammy and quick.

We make good time to Dublin then follow the coast on down to Wicklow, ticking along at a steady 8 knots, so we'll be sure of getting into the harbour before dark; being in a new boat, entering an unknown harbour, will be enough.

I'm glad to arrive. Unlike in *Fairlass*, there's only one seat (if you can call it that) in *Saoirse*'s wheelhouse so, despite the beanbag (I obviously took it for a reason) my own 'seat' hasn't been the best, given that it's on the floor and my view is pretty much up Nigel's nose. (I'd be fine on deck, obviously, but it's now nearly October – very splashy, very chilly.) As there's obviously nowhere warm and dry to sleep either, we find a cheap B&B, and the following morning, set off bright and early.

We are now faced with a decision though: weather. The forecast today is fairly fresh, but it's going to be worse tomorrow, so do we cross the Irish Sea today and head the 90 nautical miles to Milford Haven in Wales, or hug the coast to make a crossing which will land us further south, somewhere like Padstow the following day?

Having opted for Wales there's no time like the present, so we stock up on essentials in an eye-wateringly expensive local petrol station before throwing the ropes and creeping out of Wicklow's pierheads before 7 a.m. With the wind freshening from behind us we plot our passage south-east and in the space of a morning we are but a small grey 8-metre blip in the Irish Sea, surfing off waves, some of which are picking us up and pushing us along at a frantic 17 knots (bear in mind that this is over double her usual pace). It's quiet and also lonely, and very strange. There is nothing but sea behind us and nothing but sea in front and, for once, the radio is totally silent. We don't even have signal on our mobiles. This might seem a given, but for Nige and I, and all our fellow fishermen, back in Wells, the sea isn't as lonely or isolated as you might think (not least because sometimes I even have 5G a full

14 miles out.) As with all the fishing communities we've passed through on our journeys, there is a sense of connection that persists out into the sea, and normally a constant chatter from the VHF radio. Sometimes too much, in fact; the shrimpers at Lynn often conduct lengthy conversations via VHF about how the Lynnets – their football team – have performed during the week. (Lads, it really does make me want to tear my ears off.)

There is also constant chatter from all the other ships and commercial traffic, and, together with the sight of all those vessels, not to mention the towering presence of all the wind turbines, it never feels lonely – far from it. On a clear day, in fact, I can see five separate wind farms, each of which is the size of a city centre.

About which I cannot stop myself digressing. I'm not ignorant; I understand our planet's need for green energy to help combat the effect of global warming, but lost in the green agenda to clean up our world is the effect these 'giant spinning solutions' have on us fishermen. If I say the term 'spatial squeeze' to any fisherman they will know exactly what I'm talking about, but to the average person this probably carries little weight.

Spatial squeeze means exactly what you'd expect it to – we are, literally, squeezed out of the space. As these sites are constructed, something which takes years of ground surveying, resurveying for obstructions, cable laying and building to achieve, fishermen are necessarily forced out. We are usually offered a compensation package to help recoup lost earnings, but, in my experience, it never matches up with what's actually lost. Worse than that, if a fair compensation package cannot be agreed, these firms have the power (and they do use it), as a result of the green agenda, to evict us by using a high court order.

The resulting squeeze obviously has ramifications. It means multiple boats being constricted into a smaller and smaller area of the sea, as these sites continue to be identified and expanded. Plus, even once the wind farm is completed and access (albeit limited) is once again granted, it does not guarantee the ground will be as productive as it once was. Combine this with the rapid proliferation of numbers and categories of marine protected areas, the fashionable new seaweed farms that are popping up all over, the aggregate extraction industry, and the oil and gas mining platforms, and fishermen will be squeezed into an area so small that it will no longer be viable for them to put to sea. Has anybody ever stopped to consider our food security in all this? Has anybody considered that we are demolishing our country's vibrant fishing heritage? It's right that we protect eco-systems and marine life, of course it is, but is one of the endangered species here your fishermen? I would love to see wind farm companies really communicating with local fishing communities by actively supporting their modest endeavours rather than paying people off; funding small markets, ice-plants, landing derricks, shellfish-holding facilities, and so on – really working together with us so everybody gains.

Nige and I definitely feel like an endangered species right now, as in possibly the only boat in the Irish Sea today. The VHF radio is silent; there is no chitter chatter from ships or commercial traffic, and not another fishing boat to be seen. So far, in four or five hours of steaming, we have seen just three lonely wind turbines.

The day is getting sloppier and sloppier as we crunch the miles, and finally Wales comes into view. We choose to make our passage inshore of Skomer Island, which is flanked by small rocky islands with green fuzzy tops. It turns out to be a lumpy shortcut, the sea confused and roiling as the tide and waves fight against each other, and the brine crashes against the islands' weathered faces.

We round the peninsula into the Welsh estuary at around 5 p.m. and, by now exhausted after a day of being chucked about, are grateful for the sheltered waters of Milford Haven. Jack and Kenneth, who used to go whelking in the Irish Sea on a boat called *Crusader*, did so out of here and Fishguard so they know these Welsh waters well. The whelk fishing was very good here, but it made for gruelling work – they would frequently fish for three days straight, with little more than a few hours' sleep. (It's here, by the way, that that infamous car was towed away into the sea. It has a reputation for being a bit like the Wild West here.)

By 7 p.m. we have entered the marina's lock and found a berth for *Saoirse*, followed by a berth for us, above the Heart of Oak pub. We sleep well, and are out the door by 6 a.m. and back on *Saoirse*. Although I'm still the opposite side of the country to home, having done the island hop across the Irish Sea I feel we have broken the back of it. Having restocked our supplies on the walk to the B&B last night, this morning we just need to find some diesel – easy enough in a marina of this size, and possibly more difficult in the smaller Cornish harbours that are coming next.

I'm eager to get today's passage out the way; after this crossing it'll just be a case of hugging the coast all the way home, but I'm also particularly keen to reach Padstow, because my dear friend Jessie, who will hopefully have my repaired autopilot pump, will be waiting for me. Having left Norfolk not long after we both finished high school, she now calls Cornwall her home, and I miss her.

Our southbound crossing of 70 nautical miles is once again fresh and, with a moderate wind and following seas, *Saoirse* is held steadily on course as she surfs her way past the Bristol Channel, as we alternate steering her at the helm. Having posted the next leg of our journey on Instagram I start receiving numerous messages from Cornish fishermen. They are all telling me that, given the wind direction and the state of tide when we'll arrive later that afternoon, we should be wary of the sand bar that guards Padstow's harbour entrance. It's apparently called the 'Doom Bar' for good reason. I'm quickly distracted, however, when scores of dolphins visit us, cutting through the water alongside *Saoirse*, dancing and jumping in front of her. She is so small that I feel even closer to them than I did on *Fairlass*, and once again I am moved to tears.

As Cornwall appears on the horizon in front of us I am once again reminded of the messages I have received about the ominous Doom Bar, so fierce that it has its own beer named after it. Knowing the malevolence that can await you on Wells bar, and with thoughts of *Never Can Tell-A*'s breach still so fresh, we psych ourselves up on our approach (well, I do).

We enter Padstow bay and the river Camel. With sandy beaches to our left and high cliffs on the right, we take the advice given to us via the fishermen on social media and, against all our instincts, trust the channel markers as directed, even when the channel cuts in tight against the cliffs.

'Is that it?' Nige says jokingly. 'Where was it?'

'Yeah, I guess that was it,' I reply, feeling confused. Though I can see the water is shallower in places as I look back at where we've been, and that the texture on the surface is slightly different, it's nothing compared to what we're used to.

'These boys wanna come and have a go at Wells on a fresh north-westerly,' Nige chortles. 'And they get a beer named after that?'

The question is rhetorical, and I'm now distracted anyway, by the sight of the blonde girl in dungarees on the quay. Jessie! I wave frantically at her as I bustle out on deck, having not seen my childhood ride or die for over three years.

After being ping-ponged from one side of the harbour to the other (not for fun – by the harbour staff in search of a suitable berth for us) we find a pub and grab dinner with Jess. Luckily she has our autopilot pump so with the luxury of a day off, and a free pass from Nige, who is gallantly going to fit it, we plan some Cornish tourism together. Even better (as if seeing Jess *could* be bettered) we finish off with a meal at Rick Stein's flagship restaurant, thanks to a local fisherman, and social media pal, who snagged me a late booking (cheers, Murty).

Sadly, as we leave Padstow in the early morning light, we are still painfully hand-steering. Turns out the component we though was faulty wasn't the problem at all, and the luxury of having an autopilot is denied us once more. Another lumpy passage around the coast of Cornwall then ensues, and, as we

281

approach Land's End, we can make out the remnants of the old tin mines in the cliff faces. Granite rock formations with fantastical names rear up out of the sea: the Brisons, the Wrath Oar, the Armed Knight. And as we skirt round Land's End our journey hits its own landmark as we stop steaming south and now start the eastward passage home.

Our next stop is Newlyn, otherwise known (at least to me) as 'sardine town', as it's allegedly the sardine capital of England. It's also one of the busiest fishing harbours in the South-West.

The process by which they catch sardines in Newlyn is fascinating. From our B&B window I watch the seine-netters (from the Greek for drag net, not the Paris river) as they set off at dusk, to work their sardine-catching magic in Mount's Bay. It's very clever. The seine net is like a giant circular shower curtain, with floats at the top edge and weights at the bottom, and once they've found a shoal, they set it so it will encircle the sardines. They then pull a kind of drawstring at the bottom, to essentially form a purse (seine nets are also called purse nets or ring nets for that reason) then bring it closer to the boat, where they will either scoop the catch out by hand, using huge landing-style nets (it's also called brialling) or, on the bigger boats, use a giant vacuum cleaner-style apparatus to suck those wriggling *sardinia pilchardus* aboard.

Having never been aboard a seine netter, I've only seen it up close on social media, but I'm sure a trip aboard one would be thrilling. It would also be like starting over, and learning a whole new fishing skill-set; it's a reminder of just how many different talents are deployed under the umbrella term 'fishing'. Precious traditional skills that are priceless to our country's long maritime heritage.

After one day ashore, the weather gives us enough of a window to make a dash for Brixham. It's not going to be for long, though, so we leave Mount's Bay in darkness, the masthead lights of the early seine-netters dotted randomly around us, and soon melting into the mist as we head through the gaps and journey east.

The photogenic dawn doesn't last very long. As we make our way round the Lizard peninsula at around 8 a.m., I see great big swells rising up from nowhere. They're so high, fat and lazy that they block out the sky.

We need to make Brixham, and soon. There isn't long. We are being chased down by Storm Alex.

Chapter 24

'Always crush your eggshells'

An eggshell left un-smashed was thought to be used by witches as a vessel, so they could paddle out to sea and create violent storms for mariners.

You know that feeling when the air is so thick you almost feel you could touch it? When it's so heavy that you can feel it pressing down on you? That particular hairs-on-the-back-of-the-neck feeling you get sometimes, when you don't know what's coming; you just know *something* is and every sense becomes suddenly heightened; as if your whole body is now on high alert. Then, almost out of nowhere, the atmosphere changes. You notice a stiff breeze starting up, and you know a force is gathering, then – it's as instant as if a light switch has just been turned on, and the gloomy day – *this* day, in fact – is transformed into something much more malevolent. The sea darkens too now, reflecting the sky's filthy mood although, such are the contradictory feelings a storm evokes, the colour of the increasingly turbulent water is, for me, at least, one of the most beautiful – a deep greeny turquoise that exists nowhere else apart from a storm-tossed ocean. And as the wind threatens to blow the tops off the waves, their white tips now look even more strikingly white, harbingers of the maelstrom to come.

We're around 12 miles outside Brixham by now, and all around us we can see bow waves approaching. Each is being created by another boat doing exactly what we are: trying to make port before Storm Alex catches up with all of us. We already know it's going to be shit (it's been named – there's a clue there), and everything we're seeing and hearing and feeling confirms port is the place we need to be.

As we round Start Point, thankfully we're in the lee of the land, and fears of being beaten up by nature's fury recede. Though when we call the harbour authority to see where we should moor, no one answers the VHF. We go in anyway – we urgently need a safe haven – and a lad I know from social media tells me there's a visitor's pontoon, and that our best bet is to put her there till we can find someone.

It's around 6 p.m. by now, and a walk around proves fruitless, though we manage to secure a B&B close to the harbour, and get a pint in the Sprat and Mackerel. We can't find anyone to ask about moving *Saoirse*, so have no choice except to leave her out there overnight. I sleep fitfully that night, with the tempest raging all around us, and can't help worry about our plucky little boat out there on her own. Nige feels the same. By the time dawn breaks we've both given up trying to sleep, so we pull our boots on and head down to check on her.

We step outside to find Storm Alex is still doing her worst. Rigging clangs against masts, boats thrash against their moorings, and we fight our way to *Saoirse* though gale force winds, stinging rain launching spears at our faces. As predicted, she's spent the night getting beaten up by the weather and as a result even snapped one of her ropes, which has been replaced by a kind passer-by. We are clearly stuck in Brixham, but *Saoirse* can't stay here. She is too exposed. While Nige is busy manoeuvring *Saoirse* round the harbour looking for somewhere else to put her, I run back and forth in the torrential rain several times. But I see no one, so I'm not sure what to do next.

After three sodden circuits round the horseshoe-shaped harbour, and banging on their office doors, I spot a man in a hi-vis jacket, and a quick sprint to catch him up bears fruit. He does indeed work for the harbour, and tells me where we can put *Saoirse*, but his suggestion, when I run round to take a look where he's told me, seems insane. I call Nige.

'By those stone steps? In a fucking storm?' Nige fumes. 'I don't fucking think so. She'd be safer where she just was on the pontoon.'

He's right. The flight of steps where the guy's sent me look like a recipe for disaster, and that would be the case even in good weather. They are protruding from the quay wall and once the tide turns surely she has every chance of just sitting on them and keeling over? I tell Nige I'll go and ask him for an alternative, even though the guy's already disappearing, and when I turn around I see another man beckoning to me from the doorway of the adjacent café.

It's so steamed up inside that I can't actually see anything except him – he's white-haired, friendly looking, and nodding for me to go and speak to him, and when I do, he says 'Where the fuck's he just told you to go?'

'By them fucking steps,' I answer, with feeling. To which he rolls his eyes at me, which says it all.

'You're that little Cygnus, aren't you?' he then says. I nod. 'Put her next to the mussel dredge,' he continues, pointing across the horseshoe to where I've just come from. 'He's not going anywhere for a few days.' Then he grins. 'And I don't think you'll be, either.' He's right about that. We've already checked the forecast. It's apparently going to be like this for the foreseeable. 'I'll get my coat,' he adds, 'and meet you round there.'

While the man goes to get his jacket I get a blast of scents of breakfast. I've already noticed scallop and black pudding baps on the menu and my mouth's drooling at the prospect. But not until *Saoirse* is safe. So I call Nige and direct him to the berth the man has pointed out, and make my way back around to join both of them.

I'm first there, climbing down onto the sodden deck of the mussel dredge, and grab a rope off Nige as he offers her into the spot. By now the guy's come down to join us – I realise he's driven round – and tells us he'll ring the guy who owns the dredge to let him know. I also give him my number, in case he does need us to move her.

'Don't listen to the harbour staff,' the man tells us. 'They ain't got a clue. It's fishermen who run this place.'

It figures. Perhaps that's why they call it fish town.

~

But why do they call it that? Brixham has more or less always been a lucrative port for fishermen; with easy access to fish-rich grounds there has been a fleet here since medieval times. The port only really began suffering in the twenties and thirties when the North Sea became the place to be. Once again, however, Brixham is one of the most lucrative fishing ports in the country and on track to be the biggest market the UK has, thanks to its online auction, which can reach buyers all around the world. But is this a good thing?

This is where we reach the sticky middle of it all. A thriving fish market which boasts daily auctions with sales in the hundreds of thousands, and a well provisioned harbour with access to all that fish, concentrates a large chunk of the nation's industry here, not just physically with boats operating and landing in the port, but with more and more boats all along the south coast opting for landing to Brixham Market, in order to get the best value for their catch. And who can blame them for that? Of course, with business booming, this puts the South-West in a strong position for investment, and, as the saying goes, money goes to money. The richer this port gets, the richer some owners do too. And with wealth comes power. Vessel owners (who in some cases can have upwards of fifteen to twenty boats) can afford to employ people both to manage their assets and quotas, and to speak on their behalf at key fisheries management meetings – a luxury not available to the average small-scale fisherman, who has nothing like the cash, time, or resources. There are some, obviously, who care passionately about our industry, but, sadly, I have seen for myself that with the motivation for some being their own commercial interests (over and above the entire fleet's), their needs tend to dominate any discussion.

With a single port doing so well, are we not playing a dangerous game of putting all of our eggs in one basket? My cynicism aside, the strength of Brixham harbour does at least trickle downhill, with smaller boats being able to benefit from the prosperous market and its affiliated infrastructure and piggy-backing on logistics and facilities, plus better prices for their catch. However, with much of the quota privately 'owned' (in FQAs) it can make it incredibly hard for those smaller operations to expand their businesses, because they cannot access the various quota stocks available.

Remember, dear reader, that the extent of our fishing fleet is finite, because the size of the overall pie doesn't change. It sometimes also feels to me like a game of Monopoly, and that, as a small-scale fisherman, I'm stuck on the Old Kent Road. With Brexit on the horizon, will we take back the quota that has been played away into non-UK ownership? Will we deny access to our waters to non-domiciled vessels? And, if we do, what then? Are we heading for a 'land grab' by the big fleet owners?

I don't know. But I worry. Is it deliberate oppression or, deep down, am I just a little jealous that the east coast does not thrive on fish the way it once did?

I'll let you decide.

~

Five days pass till we have an opportunity to leave Brixham, which we spend tinkering with *Saoirse*, catching up with laundry, and, for the most part, just hanging around, waiting for the weather to let up. We've been stuck here so long it feels like we live here; much longer and we'll be singing Cornish sea shanties to one another. I'm certainly feeling I'm turning into a local – I have a scallop and black pudding bap every morning. But we need to get on, and on the following Monday morning we finally steam out of the harbour. The weather's still not ideal, but we both think it's doable.

It's around 8 a.m. when we leave to make our 85-nautical-mile trip to our next way point, the Isle of Wight, and, for the most part, it's pretty plain sailing. And though the almanac predicts tide and weather will create 'violent and severe seas' when crossing Portland Race, when we get there the storm has pretty much abated, and we do so unhindered.

It looks like the Isle of Wight is as far as we will be able to make it today and with strong westerlies starting to build, we plan our approach to Yarmouth harbour. We have two available options for passage into the Solent, one of which takes a course close to the shore and connects to a deeper water channel for the onward short passage to Yarmouth. Or we can go via a channel that starts near the iconic Needles lighthouse and is flanked by a shallow bank called the Shingles.

Local knowledge – another of my friends on social media – tells us that Storm Alex is likely to have moved some of the sand banks on the inshore channel. So we decide to avoid that route and, instead, approach the West Cardinal buoy that marks the start of the other passage into the channel: the point where deep water meets shallow water, and the wind will be against the tide.

Minutes later, pushed along by following seas, we are in sight of the Needles lighthouse, and though we can't see the famous partly submerged wreck of the SS *Varvassi* (she was wrecked in 1947, carrying a cargo of tangerines), we know she is there, and now a potential danger to shipping herself. As we square up to the buoy, and pull *Saoirse* round into the tide that is now screaming towards us out of the Solent, we notice our speed start to drop.

With the sea squarely behind us now, progress is slow and as we close in on the Cardinal buoy I can see the force and strength of the tide on it, as it fights to hold itself upright. Within an instant I can feel the sheer force of the sea from behind, picking us up and trying to throw us along.

And it does, literally, throw us; I can hear the sound of the empty space below *Saoirse*'s hull, as she's picked up like a surfboard on an incoming wave, and hurried along by the force of the sea. I watch, heart in mouth, as the wave rolls onward in front of us, stretching itself out, streaked with white foamy fury. Then it's gone, but no sooner have I let out the breath I've been holding than along comes its big brother, and this one's in *way* more of a hurry.

I hold my breath again, braced for our imminent destruction, and through the fog of anticipation I hear Nige tell me, 'Ash, hold on. *Now.*'

I hold on. (If he'd asked me to go out on the deck then, I would have done that instead. Such is my trust in this man.) We have been picked up so high by the next incoming wave that we are now coming down off it vertically – a bit like a cartoon boat on a cartoon wave, with the sea gnashing against *Saoirse*'s fibreglass hull. I do as instructed, and brace my hands against a step in the wheelhouse roof. Through every window in front of me all I can see is water, and we are heading downwards, straight for it. The wheelhouse floor now feels more like a wall.

I glance to my right and see Nige pull back on the controls, slowing *Saoirse* down. She is now a different beast – no longer trying to adrenaline-junkie us down the sheer face of a wave, but a calm elegant duck that lets the rest of the wave, and all its might, just roll on by underneath her.

We continue at a snail's pace for what feels like an eternity, the waves rolling beneath us, on their endless urgent pilgrimage, before slowly losing force as the channel begins to widen, allowing us to make our sedate way against the tide into Yarmouth harbour. (Though for the record, my heart is still racing. Between this and Lossiemouth, is it any wonder why following seas in shallow water make my stomach turn?)

'Fuck,' Nige says. 'She's some boat for only eight metres!' And in that moment between us I feel my heart leap a little. Not only have Nige and I got through something proper challenging together, but our little Irish lass has earned our trust as well.

We tie up at a pontoon and the waiting harbour staff member asks me, 'What's it like down on the Needles?'

I reply with feeling. 'It's shit, mate!'

Chapter 25

'Do not kill a seagull'

Seagulls are believed to be the vessels used by dead sailors to travel the seas. It is thought their squawk is the desperate cry of a dead mariner, longing to move on to heaven.

The following morning Nige reflects on yesterday's antics, and kicks himself for not taking the inshore route, which, despite that local knowledge, his own instinct yet again told him he should do. If that course would have been better, we will never know now.

We plan to head for Newhaven, and head out of Yarmouth harbour full of vigour and vim. It's a fresh westerly again and we make our way through the Solent, a very busy stretch of coastline usually, since it's *the* mecca for yachts. This morning, though, edging into the off-season period, it's mainly ferries making the crossing from Pompey.

The weather's not great, bright but pretty windy, and, sick of being beaten up by it, we call in to Langstone harbour to take refuge, deciding to push straight for Dover the following day.

It's the first time on this trip that I can drag my beanbag out on deck and finally enjoy some welcome autumn sunshine on my face.

~

We skirt round Selsey Bill, and admire the white austere cliffs of Beachy Head before they begin to slink down towards the flat, golden shingle of Dungeness. Keen to get as many miles under our belt as possible, we maintain a fair pace, and make Dover at 6 p.m. A giant basin built for large ferries then engulfs us as we journey further, moor up, and find a cheap B&B. We're really keen to get home now. We've been away for *three weeks*, living out of suitcases (well, one suitcase and a bag for life, actually) and in horrible weather. Plus the endless takeaway food, and the cheap-and-cheerful B&B vibe, are both really beginning to grate. Not least because, this being the coast, they frequently aren't very cheap, and several of them have also been far from cheerful.

I crave a bath. I am desperately *longing* for a bath. Specifically my own bath, undisturbed, for an extended period, possibly with scented candles and facepacks and bubbles. I know Nige is probably craving the Bowling Green or the Fleece, and Andy Mac, who I'm sure he's really missing (hashtag bromance). In short, we're done. We need home.

There is a weather window breaking after lunch time tomorrow, which will last until the following morning, and if we take advantage of it we can probably do the last leg to Wells in one go. So we leave Dover at 2 p.m. and steam away relentlessly, eventually turning the corner to head north for the Norfolk coast. As we do that, however, so does the weather, and as we cross the Thames estuary, for the first time on the journey, we are launching head-first into the waves. They aren't that big but they're short, sharp and frequent, shaking every bone in our bodies, a relentless slamming we're still enduring as night falls. We then run the gauntlet across Felixstowe.

The port of Felixstowe is huge. It's the UK's biggest commercial cargo harbour, being the point of entry for goods from right across the world, as well as the exit point for many of our own exports. There are a few fishing communities dotted around the estuary, but this is a place of giant container ships and lines of colossal cranes, and containers of every colour, looking like so much giant Lego, form vast Tetris grids along the wharf.

We see none of this tonight, of course, as we pass it in darkness, feeling vulnerable and exposed, just as we had back in Eyemouth. Only this time the threat feels even bigger, as the towering, monolithic ships that sit awaiting pilotage in and out of the port have little chance of seeing us from their bridges.

Being in that environment, and feeling so insignificant – like we're a tiny pimple among mountains – makes us both really alert. With the pilot boats zipping past us, often at nearly 30 knots, and with the sheer scale of the vessels that are commanding our attention, comes a kind of hyperdrive of the senses. These ships are all so vast that to apply rules-of-the-road logic to them would be insanity. We need to be constantly aware of which direction they are moving because there is no way they can get out of *our* way – and that's assuming they've even seen us in the first place. It's made harder because, in the thick, almost galactic-scale darkness, all we can see are their lights and vague vessel-shaped outlines.

By the small hours, somewhere off Southwold, Nigel is all but spent and when we swap places, I urge him to shut his eyes and rest. 'I've got this,' I tell him, once I've managed to convince him. 'I can see us through till dawn.'

The hours of darkness tick by slowly and though I know Nigel won't really *sleep*-sleep, the sense of being in charge sits very easily with me. Yes, he often leaves me to manoeuvre the boat when we're working out at sea, but this is different; it's night time, we're in unfamiliar waters, and neither of us have had a great deal of sleep. It even feels strangely liberating, and the feeling spurs me on. To keep watch, to keep a close eye on all the gauges, to be in charge of holding our onward course.

That said, I've never been so happy to see the twinkling lights of Great Yarmouth out the port side as we slink silently by. And as the night begins to brighten, and the blackness turns to inky blue, I can see the familiar blinking of Cromer lighthouse. Home turf.

I set a new waypoint for Wells and, with dawn now approaching, Nige takes over for the home straight. With the finish line in sight we have both found renewed energy for the final push.

The tide is on our side as we cruise along the North Norfolk coast, and it isn't long before *Fairlass* comes into sight, finishing her night shift with the lads. We steam to join them, and after half an hour of silly showboating, doing donuts round each other in the peachy morning light, we all sit together by the Fairway buoy, till the incoming tide can take us home.

Chapter 26

'Never say goodbye when departing'

Many mariners believed this word could doom a voyage and keep a
ship from returning home.

Now we have *Saoirse* home we need to find a home for her –
and berths are always at a premium at Wells harbour. We have a
mooring agreement for *Fairlass*, and Robert's already told us he's
happy for us to have another fishing boat at Wells, but having
a fishing boat at Wells doesn't automatically grant you a prime
quay mooring. In reality it doesn't guarantee you any sort of
mooring; it's more a case of being patient and hoping something
will come up before too long and, in the meantime, sticking your
boat wherever the harbourmaster directs. So you come in from
sea and it's a bit of a lucky dip – you just have to hope you can find
somewhere to unload.

We start off keeping *Saoirse* on one of the pontoons. Once
we're fishing with her, it'll more than likely be a case, at least for
a while, of nipping in to unload at any berth one of our fellow

fishermen isn't currently using, and then finding another one till our next departure, as some of the berths aren't conducive to unloading because they have railings, or, indeed, tourists, in the way.

Ideally we'd like to keep *Saoirse* alongside *Fairlass*, but logistically, this throws up a serious concern. It's fine when there is water there and *Fairlass* is afloat, but our worry is what might happen when she dries. *Fairlass* is a big, heavy boat and she needs to lie against the quay wall, to stop running the risk of her laying out. Since *Saoirse* is so much smaller and lighter, she would float before *Fairlass*, which means running the risk of her being caught under her bigger sister as she does so, which is something that doesn't bear thinking about. So for now she'll do as directed by Robert, and since Robert looks after all us fishermen so well, we are happy to be patient.

We spend the next ten days or so getting her ready for work. We have already ordered a custom-made riddle for her (they are usually made to measure, like Savile Row suits), and two bait box cradles, which sit on the rails, to maximise working deck space. We then set to work laying her new flooring. Every fibreglass deck needs bulwark-to-bulwark rubber covering, for what I hope by now are obvious reasons. (Wooden decks are slightly different, requiring a breathable type of mat, if any at all. A lot of bigger boats plump for an uncarpeted wooden deck option; having nature underfoot, most will readily agree, is a much more forgiving and pleasant surface to work on.)

~

By mid-October, *Saoirse* is ready to go and fish, so we have borrowed a riddle from another fisherman, Johnny, as ours is still being made. We get to grips with working a small boat that is an entirely different beast to the slow and heavy giant that is our Lass Fair. She's perfect for what we want to do, but it takes a while; we have been spoiled with never-ending space and *Saoirse* is much smaller, and the lads soon start referring to her as 'the bath toy'. (Or, maybe, just maybe, they just still can't pronounce *Saoirse*.) Nevertheless, we push her in some funny weather straight from the off. She has proved her capability, and apparently so have I: when we choose to go, and many others stay tied up, Nigel now says things to me like 'Well done Ash, you've shown a lot of lads up today.'

I feel proud, but the truth is that we push off out of necessity. If the prop isn't turning, we're not earning. And we have to earn; this boat has to wipe her own face. The boys are running *Fairlass* now (though we barely see them as, true to form, they like working the unsociable tides, so we are, literally, ships that pass in the night), and we have a big bill to pay off. So we don't have the luxury of staying tied up for too long, even if that means fishing through storms bad enough to have names.

Storm Aiden, which rocks up at the end of October, looks, from the forecast, as if it might be particularly boisterous but nevertheless we decide to turn out and, as we head out to our whelk gear, it pushes us along but luckily it's mostly from a direction off the land. Still, with gusts up to 50mph in an 8-metre boat, when we turn *Saoirse*, some 6 miles offshore, to haul our pots, it is still pretty lively.

Despite being thrown about like a toy boat in a violently churning bath tub, Nige and I grit our teeth and work through it, with a carefully curated windy playlist, featuring such classics as Bob Dylan's *Blowin' In the Wind*, and ACDC's *Highway to Hell*. It's shitty enough today that every so often we feel the odd sensation of *Saoirse*'s prop coming out of the water, as she is tossed around by Poseidon's fury. It's a split second of no momentum, the engine revving high as the blade spins in the air with no water to grip on to. Sometimes these kind of windy days are better than the ones that are only just a little bit slammy and rolly; because it's expected, you know exactly what you're in for on the way out of the harbour, and you prepare for it both practically (by tying things down and proper stowage) and mentally. When the forecast is just a bit off, however, that little bit of chip you weren't expecting ironically makes for harder work.

We fight Aiden long enough to haul four hundred pots, and have a hard-earned three quarters of a ton of whelks now on board, the sale of which will make a dent on our outstanding bill. However, we're now fighting Aiden's bad mood-made-liquid from the opposite direction, so the steam back to the harbour is both splashy and slammy.

As he sorts the deck out and cleans down, Nige puts me in charge of the controls. Essentially I am 'control-man', as he calls it, spotting for big waves that have the potential to put him on his arse if I don't ease the speed back at the right moment. He wants me to make *Saoirse* glide over them like a little duck, not like a bulldozer tearing through masonry. I'm not sure there's any substance to the old surfers' myth that waves run in sets of seven, with the seventh of the set being the most ferocious. Right now it feels like they're all number seven as I keep one eye in front of me and the other behind, on Nige, shouting 'Hold tight!' when a particularly evil one looms up in front of us and I alter the speed.

As we approach Wells again, the storm, still pretty boisterous, gradually loses its grip on us as we increasingly gain shelter from the land. Close to shore the waves have less opportunity to build up, plus the pinewoods on the beach act as a giant windbreak.

By the time we are back loading up the fish boxes, we watch in amusement as a couple of bigger boats head out on the late shift, as we're pretty sure they have been embarrassed into following our lead. It's a good feeling. *Saoirse* is one of the smallest boats in the fleet; this is why the Cygnus has such a great reputation.

It's not just about heading out while others hesitate. It's almost second nature for me now not only to follow Nige's lead, but to understand the reasons for his decisions and choices in a way I never used to before. My confidence in his leadership and experience is absolute, and his confidence in *me* makes me feel I am finally defining my own destiny.

I have changed. And not just in my growing fisherman's instincts. My outlook now is different; I have a strong sense that I have to depend on my own decisions – to own them and trust them – to get by. It's a freedom I now feel better equipped to manage, and my confidence in my decision-making grows daily. I have also embraced one of those early laws of the sea I encountered, and have a clear understanding of what it means to place your total trust in your skipper. That too, is a kind of freedom I've never before encountered. Like lots of other

303

people, I imagine, I have had periods working for people who I didn't necessarily even respect, let alone trust. It feels like such an incredible stroke of luck that I ended up on a fishing trip in Wells that random Saturday, and was booked on that trip with that apparently random man. I constantly think about the word 'if'. If I hadn't been there that day, how different would my life be now?

I have changed. My appearance now is different; I am strong. I am not remotely afraid to get dirty. I wear grotty clothes daily. I hardly ever wear make-up. I feel entirely confident in my own salty skin. I feel the last few years – particularly the last two – have been a journey of self-discovery and personal validation. How I wish I could bottle how I feel and share it with other young women – women who feel a compulsion to conform to the latest trending beauty standards, who feel afraid to take up space, who feel insufficient as the people they are. *You are enough.*

I feel privileged in every sense to have been given the gift of this opportunity, that has taken me out into the wild. Into the world. This *is* my world now and it's caught me, hook, line and sinker.

And yet.

My informal apprenticeship has not just been about self-realisation and learning new practical skills. It's also been an education into the UK fishing industry that few outside of fishing fully understand. And it is, not to put too fine a point on it, a fucking mess. I have lifted the lid on Pandora's box.

The struggle to sort it out is very real and still ongoing. It permeates every part of the job, and for everyone in the industry – a constant hum, a bit like tinnitus, which everyone carries with them day in day out. I feel the anguish of my fellow fishermen: people I *do* respect. People I *do* trust. Something has *got* to give. This community faces constant scrutiny from those that govern and control us, has to operate under ever-evolving legislation, ditto safety restrictions, making the job – such an important one – practically unworkable. And now environmental groups, too, are routinely vilifying fishermen. Natural England, for example, seeming to be pulling the strings of IFCA and the MMO, and since their sole focus is preservation of the natural environment, it makes it hard, in my humble opinion, for them to look at things truly objectively. The pressure from some vegan campaign groups is equally lacking in compassion for fishermen and fishing communities. Some peddle blatant propaganda against us. The documentary film *Seaspiracy* is a perfect example; most of the 'facts' quoted about the fishing industry have since been debunked.

Has anybody stopped to think about me and Nige? Jack and Kenneth? Our fellow fishermen in Wells? Our fellow fishermen up and down the length and breadth of our United Kingdom? I don't think so.

'Oh, fishermen, they'll just have to move. Do something else.'
'They'll have to sell their boats, find other work. It is what it is.'
'Hell, it's only, what, eleven-and-a-half-thousand people?'
'Don't fishermen realise? The environment comes first!'

I'm sure, were I to sit down and discuss it with one of their representatives, that the various bodies who govern our every move would not for a moment accept that we are being managed out of a job. But I've seen it enough times in my previous life to know what that looks like. If it walks like a duck and quacks like a duck . . .

This knowledge is beginning to weigh heavily. Now I understand this, I feel I don't just want to share it. I feel I *must*, and before it's too late. I'm not saying I have all the answers, but I do want to open this world up to a wider audience, to connect with other fishermen, to stimulate discussion, and I am passionate, really passionate, about speaking out. I have a platform, as well. Among an already endangered species, I am an even rarer (and hopefully not declining) one. A female fisherman.

I have no idea, though, that I am about to get my way.

Chapter 27

'Women on boats are bad luck'

Back in the days of sail, a woman on board was believed to be a distraction to the crew. It was thought this distraction would anger the sea and create treacherous conditions. Ironically, this could only be calmed by the bare chest of a woman. Which is why boats used naked female figureheads on the bow.

In early November our new riddle arrives, which means a day ashore, as we need to get Johnny's one back to him and our own one fitted. It's not a whole-day job but Nige also wants to replace the pound boards, and as we've really put the hours in of late, a day off – even if a work one – is a welcome reprieve.

The weather's very Novemberish; there's an annoying breeze and heavy cloud, and it's mizzling. And it's only just getting light as I pull up outside Nige's gaff in Wells. Given the weather, even though he'll be awake, I know he'll still be in bed; we're both early birds but his cue to get up is my arrival and the mug of tea I'm going to make him.

Once I've got the kettle on I can hear him moving around upstairs, and it's then only a matter of minutes before we're back out the door, Nige with his giant Sports Direct mug in his hand – he usually drinks his cuppa in the truck. Then it's a stop at the Co-op so he can run in and buy some cigarettes, before another stop at Will's of Wells, to get us both a latte, which'll set us up for a morning of small tasks.

I love these kinds of days. They are as much a part of our working lives as the long days at sea. They always start with the same rituals, including Nige's 'plan'. Nige has to have a plan, even on days we're not at sea – he's very goal-orientated like that. (Plus it gives him a chance to see exactly what needs doing and therefore how soon he can head to the pub.)

I pull in outside the Co-op so he can nip in and grab his fags, and use the time to check my Instagram.

I've been posting on Instagram as @thefemalefisherman for about a year now, sharing the highs and lows of my fishing life, and all the funny bits in between. In recent years, I've removed almost all social media from my life as it wasn't really bringing me any benefit or joy, and I was – I am – beginning to find this constant pressure to share everything intrusive, and was becoming disturbed by the idea that this was the new norm. However, I could definitely see the benefits of opening up communities like ours to a wider audience. After all, fishing isn't the kind of job where you can easily open the door to visitors to let them see how it's done, and, arguably, given everything I hope you've learned reading this book, that's something it desperately needs. And it's been fun connecting with my fellow fishermen around the country, and hearing first hand that they have the exact same concerns and fears as me. In some quarters this is taboo. The fishing world has been shrouded in mystique. And some who work within it prefer it that way. Not that I care what they think because the support and encouragement I've received, especially as a woman in a man's world, has been just amazing (cheers lads and lasses!).

I pull my phone out of my hoodie pocket and can immediately see a screen littered with notifications. Plus two missed calls from a London number. What on earth is going on?

Nige climbs back in just as I'm scrolling through all the messages. By now I've established from the comments on Insta that people seem to think there's something going down on breakfast telly that I should be a part of. It seems the broadcaster Piers Morgan, presenting on *Good Morning Britain*, has blasted the BBC for referring to fishermen as 'fisherpeople'. This has got under his skin apparently, as he sees it as yet more 'woke culture' nonsense. Someone's even sent me a clip of *Good Morning Britain*. I play it. 'Why do gender terms matter?' he's fuming. 'There are no women fishermen anyway!'

Nige lights his fag. 'Look at this lot,' I tell him, handing him my phone. 'I've had two missed calls from London as well.'

'So ring them back then,' he says. 'See what they want. You never know, you might get on with Piers!'

I call the number. It answers immediately. It's a researcher from *Good Morning Britain*. 'Are you a woman fisherman?' she asks. I tell her I am. 'So what do you think about the BBC calling fishermen "fisherpeople"?'

I tell her my thoughts. That I'm a fisherman and proud to be called one. Which is not the answer I imagine she was hoping for. I know how these things work. Controversy sells. Still, it doesn't seem to dampen her enthusiasm. She immediately asks if I'd be happy to do a live stream with the studio in ten minutes.

She's been on loudspeaker and now Nige is whispering 'Do it!' – as if I'd ever imagine *not* doing it; this is such a brilliant opportunity to put myself out there as a spokesperson for our woefully under-represented sector. Plus I might also get a few more Instagram friends. Win win!

Forgoing Will's at Wells, we drive straight over to the quay. My phone buzzes again, this time with a message from the *Fishing Daily News*, wondering if *GMB* have caught up with me. I ping a quick text back and the guy tells me that he hopes it's okay that he let them have my number – they traced me to an article I'd written for them a couple of years ago. I assure him it's fine – more than fine, in fact, as I'm going to be live on TV in ten minutes!

I have a slight qualm developing as I pull my hood up to run across to *Saoirse*. While Nige stays in the van, keeping out of the mizzle, I'm about to face Britain's most notorious journalistic rottweiler from the wheelhouse. What if he chews me up into pieces and spits me out?

Nige immediately pooh-poohs that. 'Ash, you're on the same side!' And he's right, but I still have a small fluttering of butterflies in my stomach as I head into the wheelhouse to take the video call that's been scheduled for ten minutes' time (and – eek! – is now imminent). I haven't brushed my hair in a week, am wearing the skankiest of hoodies, and am about to be seen on national TV. Then I remind myself that none of this matters. I AM ENOUGH.

I have already shared my Instagram feed (at that time my account was still private) and once the call begins I can see myself on a giant screen behind Piers Morgan and Susanna Reid. I confirm that there *are* female fishermen, albeit very few, and make my point about how proud I am to be called a 'fisherman', owing to the proud heritage and doggedness of the historically predominantly male catching sector. As we wrap up, I tell them the most important thing for me is that I do a job I love, and that's what matters most.

I finish the surreal couple of minutes wondering if I've made any sort of impact, as I imagine they were hoping for a kerfuffle. And I soon get an inkling that I might have. As I head back to Nige in the truck, with my phone in my back pocket, I feel a near-constant buzz of new notifications, and when I scroll to see what's happening I find hundreds of new follower requests.

So people *do* care. People *do* want to hear what I'm up to. I don't care what people's motivation is to follow a scruffy bird who happens to catch fish for a living – perhaps I'm just a novelty, a breath of fresh air, someone a bit different to what they might have been expecting. It doesn't matter. They want to follow me, which means I have a platform I can build on. It might not last but why would I not grab this opportunity?

I climb into the truck and grin at Nige. 'I think I'd better make my Instagram public,' I tell him. 'If that's alright with you. Anyway, how did I do?'

'You did great, babe,' he tells me. 'Well done.'

He puts his phone on the dash then and sparks up another cigarette. 'Come on,' he says. 'We've got to sort out this riddle. We need to get on and see what's what.'

'Righto,' I say, and start the engine.

Fin

Aft

At, near or towards the stern of a boat

During the writing of this book I have often felt a strong sense of 'imposter syndrome'. Yes, I'm a fisherman, and have amassed sufficient experience and knowledge to feel qualified to talk about our often misunderstood industry. However, at times, particularly when referring to my fellow fisherman, many of whom have wisdom way beyond my own, I have felt these were stories that were not mine to tell. I am only able to recount them because I have been privileged to have been given this platform. This book, therefore, is my gift to them. Perhaps its existence will help amplify their voices.

Cramming in as much as I could without turning this into a dusty old reference book was, as you can probably imagine, hard. And if you've stayed the course with me you have my sincere thanks. Thank you also for bearing with me for a little bit longer because by this point you've probably realised that our fishing industry is in one hell of a mess. I wish I could say differently, but the outlook for the future does not inspire confidence.

The MCA, to put it bluntly, is crippling the smaller boats. Its new code, two hundred pages of regulations that contradict each other regularly, is being enforced by inspectors whose interpretations seem to vary across the country and much of the fleet is being tied up for lengthy periods as a result. For example, when the MCA demanded unnecessary alterations at *Saoirse*'s latest inspection, I contested the decision. The process ended up taking three months, during which our business could not operate. We could not earn any income. And we are far from being the only fishermen with these kinds of issues.

As is the case with most of us, and probably most sectors of industry, making ends meet grows increasingly more challenging for our fishermen. Red diesel prices have tripled in a period of just a year, and the cost of bait has also rocketed, thanks to the cost of electricity to keep it frozen. The price per kilo for catch has not really risen since markets plummeted during the pandemic. With inflation as it is, margins are becoming much smaller, leaving us wondering just how we're supposed to make a living. Do we apply greater pressure on the sea? Of course not. Those stocks are our lifeline for the future. So how do our businesses stay viable?

We are also fearful that our very workplaces are disappearing. To keep our remaining fishing grounds we must constantly be in conflict, as they are increasingly threatened by the building of new windfarms in the prime, shallower grounds, nearer to the shore. The same can be said of the little seaweed farm that has just been granted a licence a few miles down the coast. Although it seems ecologically sound, the whole application process was very cloak and dagger; it was only when someone found out about the application, and lobbied hard, that the MMO agreed that the applicant must also consult with local fishermen. I am also sceptical that this 'little' seaweed farm will remain little for long.

Marine Protected Areas, which no one would deny are important to the future of our planet, creep ever more into our fishing domains too. That there is growing pressure to protect our precious oceans is inevitable, but there is a general feeling among fishermen that they too often target the weakest link in the chain, i.e. the small boats that only work in those easily accessed inshore waters. Work is being done right now to classify many long-standing fishing grounds, accessed by those small boats, as HPMAs (as discussed in Chapter 7), while there seem to be none of those offshore where the big boats are playing – and their owners have such powerful voices at the table. It's so much harder for small-boat fishermen to be heard – as we saw with the proposed Scottish HPMAs, it takes a big, concerted effort to force change. But the success of the Scottish campaign shows that when fishermen speak up and stick together, we really can help shape a better future. Everyone wants to see our ocean ecosystems protected, but thought must be given to how we can do this without destroying whole communities in the process. It often feels as if those who administer this process are standing in distant offices, throwing darts at a map, and giving scant consideration to those that make their living from them, and are *already,* since they know them and care for them and *need* to sustain them, the de facto guardians of those spaces.

Considering their past antics in 'management', many in the fishing community struggle to find a positive single thing to say about the MMO. Never have I heard a fisherman utter the words, 'Oh, didn't the MMO do that well!' Remember the IVMS fiasco I touched on in Chapter 20? How can relationships be built, or, indeed, trust be fostered, when they seem so hell bent on wasting our time and money? I hear whispers of mandatory onboard CCTV in the pipeline now too. Let's hope they remain whispers.

IFCAs (Inshore Fisheries Conservation Authorities) continue to carry out the wishes of those on high, continuing to divide the fleet with permit systems inside their precious 6-mile limits, and marching the quayside wearing body cameras and making innocent hard-working people feel like criminals. It also often feels as if they are closing the stable door after the horse has already bolted, illustrated by the frequency with which they bring in so-called 'emergency byelaws'. If they were on top of things, surely this would rarely be necessary? A prime example of this is the recent Wash Cockle Fishery Order, which, to the many fishermen who were going to be potentially put out of business as a consequence, felt like a knee-jerk response that had only come about due to years of poor fisheries management.

These unelected officials have no concept of the hard work that goes into the job, and bring in byelaws that allow them to act as judge, jury and executioner in prosecution matters, which can see fishermen ejected from 'their' districts.

The biggest joke of all, of course, is Brexit. What Brexit? Did you catch the headline in December 2022 about the UK bringing back 30,000 tonnes of fish? Call me sceptical, but even though this quota has been allocated to the non-sector pool, with the small-scale (non-sector) fishermen being managed out of the job by all other means, where will that uncaught quota end up? Back in the hands of the POs and big commercial operators, maybe? (Who I hear, by the way, are quietly very busy levelling up their businesses and building new boats . . .)

Brexit sold fishermen out. We didn't 'take back' all of our fish, nor did we 'take back' our waters. It was never going to be an easy task, but we expected more because we were promised more. Another hefty chunk added to the ever-increasing wedge between fishermen and those who claim to govern us.

~

As you will no doubt have noticed, I sometimes feel overwhelmed by the current state of play. I am desperate to make a change, and make a difference to the future of our small-scale fleets. Especially in the eastern regions, the patch of coast I call home. Back in the 1950s, Grimsby was the biggest fish market in the world. The humble fish finger was first created in Great Yarmouth. Yet these once-famous ports are no longer what they were – bustling and vibrant, the smell of diesel and fish filling the air – but tired depressing shadows of their former productive selves, a liquid landscape filled with oil, gas and windfarm support vessels, motor cruisers, sailboats and yachts. Yes, still home to fishing boats but not in any numbers and, as they dwindle, so does the supporting infrastructure: the fish markets, the couriers, the ice plants and chandlers, along with engineering fabrication, processors and wholesalers.

The loss of infrastructure on which fisherman used to depend represents a miserable *fait accompli*. For example, if we wanted to try to target a different species, let's say fish rather than shellfish, we would need to set the boat up for a new fishing method, requiring costly new fish-catching equipment and most likely modifications to the boat. I would also have to contact the MCA and probably have another survey before we could actually do any work with the new method.

But let's be positive, and say we have done that and are ready to target some fin fish. To keep the fish in top-class condition, it will need flake ice, as supplying poor-quality fish does nothing for your reputation or price per kilo. With no ice plant locally, we would have to acquire an ice machine, plus somewhere to store it that had power and water. Good luck finding those kinds of premises for rent in any small harbour setting, at least these days. But let's continue to use our imaginations. So, we have the boat all set up, have sourced some ice, and have now spent twelve hours at sea catching ourselves some fish, or hoping to. Hoping some big, foreign-owned super trawler hasn't already hoovered it all up ... In order to sell it we must now make a three-hour round trip to deliver it to our closest fish market. Sounds like pretty hard work, right?

It seems logical therefore to stick to shellfish. Thanks to the numerous other boats locally that are also landing shellfish, we at least have a supply chain in place. Despite wanting to pursue other avenues for income, not least to utilise some of that non-sector fish I'm entitled to, diversification is nigh on impossible, as there is *no longer any infrastructure to support it*. Yes, I can sell directly to local pubs, restaurants and fishmongers, but consistency for the buyer can be an insurmountable challenge as, keen as I am, I cannot personally control the weather.

I might not have been the first to think of it (though perhaps I'd better trademark it anyway) but wouldn't it be great if there was an app to address that? Not to control the weather, but a portal on which anyone could place an order for fish, which would then send a request to all the non-sector small-scale fishermen across the UK, and whoever could fulfil it, accepted and sent it. And wouldn't it also be great if the major supermarkets stopped pumping us full of anonymous pre-packaged fish (most likely caught by a non-UK-domiciled super trawler), that has spent *at least ten days* at sea before reaching the 'fresh fish' counter near you? Why not rent out your fish counters as concessions to small fish buyers? Ones scouting out the markets for the best seasonal fish from our own home-grown fishing communities? (I'm looking at you, Tesco, Morrisons, Sainsbury's, Asda and Waitrose.)

As someone who buys fish, though, you, dear reader, do hold some power. And if you want to help support small-boat fishermen my best advice, for now, is to seek out local if you can. If you're lucky enough to be near a harbour, get to know your fishermen, find out what they're catching and, crucially, when they're landing it. It doesn't matter if you don't know what to do with a whole fish or a crab, by the way. It's easier to prep seafood than many people think. Just go on good old YouTube – an infinite source of advice – then get stuck in and have a go. It will almost certainly taste better (and be cheaper) than anything in the shops. If you're land-locked, however, try one of the increasing numbers of online retailers who sell 'day boat' fish, then take the trouble to do a little research. Where is this fish coming from? Who's catching it? Can you find a boat name? Some of the best retailers will pride themselves on selling you fish with a back story. (I think they call it 'provenance' in certain circles.)

As it happens, we have started to diversify on *Saoirse* ourselves, and have made quite a splash recently with our own quayside pop-up fishmonger, selling crab, lobster, mackerel and cod, the fish being lovingly line-caught and gutted at sea, and as fresh as it's possible to be. I don't imagine we'll have the same success with our humble whelks but, hell, a girl can still dream.

It's not just about cash in our pockets, either. Just the process of interacting with the seafood-buying public is invaluable. They have so many questions, and it's great to be able to inform and to educate – both from those interactions and, later, as they follow my social media feed. Changing hearts and minds doesn't happen overnight, but each person who goes away better informed about our industry I count as a win. With so much fake news out there, getting the truth heard really matters.

You may recall that I mentioned the documentary *Seaspiracy* earlier. One of the benefits of increasing my media profile was that I had the opportunity to discuss the film with its (British) creator. I was glad to be able to take him to task about the absence of our own UK fishing industry in his excoriating attack on commercial fishing, and over some of the 'facts' presented about fishing's alleged crimes. I also invited him, while on air, to come out fishing with me and Nige, so he could see some of the responsible practices the UK uses for himself. Despite him accepting my invitation, I have yet to see him in Wells.

Thanks to that encounter, I welcomed lots of new faces to that little Instagram account of mine, giving me even greater reach in which to tell the truth about our beleaguered fishing industry. And my efforts were unexpectedly rewarded when, in May 2022, I was nominated for, and won, an actual award – the Under 10-m Fisherman of the Year. This was thrilling in itself, of course, but I was doubly excited when it was pointed out that this was the first time it had been won by a female, which really felt like the start of a revolution. And perhaps is; that same year, Isla Gale – what a great name for a fisherman – won Trainee Fisherman of the Year, and in 2023, Emma Scott (the daughter of Iain Scott, who sold us *Fairlass*) won in the same category.

Winning awards opens doors, and creates forums for discussion. When I'm not out fishing I am now busier than ever, both doing my own research about the industry, to stay current, and polishing the big crystal ball I now need to try and second-guess what the next obstacle or trend is likely to be.

The small-boat fisherman is floating slap bang in the way of 'progress' and big money, not least in the form of windfarms, which are far more lucrative for the government than we are. Is it any wonder we're always exhausted? We are fighting for our very survival and I don't think there is a magic wand that can be waved to cure all our ills.

I am scared for the future of my industry. Mostly, however, I'm in my happy place. The sea. I love my job. Correction: I *really* love my job, and I recognise that there is a need for optimism in the industry if we are going to ensure its survival. We have to work together to take a long hard look at the mistakes of the past and to forge a better, more sustainable future.

Meanwhile, if you're in Wells, please come and find me, and let's chat. Though obviously not when we're in the middle of landing, or you'll be on the receiving end of one of Nige's killer glares . . .

Ashley Mullenger, July 2023

Further reading

Online dayboat retailers

A way to know what's in season is to give https://discoverseafood.uk a look. Set up by the Fishmongers' Company's Fisheries Charitable Trust, it's full of monthly fish guides, information and recipes, and has an interactive map of fishmongers and fishermen right across the UK.

Other online dayboat retailers are:

Henderson to Home: https://hendersontohome.com/

La Mer: https://lamerltd.co.uk/

boat-2-door: https://boat2door.co.uk/

The Cornish Fishmonger: https://thecornishfishmonger.co.uk/

Flying Fish Seafoods: https://www.flyingfishseafoods.co.uk/

Mourne Fishbox: https://www.mournefishbox.com/

Weyfish: https://www.weyfish.com/

Fishbox: https://www.fishbox.co.uk/

Maps and charts

https://kingfisherrestrictions.org/fishing-restriction-map

Glossary

Administrative port	Each devolved administrator has its own designated fishing ports, e.g. King's Lynn (LN) administered by MMO, Peterhead (PD) administered by Marine Scotland. A vessel moving between devolved administrators must obtain permission from both sides.
Alongside	Tied up to a pontoon, quay wall or another vessel.
Anti-fouling	A specialist paint applied to the underside of boats to prevent growth of weed and barnacles.
Astern	The term for putting a boat in reverse.
Bar	A long ridge of sand, gravel, or other material at or near the mouth of a river or harbour entrance, often constituting an obstruction to navigation.
Bell housing	A flared casing that encloses a fly wheel and forms part of the transmission.
Bending on	The process of tying a tow to a leader, with a double sheet bend knot.
Berm	A nearly flat back portion of a beach, formed of material deposited by the action of the waves.
Berried	Of a crab or lobster, bearing eggs on her underside.
Black spot disease	Progressive degradation of a crab's shell caused by bacteria and creating black spot lesions.
Block	A part enclosing one or more freely rotating, grooved pulleys, about which ropes or chains pass to form a hoisting or hauling tackle.

Bowline	A knot that creates a loop in a piece of rope that will still be easy to undo regardless of the force applied to it.
Broadside	If a boat is broadside to something, it has one side facing in the direction of that thing.
Bulwark	An extension of a ship's sides above deck level.
Buoy	A distinctively shaped and marked float, sometimes carrying a signal or signals, anchored to mark a channel, anchorage, navigational hazard, etc., or to provide a mooring place away from the shore.
Call sign	The unique letters and numbers which identify a vessel that is broadcasting on the radio or sending messages by radio.
Cardinal buoy	A navigational buoy that shows where the safest passage is.
Careening	To rush forward in an uncontrolled way.
Cat catcher	A metal cage-like structure bolted to the transom of a boat. Often used for storing vital equipment without cluttering the working deck.
Chandlery	A place to purchase boat stuff.
Clinker/Clinked	A wooden hull constructed with each plank overlapping that below.
Cock	A male crab.
Cod Wars	The dispute over Iceland's territorial waters, 1958–1976.
Common Fisheries Policy	A set of rules for managing European fishing fleets and conserving fish stocks.
Creel	A term used instead of crab pot.
Deadwood	The lower part of a ship's stem or stern.

Deck wash	A seawater pump with a hose powered by the engine.
Decommissioning	A government-funded payment to fishermen to scrap their vessels and licences to control fleet effort.
Defra	Department for Environment, Food and Rural Affairs.
Demersal	Living in, or found near, the deepest part of a body of water.
Dhan tow	Colloquial term for the piece of rope between the surface marking can and the anchor.
Distant-water fleet	Fishing boats that target fish outside territorial waters.
Doric	Rural dialect, especially that spoken in the north-east of Scotland.
Draught	The depth of a vessel in the water, taken from the level of the waterline to the lowest point of the keel.
Ebb	To flow back or away, as the water of a tide.
Echo sounder/Sounder	A device that determines depth by sending pulses of high-frequency sound to the seabed and timing their return.
EEC	European Economic Community.
EEZ	Exclusive Economic Zone.
Entitlement	The right to licence a vessel or the right to catch certain fish stocks.
EPIRB	Emergency position-indicating radio beacon.
Fairway	A marker that indicates the start or finish of a navigable channel in a river or harbour.
Fathom	A unit of length equal to 6 feet (1.8 metres), used mainly to measure the depth of water.

Fender	A flexible bumper used in boating to keep boats from banging into docks or each other.
First sale fish	Fish offered for sale for the first time.
Fisheries officer	An enforcement officer of a fisheries administrator.
Fishing vessel register	The register of all fishing vessels in the United Kingdom, separated into over-10m and under-10m and updated monthly.
Fleet	A group of boats.
Flood	The rise or flowing-in of the tide.
Flotilla	A group of small boats or ships.
Fly wheel	A heavy wheel that is part of the engine. It regulates the engine's rotation and is crucial to the engine start-up sequence.
Following sea	A wave direction that is similar to the heading of a waterborne vessel under way.
Foredeck	The deck at the forward part of a boat.
Forward/For'd	Toward the bow or front of a vessel.
Foul	To entangle or entwine, and more generally that something is wrong or difficult.
FQA	Fixed quota allocation.
Frames	The remnants of a fish once it has been filleted.
Fresh	Windy.
Gaff	A hook at the end of a pole.
Gastropod	Scientific class of slugs and snails, including whelks.
Ghost fishing	The act of falsifying landing data; or abandoned fishing gear left at sea.

Gill net	A net suspended vertically in the water to trap fish by their gills in its meshes.
Gongoozler	A person who enjoys watching activity on the canals of the United Kingdom.
Grapple	A spiky anchor that is dragged over the seabed to find lost fishing gear.
Gunwale	The upper edge of the side or bulwark of a vessel.
Hand	Crew.
Hard eye	A hard plastic ring stitched into the entrance of a pot.
Hauler	A hydraulic powered mechanical winch.
Helm	A wheel or tiller by which a ship is steered.
Hen	Female crab.
Hipped up	Towed alongside.
Hold	The lower part of the interior of a ship's hull, especially when considered as storage space.
Hull	The main body of a ship.
Hydrostatic release	A depth-activated release device.
ICES rectangle	An area of sea in a grid developed by the International Council for the Exploration of the Sea.
IFCA	Inshore Fisheries Conservation Authority.
Inkwell	A style of crab pot.
Jack	Male crab.
Keel	A timber or steel structure that runs lengthwise along the bottom of the hull.
Knot	A unit of speed equal to one nautical mile or about 1.15 miles per hour.
Laying out	When a vessel leans away from the structure it has been tied to when not afloat.

Logbook	A mandatory log of fish caught and landed that must be submitted to the fisheries administrator (by over-10m boats).
Making fast	The act of securing a boat, or something to a boat, with a rope, wire or chain.
Marinising	Converting a product for use in a marine environment.
MCZ	Marine Conservation Zone.
Mizzen	A mast towards the stern of a boat.
MMO	Marine Management Organisation.
MMSI	Maritime Mobile Service Identities are nine-digit numbers used to identify a ship or a coast radio station.
Moult	To cast or shed a shell in the process of renewal.
Nephrops	A langoustine or Norway lobster.
NGO	Non-Governmental Organisation.
Nautical mile	1 nautical mile = 1.15 miles.
Non-sector	Describes fishing vessels not in a PO.
Parlour	A holding area inside a crab pot away from the bait.
Pelagic	Marine life living or occurring in the upper waters of the open sea.
Port	The left-hand side of or direction from a vessel, facing forward.
Port of call	A place where a ship stops during a journey.
Port of registry	The port where a ship is registered – not necessarily the home port of the vessel.
Pound	An enclosed space on deck.
Pound boards	Normally wooden and held in place by metal brackets, these act as a funnel for pots to exit the back of the boat, and stop them getting trapped in the corners. They also create a safe space if you stand behind them while shooting away.

Purse	On a female crab, the curled-under abdomen with small appendages which the eggs attach to.
Putting in	Colloquial term to mean the tides are in the cycle of getting bigger (dropping away would be used if they were approaching the lowest neap).
Quota	A measurement in weight of fish that may be caught.
Race	A location where an underwater feature or headland can affect the sea state as the tide runs around it and can create either calmer or rougher conditions than expected.
Refitting	Replacing equipment on a boat, which could be an extensive redesign or a simple replacement of instruments.
Reeds Almanac	Nautical almanac providing all the information required to navigate British and European coastal waters.
Rib	Part of a boat's structure, the ribs run from the keel up to the gunwales like bones in a ribcage.
Riddling	The process of grading whelks on a riddle.
Roe	Fish eggs.
Rule beater	A boat under 10 metres long that has the capacity to fish in heavy weather for longer periods of time.
Sacrificial anodes	Replaceable zinc blocks used to protect areas of a boat from corrosion.
Sacrificial tins	Wear plates put over the sheaves of a hauler that can be changed so as not to warp the metal.
Screw	Colloquial term for propeller.
Scupper	An opening in the bottom of a bulwark, for rapid drainage of a weather deck in heavy seas.
Shank	A string of pots.
Shickle	The processed offal of brown crab.
Skiff	A small light boat.

Slipway	A large platform that slopes down into the sea, from which boats are put into the water.
Spline	Any of a series of uniformly spaced ridges on a shaft, parallel to its axis and fitting inside corresponding grooves in the hub of a gear, etc., to transmit torque.
Sprung plank	A plank that has sprung away from the ribs.
Starboard	The right-hand side of or direction from a vessel, facing forward.
String	A string of pots.
Strop	A rope sling, as for handling cargo.
Super under-10	A boat under 10 metres long that has the capacity to fish in heavy weather for longer periods of time (see also rule beater).
TAC	Total allowable catch.
Tacking	Sailing to windward in a zigzag pattern of straight 'tacks'.
Taking the ground	A moored vessel that grounds as the tide goes out is said to 'take the ground'.
The hard	A vessel taken out of the water is 'on the hard'.
The sector	Fishing boats that have membership in a PO.
Three-bow	A style of crab pot.
Tide rip	Rough water typically caused by tides flowing in opposing ways or by a fast current over an uneven bottom.
Torque	A force that causes rotation.
Tows	The interconnecting ropes between pots.
Track record	Historical data of catch.
Transom	The flat back end of a boat.
Waypoint	A destination.

Whelk	Shellfish of the family Buccinidae, especially *Buccinum undatum,* used for food.
Windlass	A mechanical device for lifting heavy objects, which uses a motor to pull a rope or chain around a cylinder.
Xtra Tuf	Alaskan-made iconic wellie boot.

Thank Yous

I am extremely grateful for the wonderful people who have helped me throughout my life and would like to take a moment to acknowledge them. I sincerely hope I have managed to capture you all here in some way, shape or form.

Firstly, to Lynne, my ghost writer, without whom this 80 some thousand word project would have eaten me alive. You have been instrumental in creating a narrative around a very complex (and sometimes delicate) subject matter and many hours on zoom have been spent writing, reading and digressing in the creation of this manuscript. And to Andrew, my agent, who took me under his wing following a phone call from me saying 'Hi. I have a book offer. Help!' I would not have been able to navigate the bamboozling publishing landscape without you both in my corner. Thank you.

I picked up wisdom and advice from a great many people in my early working life both at Aaron Services and Zip Water. I won't reel off a list of names, but you know who you are, all of you offering me insight and skills to cope with the pressures of the working world that I still use to this day, despite the drastic occupational differences.

To all my friends, who always understand if I can't make a birthday party or a social gathering because of my work commitments. Thank you for never leaving me out on the invite, just in case I might make it and for never making me feel guilty if we haven't caught up in many months. We always pick up exactly where we left off, and you are all truly great people that I'm proud to have around me.

This new line of work of mine has meant meeting so many new people and learning a plethora of completely new information. So many of you have been incredibly patient with me; from John, Col, Larry and Johnny, back in the early days, the angling regulars, who taught me how to look after fish properly, to the engineers on various trade counters who bear with me when I try and describe some strange-looking fitting with an out-of-date thread pattern. You guys always come through for me – cheers.

I acknowledge thanks also to the wider fishing industry of our nation, to the fishermen, fishing businesses, organisations, charities and the people who buy and sell from us, who have accepted me as one of their own and brought me into the fold. You really have been instrumental in propelling me along on this crazy path I seem to be on, and without your recognition I may not have been able to achieve some of the national attention I have received in the mainstream media which has ultimately led me to this point and this book.

Thank you to the fishermen of the British Isles, I wrote this book with a dream to create a jumping-off point for discussions among the communities of governance of the British Isles and our sector, in the hope it might promote discussions for change that would make our jobs and lives easier in the future. Thank you for working hard and keeping our traditional skills alive. We are a species under threat, and on speaking to a lot of you on a regular basis we share a great many concerns that are nuanced from region to region. We *must* continue to support one another, (a special nod to Iain and 'Bob' here) if we are to fight for our beloved Industry.

Thank you also to the various communities in the town and harbour in Wells, who have shared local knowledge and supported me, with a special acknowledgement going to Robert, Tristan, Graham and Fred from the Harbour Team.

I extend that thank you further to the Fishermen in Wells (well, most of them) who have accepted me and made me feel welcome. And especially to the likes of Andy MacCallum, Horris, Carl Pickering, Andy and Martin Frary, Will Purdy, Johnny Nudds, Nicky King and their respective crews, who have always shared their help, histories and expertise in times of crisis. I try to give as much as I possibly can back to them (normally in the manner of technical support with forms, phones and computers), but feel I can never repay them for all they have done for me. They may have seemed trivial things – lending bait, fixing something mechanical, borrowing tools, providing advice, giving a tow – but it has sincerely made the world of difference at times.

To everyone that follows me on Instagram, sincerely thank you. Without you I wouldn't have had half the opportunities I have, from working closely with big brands like XtraTuf and Guy

Cotton, to being noticed by a journalist or production company. Whether you're in the fishing industry or just curious about my work, thanks for being there. Your messages, support and acceptance all mean the world to me.

To Kenneth and Jack. We've had our fair share of run-ins and cross words, but it's always water under the bridge with us when it comes to physically doing the job, and you have both taught me a great deal. (Although I'm not thankful for the time Jack tried to teach me how to put a sack over a box of whelks – that was obvious.)

To my Family; Mum, sister, grandparents, husband and in-laws. You never fail to empower me to be the best I can possibly be. You all support me in so many different ways, throughout all of my endeavours. I am grateful to all of you for your unconditional love. I hope you all know just how much I appreciate you.

And finally Nige. You know how grateful I am to you, for opening the curtain on this world for me and for taking a chance on a girl with no experience. You have the patience of a saint and I am eternally thankful for every piece of knowledge, skill and training you have given me (passed down from Elizabeth and Alan). We've shared monumental highs and rock-bottom lows and I'm sure there are more to come. Thank you for every treasured minute.

Epilogue
Feb 2025

Eighteen months on from my last entry and I feel it only right to include an update on us, our work and the ever-fluid fisheries echo chamber.

So, what's new? Well, quite a lot! I could fill another book with the highs and lows of 'My Fishing Life'. Just in case I get that opportunity, I won't allude to too many spoilers. But I can tell you that right now Nigel and I are only working with *Saoirse* and some heartbreaking circumstances have meant that we are no longer working on or own *Fairlass*.

We have really scaled back the operation. In fact, and even though our hand was forced somewhat (sorry – no spoilers), this seems to be the most responsible and productive way forward for us and our precious blue economy.

When the UK left the European Union it gave us the opportunity to self-govern our EEZ, and so the 'The Joint Fisheries Statement' (JFS) was born. This is the document that highlights the key objectives for management of our fisheries moving forward. From this, we have seen the inception of FMPs

– Fisheries Management Plans – (of which there are around forty-three). In laymen's terms, these are detailed strategies on how a specific fishery (or groups of fisheries in some cases) can be strategically managed in conjunction with the sustainability objective set out in the JFS.

So what does this mean in the real world, to me, as a fisherman? I have been involved in the Whelk Management FMP and I try to give as much of my time to it as I can, given that the measures implemented from this plan will directly affect us. (Of course, my time has to be given freely, because – even though this forum for discussion relies entirely on co-management and input from the catching sector – nobody acknowledges us as credible consultants to actually recompense for our time, knowledge and expertise.) The group is facilitated by SeaFish and attended by DEFRA, the MMO, IFCAs, members of the scientific community, and fishermen if they have/can spare the time/are engaged enough to want to be involved.

The Whelk Fishery is historically data- and science-poor so, as is fairly common practice (and is sometimes quite frustrating), precautionary measures have to be introduced until such times as we can gather more evidence for more appropriate systems to be put in place. One of the measures that is being considered is an entitlement or permit system attached to a fishing licence. I acknowledge the need to limit access to a fishery that is at risk of exploitation from any and every boat in order to conserve stocks. However, is this not us applying aforementioned plasters to a problem? And, as a result, the small-scale boats are being further divided into what they can and cannot catch? If not implemented properly and carefully this could cause a number of issues when looking to upgrade a vessel and licence as, in some cases – especially in our vulnerable small-scale fleet – fishermen would need to find a licence with Whelk and Shellfish entitlements along with a bass entitlement (which sits with the vessel and not the licence – don't ask!). This will increase the price of licences and further alienate young entrants to the industry and/or perpetuate the exploitation of other stocks due to restricted access to certain available fisheries. It will also prevent fishermen upgrading their boats to newer and safer alternatives.

~

Whilst I appreciate limiting access to the fishery has to happen, it still does not stop some vessels from having far too many pots at sea. It is my own opinion that in some regions there are far too many pots and some fisheries are suffering as a result; where there was once a time that you could work a maximum of 500 pots and earn a fair living from whelk or crab and lobster there are now boats working upwards of 850 pots in a day in order to consistently land enough to make the job pay, due to the slow rate at which the market value for fish increases.

Our energy security and clean energy dilemma is only exacerbating this issue, with global offshore wind developers paying fishermen exorbitant amounts to stay out of development sites. This money is used to invest into boats that are more capable and of course more and more pots. Don't get me wrong – there needs to be some form of compensation package for vessels that are impacted and I would be lying to you if I said we hadn't benefitted from this compensation. It has been a lifeline in some cases. However, one day I hope to be in a position to tell them to shove their payoffs where ... somewhere else.

This money could be better suited to helping our industry rebuild, to invest in what has been lost, upgrades to facilities in fishing ports, upskilling our skippers and crews, training and apprenticeships for new entrants, powering harbourside facilities like freezers, chiller rooms and processing facilities, transport and logistics networks, lobster hatcheries, data collection ... The list goes on but you understand what I'm saying: invest back into the fishing communities to compensate for what is being taken. Because resources are being taken. Just this week we have learned there is a need to increase Marine Protected Areas across our seas to compensate for the damage being done to the seabed and subsequent marine eco-systems by these giant offshore wind structures. It's something we as fishermen (and I'm sure many others) already know and yet has only just been formally acknowledged by government.[*]

An MPA doesn't necessarily fix the problem either. Fish are where fish are – you can't destroy their natural habitat and justify it by putting a marine protected area in some many miles away and say, 'That's okay, we protected the seabed over there to compensate'. That's not how natural habitats work!

We are reaching a precarious moment. Our food security is being compromised and with nobody willing to put their neck on the block I will address the elephant in the room: too many

---

[*] https://fishingnews.co.uk/news/more-mpas-to-compensate-for-wind-farm-damage

individuals are becoming increasingly wealthy. And, of course, the more money that is given, the more pots end up on the seabed as a result. When a new site is being considered for development, there are always pots in the way, and fishermen have to be paid to move them and keep them out of the area. The irony? It's highly likely those pots were paid for by the energy developer in previous years!

As for IVMS (Inshore Vessel Monitoring System), that's fallen into an abyss. It is not yet a mandatory requirement and a great many questions are starting to be asked, along with Freedom of information requests being submitted surrounding GDPR, data sharing and project cost. Radio Silence. I will caveat this by saying that the MMO are trying to turn over a new leaf, and, as a result, more productive and meaningful conversations are happening. I have raised an issue with them concerning mackerel stocks and concerns of the misalignment of landing sizes between the North Sea and the rest of the country and they are escalating this conversation with wider science. Personally, I would like to see more innovation and enforcement with regards to the issue of scrubbing berried lobsters and I know many fishermen would like them to solve the contentious issue surrounding the thriving seal populations, but nothing happens quickly, and scars of the past will endure.

The MCA continue to be as militant and unaccountable as ever. However, the industry did push back as a united front against the medical certificates and that got scrapped at the eleventh hour*. The horror stories I have both lived and hear

---

* https://fishingnews.co.uk/news/hands-up-on-ml5-industry-welcome-for-ml5-climbdown

343

with this agency could fill their own tome. I also wonder if the fishermen who have spent thousands of pounds on surgeries and specialist consultants just to get their certificates will get their money back? Or maybe even an apology?

What stings even more is that DEFRA have an aim within their implementation of policy framework to ensure that both physical and emotional wellbeing is being maintained. I will give credit where it is due: a great amount of social science is happening to understand the effects on livelihoods through the lenses of economic and non-economic factors. These studies, which look at the social aspects of fisheries and their subsequent communities, could be our last hope at actually saving an ever-declining fleet – so I have ensured that I attend any meetings, surveys and workshops that have been carried out. This included a workshop held in Whitby & Poole to look at the key contributors for the decline in the fleet and what could be put in place to help protect it, the outputs of which are being discussed by a working group I am part of at the end of the month.*

But back to us. What have we been doing and what's different? Nigel and I are very aware of the over-exploitation of some stocks and, of course, we don't want to be part of the problem. We have taken great time, care and effort in reducing the number of pots we work in a day and are ensuring that where possible we are achieving maximum value for our catch. By using my ever-growing social media accounts to showcase best practice and environmentally conscious efforts to protect stocks where we

---

* https://fishingnews.co.uk/news/shining-a-light-on-fishing-livelihoods
  https://nicre.co.uk/projects/partnership-projects/coastal-fisheries-cluster

can, we have found customers who support us and our ethos, thus enabling us to be price-makers and not just price-takers.

Last summer the commercial price for lobsters dropped to £9.50 per kilo but we remained steady at no less that £25.00 per kilo. Yes, our volume of catch may be lower than others but we are happy with what we catch, and its quality, especially as it has not sat in a pot for weeks on end degrading. We now have a lobster tank too and somewhere to keep it in Wells! Which means we can offer direct sales to the public, at reasonable prices – no middlemen to pay for! I have tried sending them in the post, too, and with great success. However, the cost of postage and packaging exceeds the cost of the lobsters, so it does not seem viable to me.

I'm also pleased to report that our community on social media continues to grow and be as supportive as ever. We regularly share the highs and lows of our work and try to educate as many people as we can about the fish in the sea and our need to get behind our country's fishermen, in the same way the public backs our nations farming communities.

I will continue to fly the flag for the small-scale fishermen of the UK. It's become a deeply rooted passion project now. We *must* save this historically important piece of our rich maritime heritage, blue economy and coastal communities, and the people and livelihoods it supports. The entire fisheries sphere starts with a person, on a boat, catching fish, and ends with seafood on a plate.

This project has opened so many doors to me, for which I am extremely grateful. I often get the opportunities to talk about our work and the fisheries space at local and national events. I even went to South Korea in November to speak at a global conference for fishing communities. I have also received an invite to Buckingham Palace's Royal Garden Party for my continued work supporting the development of fisheries. I will be visiting Parliament next week to meet with some key coastal MPs (A new government, after all, does mean some education of the nuance of our sector), and I am also consulting on a horror film in the works.

Who knows where this salty road will take both me and the industry in the future. I'm excited to find out!